Found and Lost

Found and Lost

An Adoption, An Agency and A Search for Self

Suzette J. Brownstein

ISBN-13: 9780692869970
ISBN-10: 0692869972

Dedicated to Evelyn and Samuel Gordon

All the names of the living
have been changed to protect their privacy.

Prologue

*"There is no greater agony than bearing
an untold story inside you."*

— MAYA ANGELOU

I knew for a very long time that I needed to write my story. It was a part of me that was critical to who I am, and yet, a part of my life that I rarely talked about and that caused me to struggle for many years. I am an adoptee---a product of biological parents I didn't know and adoptive parents I both know and love. Today most adoptions are "open," allowing children the opportunity to know both their history and often their biological parents.

Before though, from the 1930's to the mid-1970's, adoptions were "closed," which meant that all connections between the birth parents and the adoptive ones were sealed forever. This was believed to be the compassionate response to protect birth parents from the stigma of others knowing they had sexual relations outside of marriage. The taboos were strong at the time. It also protected the adoptee from the stigma of illegitimacy. Birth certificates in the first half of the twentieth century were actually marked "legitimate" or "illegitimate," and illegitimate children were thought of as "bastards," defective or tainted somehow, a term that most young people today would not even be able to comprehend in it's original meaning.

For the adoptive parents, the closed system meant a child of their own, with no prior or potentially disruptive future connections to the birth parents. An amended birth certificate was issued in order to give the baby a "clean slate," a fresh start. This certificate replaced the names of the birth parents with the adoptive ones, fostering the illusion of a brand-new family and thus protecting them from facing the differences between being a parent by adoption and one by birth.

The myth became that secrecy was somehow beneficial to all, and no one gave any thought to the psychological impact it might have on the child. For many adoptees, like myself, the secrecy model had unintended consequences. It created stigma and shame. "Secrecy erects barriers to forming a healthy identity. A secrecy formula encourages all the performers in the adoption drama to build their lives on the premise that an event central to the lives of all partners never occurred. Sealed records implicitly ask for an extreme form of denial. There is no school of psychotherapy today which regards denial as a positive strategy in forming a healthy sense of self," the sociologist Mary D. Howard wrote in *Adoption Resources for Mental Health Professionals* in 1986. Or in the words of the famous author John Bradshaw, "You are as sick as your secrets," and "What you don't know *can* hurt you."

In this way, I felt like I was different, and in a bad way. I wasn't the only adoptee who felt it, but of course, I didn't know that at the time. Statistics show that many adoptees from the closed system were negatively affected. In fact, mental health professionals were surprised at the alarmingly high number of their adolescent patients that were adoptees. At a 1988 Conference of the American Adoption Congress, Reuben Pannor, an adoption specialist, cited that an average of 20 to 35 percent of the young people in residential treatment centers and psychiatric hospitals were adoptees. An alarmingly high number of adoptees were also sent to disciplinary and correctional schools.

The irony was that back then, most adoptees as well as their treatment providers, made no connection to the possibility that their difficulties, at least in part, might be because they were adopted. Rather, the thinking was that adoptees would feel grateful for the families they were given and never look back. A U.S. Public Affairs pamphlet from 1969 titled "You and Your Adopted

Child" stated, "Instances of extreme curiosity and concern almost never happen…However, should a youngster ever raise the question, it is important, of course, to make it very clear that a search is unrealistic and can lead to unhappiness and disillusionment." Thus, an adoptee having knowledge of his or her ancestry and genetics was deemed irrelevant to his or her mental health, and possibly even detrimental.

Sometime in the mid-eighties, the thinking on closed adoption started to change. Too many adolescent and adult adoptees were presenting to therapists for help. When I was thirty-four years old, I came upon a book that awakened me to the whole concept of the closed system, and thus, my own story. It was Betty Jean Lifton's *Journey of the Adopted Self, a Quest for Wholeness.* As I perused the shelves of Barnes and Noble in White Plains, New York, the title jumped out at me like a jack in the box. I examined each passage, absorbing all its research, stunned and fascinated by its findings. The book exposed the impact of the closed system, a topic that until then had been taboo.

In her obituary, the *New York Times* wrote, "Betty Jean Lifton, a writer, adoptee and adoption-reform advocate whose books—searing condemnations of the secrecy that traditionally shrouded adoption—became touchstones for adoptees throughout the world. Her first book, describing her personal journey, gave momentum to the emerging adoption-reform movement, and prompted an outpouring of mail from people with similar stories. These letters, and subsequent interviews with adoptees, informed the next installments in Ms. Lifton's trilogy, in which she examined the psychological toll that closed adoption can take, and the psychological affinities many adoptees appear to share."

The findings in *Journey of the Adopted Self* were harsh; Ms. Lifton presented a large number of case studies and testimonials of adoptees who had lasting emotional damage from growing up in the closed system. It was, in many ways, painful to read. While some of it spoke directly to my experience, some did not at all. I went through a mental sifting process, trying to figure out what was true for me and what wasn't. I also came to realize that since her research pool only consisted of adoptees that presented to her for help, it was a completely one-sided presentation. There was no mention of the benefits of the adoption experience, of which there were many, nor of those who did perfectly well and thrived. In the end, and as many researchers have since noted, how any one adoptee feels about being adopted usually lies on a continuum from those who are perfectly fine and never look back (what another author called "the given side") to others who are deeply disturbed and desperate to find answers ("the taken side" of the equation). Where an adoptee falls on this continuum is based on each individual's own experiences, wiring, resilience and nature. "Most adoptees from the closed adoption era, in the end, did just fine, going on to have families of their own, careers, and fulfilling lives," Brodzinsky concluded in his more balanced and clinical treatment of the subject matter in his 1993 book *Being Adopted, The Lifelong Search for Self,* "but problems can and do occur." In the end, both were true for me.

Years later, I pulled out that book again when I started writing this memoir. The very act of putting words on paper began to give me greater clarity about the events that upended my life. But putting it out there was another matter. Who would benefit? For fellow adoptees, they could perhaps find truth and solace in my words. What about others? Then I thought about the emotions I felt along the way rather than the actual events, and I realized they were universal: fear, confusion, anger, loss, guilt and sadness, all experienced in the confines of an imperfect family, the kind we all live in. Thus, here was a common theme for everyone, the one of human frailty and resilience in dealing with what life hands us. Perhaps the appeal would be much broader than I thought.

I also knew that exposing myself in such detail would mean making myself vulnerable, and that too was scary. But I decided to be brave. If we share our humanity and the struggles we have been through, then perhaps we can all connect to each other in more meaningful ways.

I gained so much. I had been a full-time mom for twenty-three years, and the writing workshops I participated in gave me direction and confidence. Entering a room where complete strangers shared their most intimate stories of pain and challenge was a gift in itself. Pushing myself to complete this manuscript took me further than I ever had gone before. As a result of this experience, I encourage anyone with the motivation to tell his or her own story to take the plunge. The journey is challenging, yes, but filled with rewards.

After three years and countless drafts, I was finished. I was amazed I had done it. An editor told me that completing a book is "like giving birth"—what was inside is now outside. Having given birth three times over by then, she couldn't be more correct. It was a huge sense of relief and joy to finally be able to hold my baby, even if this particular one sat in a cardboard box that I picked up from the office copy store one spring day.

I hope my journey and what I learned about identity, fear and love offers either some deeper understanding of your own story and self, or of someone else's who has touched your life along the way.

$\mathcal{O}ne$

THE CALL

The music blasted, but we loved it. Jumping and twirling under the dim lights, bodies against bodies, it was a thrilling mix of new friends, potential new ones and perhaps even a lover somewhere in the crowd. When the hit song "Rock Lobster" came on, the crowd roared in delight, arms jerking, heads bobbing. The floor began to vibrate from a frenetic energy that drew us all in.

It was 1978.

I looked at Jody and Nancy, my two new roommates. Could it be only two weeks ago that I met them? On move-in day at the University of Michigan, I was nervous. Like many incoming freshmen, I had no idea what to expect. Up until then, these other students were just names typed on a letterhead that had arrived in the mail. It didn't take long for me to find out that they were easy-going, fun and bright, enabling me to breathe a sigh of relief.

The music continued to pound at the party. I moved my body to the booming beat of the B-52s. Jody handed me my second froth-filled paper cup she had retrieved from the corner keg. I looked at Jody's flushed pale cheeks and at Nancy's dark chestnut locks wet against her face, and thought how happy I was to be there. In that wild late-night moment, only two weeks since my arrival, college felt like a just-opened present, much desired and finally received. And while we were all intoxicated, it was not so much by alcohol as by the euphoria of independence, of new beginnings, of a world that was now ours for the taking as college freshmen. At least that is what we believed, what I believed.

~

Two weeks later, we were in our dorm rooms studying, bent intently over our books. The only sound is the gentle hum of the electric fan in the corner of the room.

Two pages into my anthropology chapter, the wall phone rings.

"I got it," I say. I put down my highlighter and get up.

"Hello!"

"Hello, I am looking for Suzette Gordon," says a serious and strangely accented voice.

"This is Suzette Gordon."

"*Suzette...*I have waited eighteen years for this moment."

Silence.

"I am Albert, your biological father, and I've been searching for you all your life."

Silence.

"I want you to know that I love you, and I never wanted to give you up."

Silence.

"H-hold on," I muster, as my entire body begins to spasm.

I glance at my roommates, my heart pounding, as I cup the receiver against my chest. They are looking up from their textbooks, their faces curious. "Taking this outside," I whisper, forcing a grin.

They go back to their reading, their eyes re-focusing on their books while I step into the hallway. I close the door behind me on the cord best I can. Sinking along the cement cinder block wall to the floor, I grip the phone tightly with my shaking hand.

This cannot be happening. Please, God, no. I don't want it to. What am I going to say to this man, this stranger...my father?

While I knew I was adopted since the age of six, that was all I knew, just the fact of it. It was never discussed.

"Hi, uh, I can talk now," I say with an unsteady voice.

"I'm so happy to hear your voice, Su-*zette*."

"*Okay...*"

"I guess this is sudden. Now that you are eighteen, I could call you legally. I've been waiting for this day for a long time."

I was 18 just yesterday.

"Can I ask you, where's your accent from?" I'm in complete disbelief and shock that I am talking to this man, and this is the first thing that pops into my head. *Basically, where the hell is he from so I can know where the hell I am from?*

"I'm Egyptian."

Egyptian? What? I'm Jewish! My mother told me I came from a Jewish adoption agency. Am I, a Bat Mitzvah girl from Long Island, half Arab?

I thought of the only father I ever knew, whom I used to sit next to in temple for the high holidays, stroking his blue velvet tallis bag, feeling safe and secure.

Now I didn't.

"Well, yes, but I left Egypt as a young boy and was raised in Marseilles, France."

France? So I'm French too?

"France? I... study French," I respond in a low and timid voice.

I can't believe I'm telling him something about myself. Telling him seems wrong, but I don't know why. Decades later, I'll understand that it was the closed system I grew up in playing out the only way it could.

"Ah, c'est bien! Tu parles le francais?" he asks with a deep chuckle. But it feels like sandpaper on my nerves; I don't like his familiar ease. Some unexplainable fear rises up in me.

All of a sudden, the idea that I was actually born and not just adopted, enters my being like a lighter set to gasoline, that entire black space in my mind blazing to life. It explodes inside me, burning to cinders a lifetime of denial that I actually existed before my adoption.

"Well, then I came to this country. I was young, and I met your mother."

Jeez, yeah, a mother... I have one of those too...

"My mother?"

"Yes, your mother, Pearl."

"Her name was Pearl?"

"Yes," he says, holding the word for a long time.

"But I want you to understand something. I never wanted to give you up, but I had no choice. I wanted to marry her and keep you but, well, she didn't want that. Fathers had no rights. If it were today, I could've kept you. So I was forced to give you up."

He might have kept me?

"And I have spent your entire life looking for you, *and loving you.*"

Loving?

"Wow, that's unbelievable," I say, trying not to sound too put off but feeling a tidal wave of emotion crashing down on me at the potential nightmare that is unfolding.

"It wasn't easy to find you. I had to go through a lot because the records are sealed."

Yeah, so, how'd you manage that? What was it, a shady deal?

Then some ambivalent anger wells up in me.

It wasn't his right to seek me out like this—yet why wasn't it really? I am beyond confused.

"Albert, I don't know what to say, I'm ..."

"You don't have to say anything, *cherie*, I'm just so happy to finally be on the phone with you."

Cherie?

"Yeah, well, that's...um, nice," I say, trying to stay calm. He could not know, would have no idea, how much I do not want to be on the phone with him.

"Do you remember when your parent's house was for sale this past spring?" he continues. "Well, I had friends of mine go to see it when you were home from school to pretend they were looking to buy it. They reported back to me on you, how you were..."

What?

Jeez, I do remember. Dressed in my favorite Springsteen concert tee and athletic shorts, I was studying at the kitchen table when the doorbell rang. I scrambled down the tile hallway, gripping the choke collar of my boxer Lolly, and two strangers greeted me through the screen door. One smiled and said, "I'm a broker…and here to show the house. Did your mom tell you?"

"No, she didn't, but I'm sure it's fine." I stepped back to let them in, and the house hunters stared at me intently, with an interest so bizarre for the task at hand that I still remembered it.

Now it made sense. I'm creeped out. *This is not normal.* And yet, deep inside, a very small piece of me feels touched by the intense desire of this man to find me.

"I can't believe those were your friends."

"Yes, they really helped me out. They told me how lovely you were, my dear!"

"That's, um… nice."

"Su-*zette*, I want you to come to Florida to spend time with my wife Betty and me. I have a house and a *swimming pool*, you know," he says with enthusiasm.

That's his enticement? And he seems to think coming would be as easy as a trip to the grocery store.

"I don't know, maybe, we'll see."

My mind circled back.

"Do you know what happened to my mother?"

"She was a beautiful woman, and I loved her very much," he says in a carefully measured tone. "You were a product of that love. But she became very sick after she had you, mentally…well, you know, it's not a good story, and I wouldn't go there if I was you."

I repeat the words *sick, not go there*, aloud to him, not knowing what else to say. My muscles contract. I'm already in emotional overload, so I let it lie, perhaps scared to probe anymore.

"Ok, well then, um, can I ask you what you do?"

"I have an import-export business. You know, a little of this and that."

Legitimate? I try to picture some successful enterprise that I could feel good about, but it sounds a bit strange.

"Also, I have two children, Paul and Pammy, so you have a brother and a sister!" he then announces with a present-opening-time-at-Christmas enthusiasm.

Brother and sister? He wants us to be one big happy family? I think not. I can barely accept the fact that I am even talking to my birth father, let alone think about becoming part of his family. I'm light years away from that.

"OK, we'll see...." I answer.

"But enough of me, Su-*zette*, how are you, my dear?"

"I don't know. I'm okay, I guess. I just got to school, as you know. I have two nice roommates. All's...pretty good," I tell him.

What else am I going to say? Catch him up on 18 years while sitting in the hallway of my dorm with an outstretched phone cord when I'm in complete and utter shock? It was as if an asteroid hit, one I never saw coming. And what do I owe him?

Twelve years of suppressed thoughts and emotions, building since the day I found out I was adopted, ones I never knew I had, start shooting like bottle rockets in my head. I have an overwhelming need to cry. The Pandora's box inside me, long sealed tight, opens. I am completely unequipped to deal with its contents.

"You know, I'm really sorry, but I have to go now. Why don't you give me your address and number and I'll contact you, okay?" I blurt out.

"Oh, well, sure, if you can't talk anymore."

"No, I can't, I'm sorry." I push myself up along the wall and walk back into my room on wobbly legs, clutching the phone against my chest, my head down but trying to hold it together in front of my roommates. They're just getting ready to leave, chattering about schoolwork. As they head toward the door, I turn my head away so they cannot see the strain on my face. I rip a page from a spiral notebook and grab a pen as my roommates shut the door behind them.

"Ok, you can go, I'm ready."

"My name is Albert Demachi." He spells it out very slowly lest I not get it perfectly. He dictates his address and number in Miami Beach. I scribble them down, say goodbye and hang up as fast I can. Thick tears begin to run down my cheeks, and I collapse into my chair, my brain spiraling.

What the hell just happened?

I do not ponder for long. I grab the phone off the wall again while my chest heaves and dial.

Mom and dad will know what to do. Please be home.

"Hello."

"Mom, you're not going to believe this. My *biological* father just called me."

"*What?* Noooo, he didn't!"

"Oh, yeah, he did!"

"Oh my god! Hold on, I'm gonna get dad on the phone."

"Saaaammmm, pick up the phone! He called her!"

He clicks on.

"The *SOB*, he called you?"

Wow, that was harsh. Now I am more confused. Hearing my father's venom, I burst into another round of tears.

Looking back now though, how could I have known their reaction was predictable and understandable. Growing up in the closed adoption system, parents were told to raise their children "as if they were born to you." In their minds, my brother and I were their children one hundred percent. My adoptive parents, the ones I considered my only parents, were assured the files were sealed forever. So of course there was no room for biological parents showing up, much less sharing their child.

"He called here before you left for school," my mother reveals, very agitated. "He said he wanted to call you. I begged him not to. I told him you'd be adjusting to school, and it wasn't a good time, to just wait and give you time, that's all. He said he'd think about it…"

"Yeah, well he didn't listen," I say, wiping my eyes with the back of my hand.

"What did he say to you?" my father's angry voice cuts in. I report the conversation between sobs, sucking down breaths between my words. As I speak, they douse my words with angry comments, thus escalating the trauma.

Reflecting back now, if they had said something like, "It's okay, Suzie, you don't need to be upset, this is a good thing. He just wants some connection to you. We'll work through this together," I would have been much less traumatized. Plus, I called them so hysterical that they went into protection mode, like any parent would. I did not think either to present the same case back to them, to reassure them it would be okay. We were all victims of that closed system, our beliefs on what family meant cemented into a fortress with then impenetrable walls.

"Just so you know," my mom says, "he is not in import-export. He's a *hairdresser!*"

"A *hairdresser?*"

"Yeah, a hairdresser!" my mom says in a snarly tone.

Images of visiting my mom's hairdresser Tony when I was growing up fill my head. His beauty parlor was in the neighboring town of Hicksville, on the main commercial drag of Broadway, in a strip of stores. As a young girl, I'd play with the curler carts, cone dryers, and clips while my mother got her hair done. Tony kept the two top buttons of his slinky shirts open and his greased hair back in a high pompadour. The way he laughed and flirted with the women made me leery. That's not who I wanted my biological father to be. And the way my mother said the word *hairdresser* made it even worse.

"Why would he lie about that?"

"I don't know," my father says, "but we checked him out…*definitely* a hairdresser."

"What? You checked him out?"

He was stalking me, and they were stalking him?

"We just didn't think it was a good idea at the time," my mom adds.

My dad cuts in, "I'll tell you what. You write him a letter and tell him to never call you again. That's all."

My dad is offering the perfect fix. It is what I am hoping for. He is giving me permission to close this all back up in the box so no one has to deal with it. In the moment, it makes perfect sense. "Well, um, I guess that's what I should do, Dad." And I actually start to feel better right away, taking some control back.

"Do you want us to come out there?" I tell them no.

The last thing I need is having my parents show up with melodramatic faces, rehash their anger, and treat me like a wounded puppy. Besides, it would just magnify and prolong the angst and confusion. Plus, what would I tell my roommates?

I sniff back my tears and regain some composure. My parents ask me over and over if I'll be all right. The lack of control must have been devastating for them. However, they don't even think to suggest that I speak with a therapist. No one went to therapy in the 1970s. Psychiatrists and psychologists were for "crazy" people.

After I repeatedly reassure them, my parents begrudgingly accept that I will be okay, at least for the moment, and we say goodbye. I tear a clean page from my notebook and stare at it. Do I really want to tell Albert to *never* call again? As upset as I am, and as much as I want to pretend this never happened, I don't feel right saying that either.

So I write:

Dear Albert,

I know that I'm your daughter and that you want to hear from me and to see me. But I'm asking you not to call me again. I'm sorry. I'll write you, however, letting you know how I am, but that's it. That is what I want.

Best,
Suzette

I fold it carefully and stick it in an envelope I pull from the desk drawer. The bitter taste of glue covers my tongue as I seal it tight.

Not too long after, I send him a photo, a headshot of myself. But I would not remember that I did this until thirty-five years later, when Albert showed the photo to me in his home.

On the back I wrote, "Hi Albert, here's the picture I promised you. I'm sorry it took me so long to send, Suzette." When I read my words, I suddenly remembered that I had sent it. With it, I also remembered the scared young girl who sat and deliberated over which photo to choose from her small album, one that did not reveal too much of who I was. The seeds of ambivalence that

I would carry with me for the rest of my life were planted in those moments back in my dorm room.

The telephone rings. *Must be my parents. They can't be done with this yet.* "We just called Oliver to tell him, and he wants to kill Albert," my mother blurts out. My older brother Oliver was also adopted. Smart and charismatic, he was very protective of me and angered easily. One of my parents' mantras to him over the years was, "It's not what you say, it's *how* you say it." I know getting him involved in this will be a big mistake. In that moment, I imagine him driving to Albert's home to punch him out. Oliver recently admitted to me just how right I was. "Yeah, I wanted to permanently injure the man so he wouldn't contact you again," he told me.

Taken aback, I said, "But didn't you feel any empathy for him?"

"Putting myself in his shoes, yeah, I did feel bad for the guy. It's a horrible thing to lose your own child. But my responsibility was to you." As misguided as I felt Oliver's responses were, then and now, a part of me loved how much my brother cared about me.

"Tell Oliver not to contact him, okay?" I plead with my parents, pacing the room. My mother doesn't answer.

"*Okay?*"

"Okay, okay, I'll tell him."

"And I already wrote him that letter. It's done and I'm all right now. Really." My mom doesn't believe me nor does my dad. I tell them repeatedly I will be fine, and then I tell them, "I have to go." I hang up the phone, my stomach in knots, my insides scrambled and my breathing deep. I shove my books in my backpack with jittery hands and shoot out the door, not sure where I'm going. I head outside, staring down at the sidewalk as I walk, holding back my tears.

My mind is churning in a maelstrom of confusing and crashing thoughts and emotions. Passing the rundown student houses, the row of shops, and the fast-food eateries on State Street, I am oblivious to everything. I am not able to meet anyone's gaze as my legs move forward. Mostly, I envy all the students walking by who don't have to figure out how to have two fathers and whose lives haven't just been shattered.

Two

THEY COME

Nowadays, the children come to this campus with meager belongings. Some come forlorn. Some come scared. Some come hungry. Some come angry. Some come beaten. Some come defiant. Some come resigned. Some come withdrawn. Some come confused. Some come depressed. Some come defeated.

Most of them come without hope.

Some have been slapped. Some have been beaten. Some have been tied. Some have been burned. Some have been starved. Some have been left. Some have been ignored. Some have been abandoned. Some have been fondled. Some have been raped.

Most have experienced one loss after another of anyone that has ever mattered to them. They are broken inside. Through no fault of their own, they have been dealt an incredibly cruel hand in life.

The Pleasantville Cottage School, built by the Hebrew Shelter Guardian Society (HSGS), is a 100-year-old campus in Westchester County, New York. When it was first opened on July 1st, 1912, four hundred and eighty Jewish orphans lined up on 150th Street and Broadway in Manhattan, outside their present home, the HSGS orphanage, to make the trek to their new one upstate, where over fifty acres of land and state of the art "cottages" awaited them. "Waving little American flags and sneaking excited glances at the cottage numbers pinned to their garments, traffic was rerouted as they marched, and the children stepped smartly to the music of their own band," the author Jacqueline Bernard related in her 1973 book *The Children You Gave Us, 150 Years of Service to Children, a History of the Jewish Child Care Association.* Once they arrived behind the enormous HSGS orphanage city, the column halted. They looked around. "The children, many feet deep, were not only watching the orphanage building, some were weeping." It was the only home they had ever known. The band played their final song, and the orphans marched down Broadway and across 125th Street to the New York Central Railroad to head upstate.

Arriving at the Pleasantville campus, the children were "flabbergasted, for they had never seen fields or forests like these before," stated an observer.

"We were like bugs flying all over... explorers in a new world!" said one young boy. Twenty-five "house mothers" had been hired from a large applicant pool by HSGS, a process that took over a year, to make sure that the women chosen were the best possible people for the job, taking care of those who were alone in this world.

"Our Cottage mothers were waiting for us there, their Cottage numbers also pinned to their dresses so we'd know our mothers and them their children," one child said, "and we went with them—toward Home."

Once settled, the children participated in all domestic chores. Three mandatory curriculums were established: academic, Hebrew language and Jewish history, and, the most innovative of all for its time, vocational training. By the time each child graduated, they had to have technical expertise in one area of their choosing that could lead to employment. The technical program earned unequivocal praise in 1914 from Columbia University's Teachers College.

Soon it would be deemed by the Russell Sage Foundation, one of the most prominent American foundations devoted exclusively to research in the social sciences, as "undoubtedly one of the best equipped institutions for children in the world." Childcare workers from Europe and the rest of the United States came to study its strategy. Within three years, three new institutions were built on the same model. Harvard University created a permanent exhibit in its Social Ethics Museum to highlight its groundbreaking model. The President of the United States at that time, William Howard

Taft, visited the campus. The children were left uplifted and inspired by his visit. As was he.

Today, fast forwarding one hundred years, the Cottage School could still be considered an orphanage, but of a very different kind. Now 250 inner city youth from all faiths call it home. Unlike their predecessor's from decades ago, they have experienced the most horrible kinds of abuse and neglect. Removed from their homes by the Administration for Children's Services or by a family court judge, most have been shuffled from foster care family to foster care family where each placement has failed due to the intense traumas they have suffered.

This is the end of the line; residential treatment is the only place left for them to go. Currently, according to the New York State Citizens Coalition for Children, 2,000 souls live in such institutions in New York State. There are almost 33,000 nationwide living in residential centers, according to the Adoption and Foster Care Analysis and Reporting System (AFCARS). Sadly, these children are the long shot for leading productive lives when they age out of care, meaning being able to contribute to society rather than being dependent on it. Instead, a high percentage of them end up on welfare, in prisons, homeless shelters and/or go on to suffer from high levels of substance abuse and serious mental illness.

At the Cottage Schools, a team of 552 well-trained childcare workers, social workers, psychologists and others work tirelessly around the clock to help these children recover from their traumas. There is individual and group therapy, trauma treatment, a therapeutic arts program and both on and off campus recreational activities. There are vocational programs, two well-equipped gyms and a "respite" center when a child needs time to decompress.

The staff is deeply devoted and is exceptionally caring. They work to help these children heal and give them hope for a far better life than the one they came from. In spite of the great emotional, cognitive and psychological challenges facing these youth, success stories abound.

I can state this with certainty because I have been a volunteer at the Cottage School for the past fourteen years. Moving to a neighboring town in 2002 when I was forty-two years old, I joined and became involved with my community temple to start building relationships with other families. The first two friends I made were the organizers of an annual party for the children at holiday time, sponsored by their individual temples. As one was an active member of the temple I joined, she asked if I would like to attend. I brought my husband Rich and my three children, Brian, Mallory and Asher, with me. I had no idea what to expect.

We had a hard time finding the place, as a small brown wood sign wedged between two long expanses of dense woods was the only indicator of the entrance. My family and I were shocked to discover the size of the enormous campus that lay behind it, a world onto it's own. We did not even know such places existed.

Soon I'd learned that anywhere from ten to sixteen children lived in each of these large rectangular two-story buildings called "cottages," mostly grouped by age, and there were two small public schools on the grounds, making the facility self-contained.

When we entered the recreation room, we waited in anxious anticipation for the children to arrive. I had no idea what to expect. Seven or eight boys pushed through the double doors with an energetic gust, the first to arrive. We greeted them with broad grins as they filed past us, some half awake, some with quizzical looks and some smiling back at us.

More children arrived, teen-agers in small groups, shedding their winter coats and taking in the room that we decorated with balloons and red and green tablecloths. They wore faded sweaters, t-shirts, jeans, and sneakers, typical teenager garb.

The music pumped, and soon small circles gathered on the dance floor as we watched from the sidelines. The dance floor filled in little by little, and eventually we joined them, shuffling our feet and clapping along. Some of them really began to show off their moves, and the room came to life. We handed out silly glasses, hats and necklaces and directed them to the photo booth set up in the corner.

We served pizza, soda and brownies and handed out gifts. When it was time to leave, they thanked us with warm smiles. Some even hugged us. Their bright eyes and appreciation of our presence pulled deep at my heartstrings. But it would be a while, however, before I would make any deep connections to my own beginnings. Mahatma Gandhi said, "The best way to find yourself is to lose yourself in the service of others." It ended up being star-tlingly true for me.

On the way home that day, what unsettled me most was how these children who came from extreme poverty lived side by side with children who came from substantial wealth, just minutes away from each other. The juxtaposition was so alarming. Something more should be done, I thought to myself, but I wasn't sure what that something should be. I soon found an opportunity to start volunteering there, to do my small part on the campus. Like most of us do, the small things to hopefully make some positive differences.

Three

VU IZ DER KINDA? (WHERE IS THE BABY?)

My parents, Evelyn and Samuel Gordon, met over a pickle barrel in Sam's aunt's deli on Dyckman Street in the Inwood section of Manhattan. My mom was only eight, buying a sour dill, and my dad twelve, working there after school to help his family. It was 1936, and both were the children of immigrants, their parents part of the mass exodus of Jews from Eastern Europe and Russia to escape the murderous pogroms. They became and remained childhood friends.

When World War II came, Evelyn and Sam lost touch. My dad, ineligible for battle due to eye problems, served his country by collecting wounded soldiers off the battlefields of southern France.

D-Day came, and Sam returned. Sam and Evelyn moved on with their lives and ended up engaged to different people. Then one night, they were at a mutual friend's wedding, my mom alone and my dad with his fiancé, Shirley. He saw my mom in her little sweetheart dress and platform shoes and was smitten. He proceeded to neglect his fiancé for a good chunk of the night. "He dropped Shirley home after and came to hang with me," my mom told me, to which I normally would have responded, "What a cad!" But since they were engaged three months later and married for 64 years, I guess it was meant to be.

After the wedding, my parents moved in with Isaac and Mary, Evelyn's parents. It was far from a newlywed's dream. Isaac, my grandfather, was a cold and stern man. He was critical of my mother all her life. But they did what they had to do, as one does in life, my mom gladly handing over her paycheck to help her new husband's parents, two people whom she adored but who had to move often when the rent came due. "They taught me how to love since there was no love in my own household," she explained to me. And they counted down the days until they had enough to move out.

My mom was working in her father's coat business during that time, after a long wicked bout of pneumonia forced her out of nursing school. Starting out as a presser, he had eventually taken over the whole business. So my mom grew up with means but without love.

Thanks to the GI bill, Samuel was able to work days but get his insurance and real estate licenses by night. Eventually they made it to Bayside, Queens, where Isaac gave them the money to open up their own business on Bell Boulevard, the main shopping drag in town. They hung their shingle, and became a business team in addition to a marital one.

At first, life was rosy. But Evelyn and Sam's happiness was stopped short. My mother could not get pregnant. She would write about this time in a short narrative she composed in her early eighties, wanting to document her life and inspired by my own writing.

"After years of trying, many disappointments, money going out and not enough coming in, we finally did get pregnant! We were so apprehensive, excited…almost afraid," she wrote. Unfortunately, she woke up one morning to excessive bleeding. She would go on to have a number of miscarriages before being diagnosed with what was called an "infantile uterus," one that could not hold a pregnancy. "We were devastated, heartbroken," my mom wrote in her account. She told my dad that he could leave her if he wanted, that she would certainly understand. But he wasn't going anywhere, at least not yet.

They went from doctor to doctor searching for a cure. One of the "specialists" actually infused horse urine into her, getting her hopes too high. Ironically, this same condition is now treatable, so it was an example of what the famous psychiatrist Erik Erikson called, "life history meeting history." Our lives are so often determined by the times we live in.

When they told my mother's parents about the diagnosis, Isaac was less than sensitive. "He was horrible," my mother told me, "he said to me, '*You are made of stone!*'" When her brother Saul's wife got pregnant soon after, he added insult to injury by announcing, "Guess *she'll* have to make the grandchildren for this family!" Mary, her mom, did not say a word. She abided by the unwritten rules of her generation where wives stayed silent and obeyed.

Watching other mothers pushing strollers down the boulevard, she'd go home and cry. All of her friends were having multiple children. So after years of trying and disappointment, they made the decision to adopt. "It was never should we adopt," my mother told me recently, "it was, that's what we're going to do."

My grandfather's lack of empathy, however, did not abate. He was adamantly against it. I imagine that in the world he grew up in, illegitimate children were seen as defective somehow; he would not accept someone else's blood. My mother, on the other hand, could not even try to understand his prejudices. "He made me feel so bad about myself I stopped talking to both of them," she wrote. Reading her words, I felt a wave of admiration for her, because she was able to distance herself from her abusive parents. Deep empathy and sadness filled me too, realizing that in the times she lived in self-worth was tied to fertility for women, and she was not immune.

Thankfully, the impact of my mother's insensitive parents was mitigated by my father's warm and caring ones. Sadly, my grandfather Oscar passed away before they adopted my brother, so he never got to meet my brother nor me. When they told my grandmother Sarah their plans, she said, "You *want* a baby, so you *get* a baby!" in her thick Yiddish accent, pleased as all punch.

They went to the only Jewish adoption agency in the area, Louise Wise, on East 92nd Street, to begin the process. Louise Waterman Wise, the founder, wrote, "The child of an unmarried mother rarely has a chance. It is whipped from pillar to post and denied that place in life to which every human being is entitled whether its parents be married or not." She was typical of that era, believing a child was better off being given away rather than being raised by a single parent, and given the mores and values of that time, she was probably right. Interestingly enough, she was also the wife of Stephen Wise, the most prominent leader of the American Jewish community in New York in the 1930s and 40s, president of the American Jewish Congress and World Jewish Congress, board member of the NAACP, and good friend and advisor to President Roosevelt. Quite an impressive guy, yes, but some of his peers would rather have him relegated to the trash heap of history for not doing more than he did to help the Jews during the Holocaust. He did, after all, have Roosevelt's ear. Still, the synagogue bearing his name still stands on the upper west side of Manhattan, and the congregation is alive and vibrant.

⌒

When my parents went to Louise Wise, the demand for infants was high. Infertility treatments were only starting to be discovered. Many couples remained childless. So my parents were crestfallen to hear that the waiting list was four years. Returning home, they found wispy Sarah dressed up in her best temple clothes waiting for the baby's arrival. She asked in Yiddish, "*Vu iz der kinda?*" (Where's the child?), not understanding that it wasn't as simple as going to the supermarket to pick up a loaf of bread.

My parents wished it were that simple too. They decided to go to another well-known agency in the hopes of a shorter wait, but they were shocked to find out from the social worker there that "Jewish parents cannot adopt Christian children." So back to Louise Wise they went, and the second part of their ordeal began. There were extensive interviews, parenting classes and home visits, to hear my mom describe it, more of an inquisition than a screening process. Ironically, the social worker, a black woman whom my mother very much liked, asked her how she would feel if she was given a black baby. My mom answered, "Well, since you're telling us to treat the child as our own, then I think a black child would have a hard time with that," she paused, "but I'd take one, yes." She left feeling like it was the end for them, that she'd ruined their chances by expressing any negativity, but much to her surprise, they were approved for the next phase.

The next big hurdle was their bank account. They had little money and adoption required lots of it. My parents would always struggle in this regard, but growing up, I had all the basics a child needed. When my father eventually transferred his real estate and insurance business from Bayside to Jericho, where they moved when my brother was three, they had high hopes. When business began to fizzle, they decided to go into retail together, buying The Card and Party Gallery in Rockville Center, New York. It was Hallmark at its finest. I loved working there on the weekends, and my dad would let me take home much of the seventies ephemera, tchotchkes and stuffed animals, more than he should have. He could never say no to me.

My dad ended up buying a second store when I was growing up, so their fortunes turned a bit for the better. The store was in a town called Locust Valley, land of ancestors from the Mayflower. He bought a longer gold chain for his Jewish Chai so it would hang under his shirt where no one could see it and took to wearing green, pink and plaids. It was the first time I learned that others may have prejudice against the Jewish people. Better to blend in than advertise, I guess my dad thought, worried that some of his clientele might not look favorably on a Jewish shopkeeper in their midst. While he might have been wrong, it was the first time in my life, at 13, I thought about what it meant to be Jewish. I looked at my religion as just a part of who I was before then, unquestioningly, which is easy when you live in a town were you are in the majority. The prejudice was uncomfortable to think about, but I didn't dwell on it. It was my father's devotion to Judaism that probably helped cement my own later in life. But the question of religion as birthright, being what you are because that is what you are born as, would be overturned for me with Albert's call.

$\mathcal{W}$ondering how they would get the cash to be eligible to adopt and knowing they would never ask my mother's father, they went to their good friends, Thelma and Seymour. A rotund and jolly couple that they met at their temple in Bayside, Thelma and Seymour said yes without hesitation. To clear the process, my parents had to pretend that the money was really theirs, that they had enough to support a child. It worked, and they gave it all back to Thelma and Seymour once the adoption was approved. My mom and dad were forever grateful. My mother still visits Thelma to this day and while she is sharp at 94 years old, she has no memory of this generous act that changed my parent's lives and my life forever.

The waiting game began, and that too was stressful. I was astounded to read in my mom's narrative that it was so unnerving that my dad moved out at one point. My mother was "convinced that it was the end of my marriage," because my father wasn't sure he even wanted to adopt anymore. She thought that he would find someone else to marry so he could have children, biological children.

After my dad moved out, my mother had to call Louise Wise. "Telling them to take us off the list was the hardest thing I had to do," she wrote. "I was so embarrassed to call our social worker after all we had gone through with them. I lied and told them that we had financial setbacks." She could not bear to tell them that my father had left her, which would have instantly disqualified them. She was despondent.

My father returned to her after three months of living apart; and of course I would not be here writing this tale if he did not. My parents' rabbi was the one to convince him. Clergy were the closest thing anyone had to therapists back then, a person to share your troubles with behind closed doors and hopefully get the advice you needed. The rabbi must have done a good job, because my dad not only returned to my mom, he also told her how deeply sorry he was, and that "he was ready, really ready." My mother, hurt yet happy, made *him* call the social worker to tell her, "We're okay now." Thankfully, the agency returned them to their original spot on the waiting list for babies.

Soon thereafter, in the fall of 1956, they got the call they had waited seven years to receive. The "We have a baby for you!" one. It was my brother

Oliver, named with an O for Oscar, my dad's father. They were bursting with happiness. But first they had to move to be eligible to take him home. Adopted babies had to have rooms of their own. So they scrambled to find a two-bedroom apartment to move into, something they could ill afford. But no matter what they had to do, they would make it happen.

Out of her intense joy, my mom called her parents in Miami, where they'd moved because her dad had retired. She hoped that he might have come around. "I was still seeking his validation," she told me. They hadn't spoken for years, and while my grandmother seemed genuinely happy with the news, she said, "Don't tell your father." Learning this, I had empathy for my grandmother as well that she had to abide by a man who distanced her from her daughter.

When my brother turned eighteen months old, my mother was finally legally allowed to take him out of state. She wanted to bring him to her parents, again hoping that my grandfather might have softened and still seeking his validation. She called her mother and asked if she could come. My grandmother told her that her dad said it was okay. She was thrilled.

"On the ride home from the airport, my father started in right away about us adopting, all the bad stuff…" my mother explained, "and Oliver could hear it all. Since he was starting to understand things, I was so upset." As soon as they arrived at the house, she called my dad to tell him. "He told me to turn around and come home," she told me, "that I didn't need to put up with that!" And that's what she did. I had to give my mother credit. I knew she was a strong woman, but I saw her then in an even brighter light. I was sure that it must have been horrendously painful for her, her father's rejection of the child they had wanted for so long.

Four years later, after going through the same difficult process and adopting me, she was still not speaking to her father. He came to New York on a business trip and surprised her with a phone call. They met for lunch, and he seemed pleasant and receptive for the first time. He actually offered to buy Oliver a bedroom set, as she and Sam had been unable to afford one yet, having just bought their home in Jericho. He wanted her to visit them in Florida again, this time with Oliver and me. She warned him that she would turn around and leave again "if he started in."

He promised her he wouldn't. "The first night there, I woke up to you crying in your crib. I got up, put on my robe and walked down the hall to check on you," she told me. "I stopped—there was my father, standing in your doorway, talking to you in the sweetest voice, trying to calm you. I knew at that point he had finally come around."

I pulled out my photo album recently and found the black and white pictures from that visit. There was one where I am standing on a chair between my grandmother and grandfather in front of their Florida home. I was wearing a white linen dress with cap sleeves that puffed out from the waist and black patent leather shoes; my mother had no doubt wanted me to look extra nice. I was holding both their hands, smiling. There were photos of my brother and grandparents too.

I showed the picture to my mother, wanting to know more about that day. She told me that she took them right before we left for the airport, and that her parents were both pleasant and accepting of Oliver and me. "And then three days later we got the call," she said, "that my dad had a massive heart attack and died." Isaac's moment of redemption came just in time, and with it, he gave my mother the most significant parting gift he ever could have given her, the one of acceptance of her adopted children.

Right after my parents adopted my brother, the agency told them they would have to wait four years before they could put in an application for a second child. They turned theirs in four years to the day. "We weren't very hopeful since we already had a child, and the waiting list was still long," she explained.

In November of 1960, just two months after submitting the paper work, the phone rang. It was Louise Wise. The second, "We have a baby for you!" call arrived, shocking them both.

When my parents arrived at Louise Wise to set their eyes on me for the first time, my mother told me that my father was utterly speechless. When he finally found his voice, he choked out in awe, "She's *beautiful…*" He refused to wait the mandatory twenty-four hour period required before parents could bring their baby home. Sending my mother out to put more change in the meter on East 92nd Street, he cajoled, argued and demanded, so much so that for the first time in the history of the agency, they gave in.

That day, Sam and Evelyn took home their second adopted child, the one they named Suzette, the one that was me.

Four

THE DAMAGE

In those months after Albert's call, I could no longer shut the Pandora's box inside me he had so cluelessly opened. All the shame I had locked inside me bubbled out and covered me like some toxic potion. A big part of this caustic brew was the question I could no longer suppress: "Who the hell am I?" Before I had not allowed this thought to seep in very far, but now I couldn't escape it. A huge psychological upheaval erupted inside me. The mixture of Albert's half-revealed facts and my parents' extreme outburst buzzed through my head each day: Arab, French, Florida, liar, weirdo, stalker, hair dresser, insane, ill. And if I was half Muslim, what did that mean? Did I now need to reevaluate my religious beliefs, seeing them solely as how I was raised rather than who I was? Given the history of the Arab-Jewish conflict, and my parents' strong Zionist bent, these issues were too complicated and anxiety provoking for me to even go there. I felt like I was just put on the opposing team in the Israeli-Arab Six Day War. Eighteen years old and vulnerable, I was not sure what to think anymore.

As I look back, I think of how Lifton poetically described what happened to me. She said that "found adoptees [as opposed to ones who initiate the search] are often still in their deep sleep, and thus not even there to be found." So once they are awakened, they might feel like they are "falling through a trapdoor of the self into the dark pit of unconsciousness, the one they had so painstakingly split off…to never be the same again." As much as I hated to admit it and as harsh as these words were, the description she wrote matched my experience all too well.

To make matters worse, what I didn't know then, but do know now, was that Albert called me at the worst time possible. I was in the psychologically critical stage of adolescent identity formation, which is a tough job for any teenager, especially without the extra complications of being an adoptee. On top of that, this happened to me during one of the most challenging times of this process, when a child leaves home to go to college. The rupture of the parental bond and the forced need for the child to achieve full independence can lead to immense vulnerability; children must figure out who they are in a world that is not only unfamiliar but with new unexpected pressures – to make friends (before social media existed), choose a career, and adapt to a completely new lifestyle.

It is not surprising then that Albert's call sent me into a tailspin; it was a time that could be difficult for anyone, even without the years of secrecy, stigma and shame I stuffed away and was then forced to confront.

Since as a study tool in college I liked to use acronyms, I came up with this one recently that summarized the ensuing D-A-M-A-G-E:

DEPRESSION: Sullen and withdrawn, I hid and studied for hours in the stacks of the libraries on campus. Their musty odor, hidden spaces, and dim lighting offered me solace, predictability, and a chance to crowd my mind with schoolwork thus helping me push away thoughts of Albert.

ANXIETY: I felt self-conscious around the peppy, confident, and fun-loving people I would have normally sought out. I stuck with the quieter types, the girls I didn't have to work hard to keep up with socially. It became easier to not like people before they might not like me. I became extra shy around guys I liked, finding myself at a loss for words.

MENSTRUATION: It stopped. "The lack of menses is part of your being so underweight," the doctor told me when I went to see him during my winter break. He didn't ask what caused my weight loss, not that I would have told him. I wasn't sure I understood it myself.

ALLOPECIA ARREATA: the medical term for hair loss, which I discovered when blow-drying my hair during Thanksgiving break. I stared in disbelief at a perfect silver dollar sized circle of flesh in the back of my head.

"Mommm, come heeere now! I'm freaking out!" I screamed from the bathroom. The doctor, behind his big mahogany desk polka dotted with lots of diplomas said, "We're not sure what causes it."

"Well, will it grow back?" I panicked.

"We don't know. Have you been under any stress?" Tears began to pool in my eyes. I told him, "Well, I just started college, and I'm a biology major…"

"Well that could do it," he shrugged, handing me a tube of useless cream.

GAUNT: How I looked. When I opened my dorm room door to welcome my parents for parent's weekend, my mom said after hugging me, "You look good, but wow, you got so thin! Don't you think so, Sam?" My dad looked me up and down and nodded his head yes, his face showing a hesitancy to think there could be anything wrong with me. I looked down at my form fitting sweater and jeans and didn't see what all the fuss was about.

"I don't know, yeah, maybe a little," I admitted. I didn't tell them I was on a mission to not gain the "freshman 15," an excuse for me to eat very little. When we went to the football game that weekend, where the tradition was having guys grab girls and lift them in the air to pass them up to the top of the stadium, the guys behind me asked me if I wanted to participate. "*Me?* Nooooo way!" I exclaimed. Plus, I thought it was reserved for shapely blonds, not petite thin brunettes. Well, my words held no weight, because I was grabbed, lifted, and propelled from person to person up to the top of the stadium, my body ironing board stiff and my brain terrified. On the way down, everyone was cheering; I was mortified. "Never saw a girl go up that fast," said the guy who first grabbed me. While the rest of the game was a blur, my speedy ascent stuck in my head.

Back at the dorm, I borrowed my across-the-hall neighbor's scale. The dial spun around and settled on 94 pounds on my 5'2" frame. I hadn't gained the "freshman 15"; I'd lost it.

ESTEEM: of the "self" kind that is. Looking back now, I can see how a lot of mine was destroyed.

In spite of all this, I knew I wanted to succeed in college. Dropping out was never an option for me. Trauma usually ends in a fight or flight response, and I chose to fight. Survival skills kicked in. I tried to shove the call and all that went with it back into the box where it was before.

I had no idea it could no longer fit.

Before my parents left that weekend, my mom looked at me and said, "You feeling all right, Suzie?"

"Yeah, of course. Why?"

"You just don't seem yourself, that's all," she said, "You seem kind of down...different."

I assured her I was okay. My dad ignored the exchange. They must have considered Albert's call, but no one mentioned his name. Instead, the call hung like a transparent flag flapping loudly right in front of us. And since my parents' flight was out of Detroit early the next morning, we simply kissed good-bye. When I pulled away, I noticed the deep grooves on their foreheads and worried concern in their gazes.

I clearly was not the master of disguise I thought I was.

When I arrived home for Thanksgiving break, three months after Albert's call, it wasn't to the suburban home I grew up in on Long Island. My parents had moved to central New Jersey, to a new over-55 condo community that sat in the middle of tomato farms and dark roadside bars with restaurants attached. The two Hallmark card shops my dad owned had taken a toll on him. He was a worrywart of epic proportions. My mom used to say, "if Dad had to shovel shit in the street, he's worry there wasn't enough shit to shovel." His nerves were shot.

So when my uncle offered him a desk job at his company, he took it. But the commute was two hours each way. So when I left for college, they packed up and moved to be near his job.

That short Thanksgiving break in New Jersey, and the breaks to come after, weren't ideal given the state I was in. I knew no one in that rural area and was far from the security and friendships of the town I grew up in. But I never thought to complain.

Gratitude was always my default mode as an adoptee. So I just felt happy to be back in the safety and security of my parent's nest.

It wasn't easy for my mom and dad to move either, leaving a town they loved. But my mom always seemed to know that life wasn't about getting what you want but wanting what you get, the self-proclaimed "everlasting optimist." My dad was just relieved to not have to keep pushing the pedal to the metal, walking in to our home covered in the ash of the cigarettes he smoked, pouring the same Scotch on the rocks with a splash of milk, to soothe his ulcer, as he always did before.

My dad had his first major heart attack over the summer following my freshman year. It occurred in the middle of the night. I was sleeping soundly in my bedroom that sat across from theirs in the condominium in New Jersey they had moved to. When the paramedics arrived, my mother shushed them to be as quiet as possible so they wouldn't wake me. I woke up anyway when I heard voices and movement in the hallway. Opening the door, the paramedics looked up at me with startled faces while they were wheeling my father past my door. My mother said in almost a whisper, "Dad's having some chest pain…he's okay…I didn't want to wake you. Just go back to sleep…"

I stared at her in disbelief.

"*What?* Are you *kidding* me?" I blurted out. "Give me the keys! I'm driving us to the hospital!" Thankfully, my father survived.

And when my dad had his second heart attack, a massive one, during my sophomore year, he lay in the ICU at death's door for weeks, but they didn't tell me because "we didn't want to worry you," they explained. I found out after that my dad cajoled the nurses each week into wheeling his bed down the hallway to the payphone for our Sunday night phone calls, all the while attached to IV bags and tubes. He told them, "If you don't take me, I'll pull everything out and go myself." Nothing in his voice on the phone with me ever gave away the dire circumstances of his health.

Perhaps after Albert, they couldn't bear giving me anything else to worry about.

Back at school, taking a class in sociobiology brought new gyrations. It was all about how people try to maximize their genes in today's modern world, Darwin's theories still alive and well. Some of it was pretty controversial, but there were a number of pages in the textbook, one my professor had written, on adoptees. It said that adoptees, who represent a unique case, will act as if their genes were the same as their adoptive families, so they will mimic the "enhancing behaviors" to their relatives. Basically, this meant adoptees will support and be there for their adoptive family as if they were their biological one. While this theory seemed right, in spite of my being a real-life case example, I did not think to raise my hand or say a word to my professor after class.

The secret of my adoption continued to stay buried deep. I was still years away from coming out.

Five

THE WAY IT WAS

I'm seven years old with a bowl-and-bangs haircut, shorts and a cropped top, playing outside. It's 1967 and modest two-story colonial and split-level houses are set back from the sidewalks on small well-manicured yards. It's a warm and balmy summer night, not yet dark. A game of kickball is in progress in the street and all the kids from the block are there. Parents are tucked away in their houses, moms washing up dinner dishes while dads lounge on recliners puffing on cigarettes, watching Ed Sullivan. Their presence isn't needed outside because bad things didn't happen in places like that yet.

I remember it like this: Jay, a tall and gangly boy, pedals his bike over to us. He lives on one of the connecting streets, which is almost a whole other universe to me. "Can I play?" he asks, setting his bike down on the cement curb.

He and the older kids argue back and forth about why he can't, because the game was already underway and games were not to be taken lightly. Jay's not happy, and when I jump in to offer my own rejection, his anger boils over.

"Your parents aren't your real parents and your brother isn't your real brother."

"*What?*"

"You heard me!"

"That isn't true!" I yell, horrified.

"Oh, yes it is. It sure is."

I freeze at Jay's assurance. *What could he be talking about?*

My brain starts to short circuit as if the wires were unplugging from a switchboard. Without saying another word and certainly without looking over at my friends, I turn and run as fast as my sneakers can carry me. My spindly legs leap up the three concrete steps and I push open the front door with all the force I can muster. Racing across the tiled floor, I scream for my parents. At the sound of my panicked voice, they hurry to me. I am weeping loudly as I blurt out what Jay said, knowing they would reassure me that his ridiculous words weren't true.

Both my parents wrap their arms around me, and their embrace gives me some temporary comfort. But I know instantly something isn't right. Their faces look pained and suddenly both my mom and dad start to speak in a torrent of words. I don't remember much. No doubt the story was wrapped and tied with a beautiful bow about how both my brother and I came to them from other mothers and fathers who could not take care of us -- but without any mention of whom those parents were. What I do remember is their simple reassurance that yes, my brother is my brother and that they are my parents in spite of the fact that I was adopted.

After the penetrating shock of their confession, my heart filled with relief, but I'm confused. Even though my parents said Jay was wrong, that it didn't change anything, he was right too, and in some incredibly disturbing way.

At the end, my father added, "and the rest is nobody's business."

I shook my head yes, looking up into his comforting eyes.

His words gave me relief. They meant I never had to speak of this truth again.

But if I could not talk about it, what did that mean? Was it something bad?

It must be.

I felt shame.

I left the kitchen, to go where I don't remember. Probably up the shag covered steps to my room, to be surrounded by the things that made me feel secure.

I made a decision to not think about it, to push it all away in some dark forbidden space in my child's mind where it couldn't hurt me. My parents were 100% my parents and that was all there was to it.

The next time I pulled the door open to go play with the neighborhood kids, I was nervous. Were they all going to look at me differently now? Would they have sympathy or just be glad that they themselves weren't like me, someone who was *adopted*?

No one said a word.

From then on, being adopted became my secret.

I was now different from every other kid I knew. And feeling different in childhood is never good, no matter what that difference is.

Days later, I was playing on the front lawn. Our next-door neighbor's paneled station wagon pulled up into their driveway. Mom walked across our lawn, the sun beating down, to greet her good friend Ruby. I watched them chat and saw mom smile and hug her. Walking back after a few minutes, she said to me with a huge smile, "The rabbit died... Ruby's pregnant!" I smiled too. Ruby's daughter Leslie was my best friend, so we would now have a baby brother or sister to play with. That sounded great.

But then I wondered about that rabbit situation. If my mom never had a rabbit die too, did that upset her? It never dawned on me to think that there was a woman out there who actually did.

Of course, I did not say a word.

When baby Laura was born, everyone announced, "She looks just like Ruby!" Their faces all beamed, filled with the wonder and power of genetics. I beamed too.

Who did I look like, I wondered?

As I grew up, my mom played the upright piano in my living room beautifully, while I was one of the few in fourth grade to fail the flutophone test for musical ability. I excelled in art while neither she nor my father could draw a straight line. I never allowed myself to go there.

For everyone else, making such comparisons was natural as the air they breathed. For our family, for many adoptees from the closed system for that matter, it was the elephant in the room. And even if my parents wanted to make a comparison to my birth parents, they weren't even allowed to know who they were.

When people would comment on how my brother was so tall and I was so small, for me, it wasn't the comment that was so bad actually, but the conspiratorial glances, reddened faces, and fake smiles my parents, brother and I, exchanged in response to them. "Yeah, well…." one of us inevitably answered, and would then change the subject.

My father's earlier words would always echo in my ears: "It's no one's business." I never even thought to ask why that was.

The closed system created what Lifton describes as a "conspiracy of silence" amongst family members, or what I liken to as an unspoken set of rules. "The conspiracy didn't have to be agreed upon verbally," she states, "but was unconsciously communicated. It demanded loyalty and submission by the adopted child. Any natural curiosity a child might have about their biological parents was suppressed. To ask about the biological parents," she continued, "the child would fear putting the love of the adoptive parents at risk."

The child goes into what she calls the "adoption fog or sleep," or what Joe Soll refers to as a "state of limbo" in his book *Adoption Healing*. In that state, "the child not only cuts themselves off from any thoughts or feelings they might have on the matter, *they don't even know they have them.*" The adoptee "may appear just fine…both for her parents who she doesn't want to disappoint by being unhappy and for herself, so that she can continue to repress that big ball of emotion. Later in life, it will be very difficult for the adoptee to talk about it because this fabric of tangled emotions is so painful and so difficult to unravel."

The summer after fourth grade, I actually decided to test the waters with my secret, the one and only time. At camp, walking the path side to side to our bunk, I confided in my best friend, Diane.

"I have a secret that I can *never* tell anyone about."

"Really, why?" she asked.

"Because I just can't, ever…"

I held her stare for a second or two and then had to look away. And while I felt empowered for that brief moment, I was relieved that she did not press further, not that I would have confessed. I felt that somehow if I told, people would never look at me the same, much like Hester Prynne in the Scarlet Letter, and it would be irrevocable.

⟜⟶

*T*he secrecy that defined the closed adoption system, that conspiracy of silence that encircled us all, played out in my little suburban neighborhood in many other ways, I'd learn as an adult. My neighbor, Cindy, and I played a lot. Barbie dolls and cartwheels on the lawn was the order of the day. She was adopted too, but I never knew. Her mom knocked on my door when they moved in and said to my mom, "I heard your kids are adopted… so are mine, but they don't know…so please never say anything."

My mom was in shock that someone from the neighborhood had filled her in on this fact.

"My kids know," she responded, "but I'd never say anything of course."

I lost touch with Cindy after we moved away, so to this day I don't know if she ever learned the truth.

One of my mom's best friends, Marilyn, lived around the corner. She had a son who was also adopted. He did not know it either. His parents told him when he was an adult. Marilyn shared the story with my mother. He reacted with such intense anger that he did not talk to his parents for years.

An adopted friend confided to me recently, "my parents told me that my biological parents died in a car accident when I was born." She, of course, accepted this lie, but her birth mother called her when she was twenty-three, exposing the true story.

Learning about my secret early, even if it wasn't discussed again, was much better than being lied to or not knowing at all. At least I had the truth.

My first life memory is of the night before kindergarten. Not being able to remember how to spell my name, I sit in the living room and cry. "Mommy, how could you give me such a long name? I can't spell it…what will I do when the teacher asks?"

"She won't make you."

But I don't believe her, so I made her practice with me over and over. In first grade, I made flash cards to remember my spelling words. One day the entire year's cards came tumbling out of my school bag. The other children looked on in amazement. "You keep all those cards?" said one girl. My embarrassment led to panic and fear. "Yeah, but I don't look at them. I just keep them there." I scooped them up as fast as I can.

As long as I can remember, I wanted to do well in school and make my parents proud, to be a good girl.

It might have been part of my natural inclination, I don't know, but I believe being adopted certainly egged it along. I was not alone either. This desire to be the "good adoptee," I later learned, was a common response to being adopted. "She is likely to be acquiescent, a people pleaser, a grateful daughter, happy go-lucky teen, but inside she is confused and needs help," Soll wrote.

"Can you keep quiet? I'm trying to study!" I'd yell to my mom from over the iron railing upstairs outside my bedroom door. I was in junior high. In the early evenings or on Sundays, her friends would often stop by for a coffee and cigarette, and their voices were loud. I needed to get straight A's.

"You're your own worst enemy," my mom used to tell me of my growing perfectionism.

Maybe deep inside, I was afraid I could be given back.

Stomachaches would come and go, with no apparent reason. Doctors would say I had a "spastic stomach," probably from nerves. No one, including me, thought to consider a possible connection between the growing pressure I put on myself and being adopted. The impact it might have had was simply not on anyone's seventies' radar screen.

The flip side of the equation, across from the "good adoptee" like me, was the "bad one," those who acted out. Some doctors, confronted with the most extreme cases at the time, actually believed there was an "adopted child syndrome," a controversial term even back then. It was said to cause attachment disorders, defiance of authority, and in more limited cases, acts of violence.

I remembered when the notorious serial killer David Berkowitz, Son of Sam, terrorized Long Island in the late 1970s. His dark blank eyes peered out at me from the cover of Newsday one day. It said that he was adopted. It sent a shiver down me, when I saw that in print, that I might have anything in common with him.

The defense lawyers used this "adopted child syndrome," in his defense.

Years later, I read on the internet that serial killers in the United States are twice as likely to be adoptees than are present in the general population, according to Mirah Riben author of *Shedding Light on the Dark Side of Adoption*. They include Joel Rifkin, Ted Bundy, and the "Hillside Strangler" Kenneth Bianchi, among others. And while of course these examples are the most extreme of the extreme, and adoption only one small piece of the myriad genetic and environmental influences that can lead a human being to commit such horrific acts, Riben concludes that in criminology, "because some adopted persons deal with these very real issues of loss, abandonment, rejection, and anger, we cannot ignore their existence as contributing factors when an adopted person commits murder." Heavy stuff.

When my parents sat my brother down and told him he was adopted, he answered, "Is that it?" and went off and played. It was barely a blip on his radar. He never brought it up again, and we never talked about it to each other growing up. He told me as an adult that he never cared about being adopted. "We had mom and pop so..." Whether that was the brainwashing of the closed system or he truly did not care, I do not know. But knowing my brother like I do, I imagine it was the latter.

I recently had dinner with a new friend who adopted two children in the 1970s, a boy and a girl. She then went on to have a biological son. Her adopted son was troubled as an adolescent, and she did everything within her power to help him. Sadly, once an adult, he slowly severed his ties with her and his siblings even though they tried hard to keep up a relationship. Needless to say, it broke her heart. As of now, they are fully estranged.

When his 35th birthday came a few years back, she told me she decided to call him to wish him a happy birthday, to reach out in this small way. When he didn't pick up, she left a message. He emailed her back to say, "If you knew me at all you would know I hate my birthday…not a celebration of being born, but a reminder of the family I didn't chose and the one I didn't get to know…"

That stabbed at my heart. I can't imagine how much it stabbed at hers. Obviously this was a man in pain about his adoption experience and on the opposite end of the spectrum from my brother and me, as well as so many other adoptees I knew. But he isn't alone. There are others out there like him, and they've formed several grassroots activist organizations, including Parents for Ethical Adoption Reform, Origins-USA, and Concerned United Birthparents. Some call themselves adoption reformers. Others prefer terms such as "adoption truth advocate." A few will come straight out and say they're anti-adoption. That said, very few of these activists claim that adoption shouldn't be an option at all, but they believe that adoption is far from the perfect win-win situation it was so long perceived to be. They fight for fair and ethical adoption laws, policies, and practices for all the parties involved.

"I would rather see us live in a society where we say to struggling pregnant women, 'Okay you have a problem, we should try to fix the whole situation, rather than remove the child and leave the mother in crisis'" says Claudia Corrigan D'Arcy, one of these online activists for adoption reform. Her words make sense. Mothers relinquish children because of a lack of resources rather than a lack of love. If you can help a birth mother to keep her child, that would be the most ideal solution. But Ms. D'Arcy also admits, "I do understand that there are times when children must be removed from their biological families for real reasons, and that is a terrible tragedy that a child should never suffer."

But many do, like the children who end up in places like the Pleasantville Cottage School.

*W*hile secrecy shrouded my adoption, my parents had still another secret: my biological father Albert called the adoption agency looking for me when I was two. He said he was doing estate planning and wanted to include his daughter in his will. The director knew it was a ruse to find my whereabouts and wanted to warn my parents. She assured them that there was no way possible he could ever have access to my records.

Albert wrote the agency a letter after that inquiry, one that the agency copied and shared with my parents, that said, "Louise Wise cannot tell me what I can and cannot do." Of course, his name was blacked out, so my parents couldn't even consider contacting him to have some kind of meaningful discussion. They actually asked Louise Wise if they could have his name, but the social worker was adamant when she said no.

My mother confessed, "From that time forward, we were afraid, waiting for the other shoe to drop," meaning it would only be a matter of time before Albert found me and entered all of our lives.

"What were you so afraid of?" I asked her as I started writing this narrative. We were driving to the movies from her condo in Florida one night. I wanted to get to the bottom of it.

"That our lives would never be the same," she said with anguish and a sense of doom, thus meaning that their lives would be a lot worse. "And dad thought he'd lose you."

"Lose me, lose me? Like I wouldn't be his daughter anymore?"

"Yes, he even said once, 'She might not go shopping with me anymore.'"

I thought back to our mid-week shopping jaunts, where he delighted in taking me to department stores after we finished supper. He'd pull clothes off the racks to show me, and even though I usually said "Yuck," or "Gross," he never gave up. When I found something I liked, he made me come out of the dressing room to show him. His face always beamed, and he'd say "gorgeous!" no matter how ill fitting the garment was.

Did he feel insecure about his place with me his entire life? I hated to think it.

"He didn't get it that no matter what happened with Albert nothing would change between us?" I asked her in disbelief.

"I did, but he didn't." I found out he was not unlike other adoptive parents from the era who became very irrational in this regard. "It's common to worry that our kids will seek reunions with their birth parents and then desert us altogether," Marilyn Schoettle wrote about adoptive parents in *The Adoptee Search: Looking for the Missing Piece.*

Due to this fear, my father, in fact, was the proverbial ostrich with his head in the sand. He never brought up my adoption to me, not once, in all the years of his life until he passed at 85 years old. He could never even mention the word when I was grown, let alone have a meaningful conversation.

"So *you* never felt that way?" I asked my mom.

"No." I was skeptical. While she might not have feared losing me completely like my dad, being forced to create a new blended family of sorts, where she would have to share her daughter with a stranger, I am sure was frightful to her. But it was okay if she didn't want to admit it. My mother, always the rock, my rock, was not exposing any vulnerability, at least not yet.

The fear my parents lived with played out in other ways. Mom elaborated on the comment she made right after his call to me at college: "We checked him out…he's a hairdresser." It ends up that she, my dad, and two couples they were friends with, drove to Albert's hair salon in Miami one day to see what they were dealing with. This was right after he called them when I was a senior in high school.

My parents were hesitant to enter, so one of the wives, Marian, offered to do it. Marian, quite the pistol, must have marched in there head held high, concocting some story with dramatic flare about needing to find Albert. As it ends up, Albert went by the name "Pierre" at the salon, because when he was hired, there was another Albert who had left the salon who had a bad reputation. So the owner asked Albert to go by a different name, to which he agreed. I thought it a bit strange to go your entire life with two different names, but he didn't seem to think so. And of course, I imagine this was the reason Marian left disappointed when they said, "no Albert here." He could have possibly been standing just a few feet away.

My mother confessed to me recently that Sy, the man who lent my parents the money for Oliver's adoption, offered to "hire a hit man to take care of Albert." He was in the metal plating business and told her "he knew some people." Also, our neighbor across the street Marty, a close friend who was employed in the garment industry, told my parents he too "knew some guys," my mom assumed Mafia, "who could at least break his legs if they wanted." Even if both men weren't *really* serious, behind their offers was the obvious evidence of my parents' distraught mental state and the wish that Albert would just disappear.

Albert actually found me when I was in the eleventh grade, thus accomplishing Mission Impossible. I asked him point blank recently, "How'd you actually do it?" He said that a lawyer friend of his, sympathetic to his cause, "went to some bureau or another on my behalf," and that together they "worked hard at it for years." A sympathetic judge eventually relented and told the lawyer who I had become. He did not remember any more details, so given his fuzzy recollection, and knowing that thousands of adoptees today in New York are still trying without success to do what he did, I have to imagine there is more to the story. In any event, it was an incredible feat to accomplish in a day when parents were guaranteed complete anonymity by law.

When I was in twelfth grade, only six months or so before he called me in my dorm room, the phone rang one Friday night at my home in Jericho. It was then that all my parents' fears became a reality. "I'll never forget it," my mom told me, sitting in her Florida condo at the age of 84. "I got a call from someone named Rachel at 5 pm. Dad wasn't home from work yet. I knew immediately when I heard this strange voice that it had to do with you. She told us Albert had found you, and was going to call that night, preparing us." It was the call she had dreaded for fifteen years.

"I hung up, really afraid, panicked, because I knew you'd be coming home. You arrived with a group of friends to change your clothes for the night. Dad walked in from work right after. You went up to your room with them, and I put down dad's dinner, not wanting to say anything while you were home. He kept asking, 'Is something wrong?' He knew me so well. So I told him quickly while you were upstairs. His face turned white. Then you and your friends came running down the steps, and you all ran out the front door. Literally two minutes after the door slammed, the phone rang. It was Albert. I couldn't believe the timing."

He told my mom he was going to call me when I turned 18, that it was his right. And that, after all, "she could end up marrying her own half brother or sister otherwise," he argued.

"Can you imagine?" she said and rolled her eyes. Mom pleaded with him not to call me, because I'd be adjusting to school. "We were just trying to buy time," she said with a clenched face. "We knew that no matter what, he'd never stay out of your life."

I imagined the scene playing out in my childhood home. Me, in my Huck-a-poo blouse and bell-bottom jeans, running down the burnt orange shag carpeted steps with a herd of my friends and out the door, the screen door slamming. Albert calling and them speaking to him with an authority that was masking their terror. Them hanging up their receivers on separate phones in shock. My father joining my mother in the kitchen where he pours himself a double Scotch. My mom striking a match and lighting a cigarette while her hands are shaking, inhaling deep.

"What the hell are we going to do?" she asks him in the haze of smoke from her Virginia Slim.

The next day, now frantic, they called the high school to warn them that Albert could show up there. I wonder to this day if there were teachers and staff keeping an extra close eye on me. Of course, I was oblivious to all of it. While Albert never did appear, he did manage to secure a copy of my yearbook so he could see my graduation photo. My parents never got over that one when they found out, furious at the school for years.

He recently announced to me, "You know, when you were back in high school, I got your yearbook!" his face beaming with a devilish pride.

"You sure did," was all I could think to answer.

⌐⌐

Looking back now, the adoption fog served its purpose well over all those years until I got to college. I can remember sitting at my desk one day during my senior year in high school and writing a poem, something I liked to do. I don't remember the specific words, but I do remember the title:

"What Can Be Better than Life at 17?" So in spite of all that was suppressed, in my "adoption sleep," I was happy.

But one day that spring, my parents came over to me and said, "We need to talk." I sat down next with them at the kitchen table, my eyes were open wide, curious as to what they might have to say.

"I was wondering if you have any questions you want to ask me about, you know, being... *adopted?*" my mom asked. It was the only time, at least that I can remember, that she ever brought it up. The word came forth from her quivering lips with such a hushed tone of seriousness that my chest squeezed and my insides clenched. I knew inside she was just trying to be a responsible parent, but it felt as if she wanted to walk me into some dark cave where scary ghosts lived. There was no way I was entering.

She told me that Albert had called and that he might try to contact me in college. She wanted to prepare me. But, and this is the crazy part, that day when Albert called me in the dorm room, I had no memory of her telling me. It was if he had called out of the blue. It reminded me of what my writing teacher Cullen once said—that memory is not only a fluid thing that allows us to see things how we want to see them, "but it is also sometimes lost to us because we do not wish to see at all."

What I do remember is that I looked down at the faux marble pattern on our kitchen table, shifted in my chair, and said, "No questions, Mom... I'm fine, really fine." I wanted to remove myself as fast as possible from the conversation.

I asked her recently what I said after that. "I'll never forget," she recalled. "You looked at dad and said, 'Let's go shopping.'"

"Shopping?"

"Yes, so we thought you didn't care." My mouth was agape. But it wasn't surprising that I would want to escape and do the thing I loved most with my dad, that he loved most. "I guess I just couldn't deal," I said.

The truth was none of us could.

The next day, trying to push my mother's words out of my head, where they were still ringing, I pulled out my paisley-covered journal hidden in the bottom drawer of my desk where I copied my favorite poems with a calligraphy pen. I would read them every so often, when I felt introspective or down, taking in their lovely prose and universal truths, from Frost to Whitman to Browne. They calmed me somehow, by connecting me to something greater than myself, perhaps because I was a deep-thinking adolescent as many are, but perhaps also because I was unsure of my own place.

I read a few of them, put the book down and headed down the stairs. "Mom, I'm going out for a bit. I'll be home soon...just want to get out a little."

Throwing on my coat, I drove off to a bay beach on the north shore that I hadn't been to in a long time. Something inside me wanted to look out at the water, which I knew would have a calming affect. Pulling into the empty dirt parking lot, the car bounced across the small rocks and potholes. Where the sand started, I slipped off my clogs and socks and picked them up. I walked along the pebbly beach taking in the expanse ahead. The wind blew my hair across my face, and I deeply breathed in the briny air. I sat down on a smooth patch of sand and spotted a small round and shiny rock. Picking it up, I rolled it through my fingers, the damp sand granules tickling my skin, while my thoughts circulated fast.

A damp breeze blew hard, chilling me, and I wrapped my coat tighter around me and curled my arms around my legs. I sat and watched the waves spread out on the shore, creating small detergent like bubbles over the decaying seaweed, and then flow back again with their predictable mesmerizing rhythm.

I looked up at the overcast sky, and I asked myself, *Who am I really?*

Six

JAZZ NOTES AND A PLAN

*D*riving on to the campus of the Pleasantville Cottage School for the second time, after my initial visit for the temple party, I stopped at the small brick gatehouse at the entrance and told the bearded man inside the purpose of my visit. "I'm here for an orientation with Phina Geiger," I said. The gate lifted, and I proceeded down the wooded road to where I could eventually see the identical cream-colored stucco buildings emerge between the barren trees, the "cottages" that the children lived in, the ones I took in the last time.

This time however, I slowed down. I leaned over the steering wheel to examine them more closely: the thick white columns in front, the tile inlay that formed large decorative squares along the top floor and the carved white wood trellis that sat under the rooflines. It became evident to me that the Jewish philanthropists who built this place put a lot of time, thought, and money into its construction and design.

Once parked, I turned to take in the campus from this central vantage point. It was an expansive and open grassy square with the residential buildings placed evenly around the perimeter, facing onto it. An American flag flapped above me. I thought to myself this could be a military compound, or a camp of sorts, if you didn't know better.

Approaching the massive dark metal trellis door of the large Administration Building, I saw the letters HSGS inscribed on top, not yet knowing what they meant. Inside, Phina, the director of volunteers, was waiting for me for the orientation she had planned. A petite woman with short side-swept hair, she wore thick-framed oval glasses and a colorful scarf matched only by her bright and welcoming smile.

"I can't thank you enough for starting this volunteer group," she said to me. "Who would've thought that I would've gotten another group out of that lunch?" It was just a month earlier at a UJA-Federation lunch, an agency that I had been involved with since moving to Westchester, that I had been so taken with the words spoken by two girls from the Pleasantville campus. They were brought there by Phina to speak about the value of volunteers in their lives. The luncheon was to honor these volunteers, a small group of women who were going at lunchtime every couple of months, since UJA-Federation helped to support the campus financially under their large umbrella of agencies.

The girls stood before the podium microphone. One girl, tall and lanky, turned her gaze downward while Phina introduced her; the other, heavy set with streaks of dyed burgundy hair, stood to the side nervously looking over the large group of seated women.

"We love when the volunteers come," said the first girl into the microphone while tugging on her ill-fitting dress. "They make our day and make us feel special."

"They do fun things with us, and we look forward to them coming. They care about us," the second girl added, reading from a sheet of paper she unfolded.

I looked away briefly from the speaker dais and around the room: the crystal chandeliers, the crisp white tablecloths and the elegant china embossed with the country club's name. What could these girls be thinking, watching elegantly dressed guests being served by men and women in uniforms who wordlessly placed salmon fillets and tied-up asparagus bundles on their plates? This is a world the girls did not know and probably never would. The dichotomy of it, who we were and who they were, stuck to my ribs in discomfort, along with the saffron rice.

At the end of lunch, I approached Phina, smoothing my grey suit. "Phina, you remember me right? I was at the holiday party with the temple. Can I start a group of my own and come as well?" I was so moved by the girl's words of appreciation that I knew that this was the opportunity I was waiting for to be an actual continued presence on the campus. "Are you kidding, I'd be thrilled!" she said. Once home, I went right to my computer and emailed the following to a number of friends.

Hi Guys: some of you are aware of the Pleasantville Cottage School just a few miles from our homes. For those of you who don't know, it's a campus you have probably passed hundreds of times and not realized. Living there are over 250 boys and girls from the inner city who come from the worst kind of poverty, abuse and neglect. I'd love to get a group together to start volunteering there once a month to brighten their lives a little. Would you join me?

The emails came back, a yes from ten out of ten.

Phina led us up a staircase to a conference room on the second floor for our orientation. She thanked us for our willingness to volunteer. Explaining the history of the campus as a Jewish orphanage, she told us that in the sixties, due to the dwindling number of orphans combined with a child-care crisis in the city, the agency opened itself up to *all* children, regardless of faith or color. This decision, I would later come to understand, was made by the directors at that time based on the Jewish mandate of *tikkun olam*, Hebrew for "to heal the world." And that means everyone.

Once it became open to all, the state started giving funds to the agency, Phina explained. "Who's this *agency*?" I asked.

"Oh, the JCCA, the Jewish Child Care Association. This is the group that runs our campus...they have lots of other programs too." They had over thirty of them, I'd soon discover, everything from foster care to mental health programs to day care, spread throughout the five boroughs, serving the most needy populations of New York. Today there are over 16,000 children and families in their care.

Phina went on to explain, "Many of our youth have been in and out of foster care homes and have not been successful," she said. "They need too much help." The three programs on the campus were Pleasantville Cottage, Edenwald, and Diagnostic. Diagnostic was where children were placed for shorter-term assessment (now called START), Pleasantville for the children with IQs above 70, and Edenwald for those who fell below. Soon they would add Gateways, the first residential program for commercially and sexually exploited children, some as young as 11 and 12. It is commonly referred to as CSEC.

On that last point, it wasn't until the passage of the Safe Harbor Act in 2008 by then Governor David Paterson that children under the age of 16 who were engaged in prostitution were finally seen as victims rather than criminals. With this long overdue law, these girls would be given state protection and social services rather than placed in jails and detention halls. With its passage, the JCCA stepped in to construct Gateways, the first and only residential program that exists in New York State today. It is transforming lives every day.

"Are any of the children happy to come here?" my friend Lisa asked.

"Some are, sure, for the first time they can sleep at night. But most aren't. They never wanted to leave their families to begin with, even if they were abused or neglected." I thought of the movie Shiloh, where the beagle keeps returning to his owner who kicks and starves him. "It's all these children know," she added, "It's better to belong to someone than to no one at all." We all looked at each other with somber faces.

Years later, I came to better understand this concept of belonging. It is an all-important human need that most of us take for granted, including me. The incredible author Brene Brown said it best, "We're biologically, cognitively, physically, and spiritually wired to love, to be loved, and *to belong*. When these needs are not met, we don't function as we were meant to. We break. We fall apart. We numb. We ache. We hurt others. We get sick." That in a nutshell, described the Cottage School kids well.

"How long do they stay?" my former college roommate Nancy who now lived nearby asked.

"The average stay is two years," Phina said, "and to place them afterward, the social workers work hard to get them back to their homes, or if that's not possible, to another relative or another foster care family..."

"Wait, I don't get it," I said, "why would you return them to a parent who was abusive."

"Well, we wouldn't, but the JCCA works with the *family* too. The goal is to help the parent get better so that they can get their child back." Many of the parents suffer from mental illness or with substance abuse, so they too desperately need help.

I'd later learn that in the early days of child welfare, the goal was to remove the child for good and work with him or her in isolation, thinking that was the best method to help them heal. But now we know differently. Ideally, a child would always be returned to a parent because it is now understood that the loss of a parent is one of the most traumatic and distressing experiences that a child can undergo, even if that parent was abusive or neglectful.

Studies show the intense grief of being removed from one's home can be unbearable. In Meeting the Challenges of Contemporary Foster Care, the author's state, "Children in care face enormous emotional and psychological challenges as they try to adjust to new and often changeable environments. Within three months of placement, many children exhibit signs of depression, aggression, or withdrawal. The loss can stunt development, lead to feelings of instability and a loss of control." So JCCA and other social service agencies do their best to put services into the home to keep children with their family if at all possible. By providing wrap around therapeutic and medical services to *all* family members, a preventative services model is now seen as the best course of action. If that doesn't work or if the abuse is putting a child at risk, the child is then of course removed.

Due to this new philosophy, the number of children in foster care in New York State has decreased from 53,902 children in 1995 to 20,539 as of December 31, 2012. There are still plenty of children who cannot stay in their homes, and for them, foster care is the answer. Done right, it can have positive outcomes too; many foster parents provide wonderful environments for children, and children can and do thrive there. It is often the best solution to a difficult and heartbreaking problem. The same can be said for residential care as I have witnessed at the Cottage School. Placing a child in an environment where there are few choices, lots of structure, and plenty of therapeutic care can be the right choice for the child that is unable to function in society.

"While we help them heal, in the end, it's still an institution," Phina continued, "and that's where you guys come in." I smiled. I saw my friends' faces perk up as well. The mood in the room lifted.

"You see, everyone they know in the system so far has been paid to take care of them. As volunteers, you're here because you *want to be.* You let them know that people care about them and want to help for no reason other than they matter. Even though the amount of time you spend here is short, it means an enormous amount to them. You're also role models, showing them there's a better way to be."

I hadn't thought of that. What role models could they have had during their childhoods? I took for granted that my mom and dad taught me those essential life lessons: that I have value in this world and that I'm worthy of love, through their praise, their hugs and their support. If no one had taught or demonstrated this to them, how would they know it?

When Phina told us that we would be placed in Cottage 10, home to the most emotionally fragile girls, we asked if we would learn their individual stories. She told us no. Legally, their privacy needed to be protected. She added that "you really don't want to know anyway…are better off not…since the stories are horrible."

"What if they can't find anyone to take a child that's here?" one of the women in the group asked.

"They usually do. If the parents relinquish rights though, the children are put up for *adoption.*"

And there, in that moment, my first deeply personal connection to the children at the Cottage School was made. I suddenly felt a kinship with them, albeit a weird one, knowing that there was a huge and painful difference: these children were older, traumatized, and in and out of foster care. Their chance for a blissful childhood was long gone. I had won the adoptive parents lottery with Evelyn and Sam as my parents. I knew before that I was lucky. Now that took on a new level of meaning.

I left the orientation meeting, my mind abuzz with all this new information as I headed to the local Starbucks. The soft lights and upholstered chairs, the jazz notes that filled the air, and the deep aroma of roasted coffee seemed as far removed from the Cottage School as possible. A feeling of immense gratitude overcame me for the freedom of even being able to walk into a Starbucks and buy whatever I wanted, plus having a car to take me there.

Everything I just heard at orientation whirled in my head. So did the newly realized connection to my own beginnings even though I was beyond fortunate to be spared the path the children at the Cottage School endured.

Inspired by Phina's words, I started to formulate a plan for how our group might contribute. I thought it would be a good idea to pick the dates for the entire year in advance, increasing the likelihood that we could all be there. And because I wanted to make it as easy as possible, I figured that this could best be accomplished by assigning one person to each month; whoever that person was would be responsible for bringing everything. That way the other volunteers could just show up without anything else to think about. I thought of the line from *Field of Dreams*, "Build it and they will come," and replaced it with "Keep it easy and they will come," and smiled.

I suggested we bring a lunch, a craft, game or activity to do with the children, a birthday cake, and a gift for the children who were celebrating that month. We would also bring a small gift for each child, so no one in the cottage would walk away empty handed. I grinned - a veritable birthday party - not unlike those my parents threw for me, I threw for my own kids and I had attended for so many others. The ones that made a child feel special.

Once home and happy with all the details, I typed up my initial plan, a calendar, a "to bring" list, and contact numbers, and I emailed them to everyone. They all seemed good with it, so I was pleased.

My first cottage volunteer group, or "lunch bunch," as it was later called, was ready to go.

Seven

A Geographical Cure

By the time junior year of college arrived, I was ready for a break or possibly, an escape, from the demands of being a biology major, the Michigan snow and cold, the last two summers stuck in rural New Jersey, and most of all, from a place where the rest of my identity, and with it my self-worth, was still locked up tight two years after Albert's call.

Escape was easy, especially when I was headed for an adventure. I arrived in the City of Lights for the now common junior year semester abroad, but back then one of my housemate's boyfriend and I were the only ones I knew doing such a thing. Just a few days before I was to leave for France, Albert's accented voice blew into my thoughts with a stronger gust than usual. One of my mother's other comments also reverberated in my head:

"Any dog can make a baby. It's the raising that counts."

She was right of course.

But knowing now that Albert had wanted to raise me, his words echoed in my head: "I wanted to keep you," he said, "but I wasn't allowed. Fathers had no rights then." And with this knowledge, a wave of guilt grew inside me. My conscience said, "Go there," which meant contacting him. It was time.

I wrote him a letter telling him I was fine since we last communicated, but reiterating not to call me. I have no memory of what else I wrote, but I do remember this: it was a lot easier to do right before boarding a transatlantic flight.

A few weeks in to my escape, I spotted Alain. He was descending the steps of the dorm where I was placed. Tall and lanky, with long dark bangs that swept across his forehead, he had an aura and confidence that pulled me towards him. I couldn't help but stare; I was immediately attracted. I was standing there with my new American friend Dee, in my deep red ruffled button down blouse, high-waist jeans, and sneakers. He came over to me, looked deep into my eyes, and said in a soft voice, "Americaine?"

"Oui," I said and melted. Much to my surprise, the attraction ended up being mutual.

This brief encounter would soon lead to the beginning of a romance, not only with a man but with a country, but I am not sure if the two were really distinguishable at that point. It was the first time I had ever fallen in love, and it was movie magical. When I walked down the streets, my feet were elevated above the bustling Parisian sidewalks.

Alain and I spent a lot of time together, and ironically, it was my lack of ability to be loquacious in the language that served as a perfect opportunity to get close to him without having to be witty, endearing, or quick. I had not left my insecurities behind, but our butchered language skills led to delicious and flirtatious laughter. I felt light and unburdened.

I was discovering so much too. By learning the genius of Sartre, Camus, Resnais, Truffaut and Malle in books and films for class, combined with European travel, my mind was expanding. Thoughts of adoption and Albert were as distant as I was from home. Between Alain and the excitement of this magnificent city, this geographical cure was actually working.

Not long after classes began, my friend Dee and I left on an excursion one Saturday for a project we were assigned for our art class. Dee, prone to wearing overalls and eating a daily Nestle Crunch bar, rushed under the ornate black iron Art Deco metro sign that read Alexandre Dumas to head to the Musée d'Orsay. We had to choose an artist to study and chose this magnificent museum full of Impressionist paintings for our hunt.

When we emerged, a misty rain began to fall. We stopped for warm croissants at a boulangerie and were engulfed in the sweetness of the hot flaky dough. We walked along the banks of the Seine taking in the majestic architecture as the small fine droplets of water fell on our flushed cheeks. Taxis whirled by the traffic circles and tourists cowered under umbrellas in raincoats with eager eyes. Even with the light wet fog and chill, Paris was beautiful!

Entering the great hall at the museum, shaking out our hair and our coats, our eyes moved rapidly, taking in the colors, hues and brush strokes of the masterpieces it held. My eyes were wide and filled with wonder. I turned a corner, looked up and stopped. I stared at a painting of a mother holding an infant. It was breathtaking. The soothing pastel hues contrasted against their cream colored garments gave it an ethereal quality. But it was the eyes that got to me the most; the intimate and loving gaze of the mother toward the child. The child looked out at me, with a peaceful but inquisitive stare that asked, "Who are you?"

"Dee, come look. I found my artist."

"That's beautiful!"

"Mary Cassatt," I said aloud as I leaned over to the placard. Over the next few days, I spent hours at the Paris library with art books opened around me, feverishly taking notes. I learned Cassatt was an American who came to Paris in the late 1800's to paint. She was 22 and befriended Degas. I was 20 and couldn't imagine the courage it took to leave home back then. Cassatt was looking for a place to become who she needed to be, or perhaps to escape who she was admonished she must be, a timeless tale of youth's rebellion and trying to find their own meaning.

Many of her other paintings were of the tenderness between mother and child as well. I was drawn to all of them. I went into the gift store and splurged on an art book of her work, clutching the paper bag close to my chest as Dee and I left the museum.

Fast-forward thirty years. I pull that same book off the shelf of a wall unit in my home in Westchester and lower myself crisscross on the carpeted floor, now a mother with three children. I run my hand across its glossy but faded cover and leaf through the pages. The sweet dusty smell of books long neglected wafted up to my nose. Staring at the beauty of not only the art but of the love caught in Cassatt's images, I remember the young twenty year old who stood in that bookstore and purchased it. I wonder why I was so drawn to these paintings. Was it a suppressed longing to know who my birth mother was? Did it speak to the significance of that bond and the level of sacrifice I inherently knew she had to make?

I thought of the Bible story of King Solomon. There were two mothers who knew each other well, both with newborn infants. One of the infant's died, and the grieving mother, out of desperation, claimed that the other women's baby was actually her own. They went to the king to settle the matter. In his wisdom, the king told them then he would just cut the child in two and give them each half. The first woman before him shouted, "Go ahead and cut him in half. Then neither of us will have the baby."

"Your Majesty, I love him very much," said the second woman, "but give him to her. Just don't kill him." He knew that the mother willing to give her child away rather than see him killed was the true one. This was not unlike the sacrifice Pearl, my own birth mother, had made for me at the time of relinquishment.

⌁

When it was time to pack up my suitcases to return to Michigan, I embraced Alain with not only tears, but with mutual promises of back and forth visits, wondering how long those promises would actually last. During the years after my graduation, they did. I made extended visits to Alain's family home outside Toulouse and him to me in Chicago, where I had moved after graduating.

Nestled in the southwest, removed from mountains and sea, Toulouse was a place few American tourists ever visited. It was a picturesque city, also known as "La Ville Rose" (The Pink City), because of the colors of the bricks used to build it. The narrow alleyways and cobblestone streets, the year-round sunshine and the flow of people, welcoming and kind, made it an idyllic place to live.

"Tu es *Americaine?*" Alain's friends asked whenever I opened my mouth.

"Oui, Americaine!" I'd smile back.

"Ahhhh, c'est formidable!!! Su-pare!" and then they stared at me like I was a mirage in their semi-provincial desert. Being that it was 1981, television shows like Dynasty and Dallas were playing on French airways. These shows portrayed America in all its excess, yet they were a common reference point for many young people. So people seemed as enamored with America as I was with France. I had to laugh, for as the saying goes, "the grass is always greener."

Whenever I was there, at some point, I started forming a new identity, some French-American version of myself. It felt like putting on a brand new suit. I was no longer the little girl in ruffles who met Alain in the dorm lobby. More confident, I began to dress like the chic women that surrounded me. I became fluent in the language. Alain's family embraced me. Since Albert, my birth father, had spent part of his life in France, it made me feel, in an odd way, that I was somehow French as well. It gave me a sense of belonging.

I could have been born there, I sometimes thought. But I could have been born anywhere, for that matter, I thought too. Being adopted changes the lens in which you look at the world. Belonging becomes complicated, and while you cling to the parents who took you in, you also know that you ended up with them because of a random alignment of a list in an adoption agency. Ending up in Toulouse with Alain seemed no more precarious and unpredictable than ending up on Long Island with the adoptive parents I had. I started to believe that belonging wasn't about genetics or family then, but simply establishing roots in the place where you are the happiest.

While my identity was morphing into some French-American version when I was there, Alain was fiercely proud of his Italian one. He clung to it like a dog to its bone. His parents were immigrants from Northern Italy. They packed their car and left in a hurry to escape Mussolini during World War II. "I'm really Italian even though I was raised in France," he'd say with pride.

"Okay, great," I would answer, without much enthusiasm. Not knowing my real heritage, I tended to downplay the importance of it.

"Where were your parents from?" he asked once.

"My parents were born in the U.S., but my grandparents were from Russia," I answered. "My grandparents hid in basements in their village as the Cossacks rode by on their horses with swords in hand, wanting to kill Jews, but my grandparents escaped and made their way to the U.S."

But at some point later, I told him the truth, that there was more to this story.

I told him I was adopted.

It was the first time I ever said those words to another soul. We were standing outside his parents' house, him leaning on his old silver dusty Peugeot, and me in front of him, the warm summer sun low in the sky. I don't know what provoked me to say it, perhaps it was another conversation about his heritage. Saying them in a foreign language, *je suis adoptee,* felt odd as well as frightening. It was all I could do to force them off my tongue. My body clenched after the words tumbled out, waiting for his response.

Ironically, it was only recently that I even remembered telling Alain, something in the writing process flipping a switch in my memory bank. Examining it now, I believe that because I was living in the bubble *francaise,* an entire ocean separating me from the players in my adoption tale, that I had the courage I needed to do so. But I did not go on to tell him any details of my adoption story, about Albert's call or about Pearl, because I was far from being that comfortable yet.

Alain was shocked at first to hear it, but soon he seemed to forget it. It became a detail he stored away on his own mental shelf and from what I could gather, it was not that important to him. Looking back now, it should have been a light bulb moment for me. The stigma was not as bad as I had imagined. Unfortunately, it took many years until I would fully absorb that lesson.

About two years into our back-and-forth love affair, after a dinner of ratatouille and fish in sauce béchamel with his family, we watched the Olympique football match that was taking place in Marseille. When I heard Marseille, my ears perked up, remembering that Albert lived there during his time in France. "What kind of place is Marseille?" I asked Alain.

"It's OK, kind of gritty, lots of immigrants -- a lot of crime there," he answered as he stared ahead at the players. "Why?"

"No reason." My heart squeezed, unwilling to give him even that tiny detail. I smiled at him but wondered why I felt bad about this. The life altering question that I never allowed myself to think about swirled through my head: was a person defined by where he or she comes from? Was I a half-Muslim, half-Jewish girl, with some French culture in me, from poor compromised beginnings, pretending to be a middle class Long Island Jewish girl of Eastern European descent?

Even though Albert had "crossed me over," as Lifton said, into the reality of my biological world when he called, I had, for the most part, shut it off again. I didn't like being reminded that the other world even existed. Wanting to wash away these uncomfortable thoughts, I got up to help Alain's mother wash dishes. I wanted my feelings of uncertainty to swirl down the drain quickly. If only it was that simple.

During the three years Alain and I flew back and forth to visit each other after college, I did not ignore Albert completely. When I thought about him, I felt tremendous guilt about having pushed him so far away. I didn't know exactly what I owed him, but I felt I owed him something. So I would force myself to pick up the phone. I called a few times, maybe three or four in all, I cannot remember.

I always called from a pay phone. Pay phones were impersonal, cold and detached. It made it easier to pick up the receiver. Pushing the square metal buttons while gripping my phonebook on the street, there would always be a gigantic pit in my stomach. My heart would beat fast. I would pray he wouldn't answer. But he always did.

"Hi, Albert, it's me Suzette."

"Suuu-*zette*!" he would respond in his elated but off-tempo sing-song way, followed by a dramatic, "Hello there, *ma* cher-*eee*."

I'd clench inside and he would begin to chat, filling me in with short snippets about his family, interspersed with simple clichés like "c'est la vie" and "que sera." I didn't offer much in return, nor did he ever ask. I remember there were inappropriate, at least to me, avowals of love and comments that I thought were naïve. I cannot recall what they were now but only that they made my eyes roll. Once, he even referred to me as his "doll," which made me cringe. His indefinably strange accent and his deep repetitive laugh grated on my pulsing nerves. I was so far from ready to have him in my life.

These sporadic phone calls were all I could manage, even though he wanted to have a real relationship.

I did not tell my parents about those calls, but at some point my mother asked, "Have you ever heard again from Albert?"

"Yes, I have," I answered, her face turning ashen. I felt a sense of betrayal even telling her. "We just had a few quick phone calls...that's all," I told her with a flippant tone. I was trying to minimize it as best I could because I knew that behind her question was a threatened heart and unresolved anger, even though she would not admit it, the closed system still holding us firm. I did not want to upset or hurt her. She said, "Okay then" shaking her head with a half smile, trying not to look too unhappy. Then I changed the subject.

My transatlantic romance with Alain lasted from age 21 to 24. I worked at various jobs when I was back in America, unsure of what I wanted for a career. I bounced around ideas from public health to biological research to education and filled out some applications for graduate school and even attended classes. I pondered, *how do you pick one thing to be forever?* Adoptees, in fact, can have a hard time settling, since "not knowing who they are can make it more difficult to figure out who they want to be," Brodzinsky stated in *Being Adopted*. I don't know if that was the reason I struggled in this regard, obviously many college graduates do, but looking back, I think it played a part. I would end up getting a Master's in Education but not until years later after my first two children were born.

Though my heart remained in France, I dated during that time too, knowing it would be foolish to cut myself off from other romantic possibilities. No one I met meant enough to me to consider breaking off my relationship with Alain. After three years of back and forth, I decided to try living there on a more permanent basis. Alain took an apartment in the only high rise in Toulouse, to make me feel more "at home." I started a tutoring business, posted flyers around, and taking on students. We were living like a married couple. I was happy, at first. But as Frost says in his poem, "nothing gold can stay," nor could this relationship. When I watched the news on television about America, my heart began to ache. When I went to see American movies, I started to miss home in deeper ways than I ever did before.

"I want to get you an engagement ring," Alain said one day.

"I'm not ready," I answered.

It wasn't only about becoming an ex-pat. I realized how attached I was to my family, the same as he was to his. I didn't want to spend my life without them nor hurt them. My mother told me, "I have nightmares about you moving to France and us coming to visit our grandchildren…they run up to us but they only speak French and I can't talk to them." I tried to assure her that it would never happen, but her nightmare kept recurring.

Did being the good adoptee as a child also mean being the good adoptee as an adult? Or was it all just normal for me to want to be with my parents and brother, plain and simple?

Also, what happened if Alain and I had children and our love boat sailed away? I would have to stay there forever. Maybe the Beatles got it wrong; love wasn't all you need.

After many sleepless nights and a newly developed painful ulcer, the time came when I knew I had to let go of Alain. I broke his heart. But mine ached too. I guess I figured out that what I needed at age 21 and what I wanted at 24 were not the same. I realized love and adventures in a foreign land had been a perfect elixir as they helped me heal from the trauma of Albert's call, lifted me out of my depression, and allowed me to regain confidence and self-esteem. But the sense of brokenness was still there, buried deep—and with it, though I didn't know it at the time, the building blocks of the self that I still needed if I was going to become whole.

Eight

LOVE AND COOKIES

"Hey there, I'm Rich!" said the handsome guy who introduced himself to me after I accidentally got pushed into his good friend. I was with my childhood friend and roommate Melanie at New York's Cadillac Bar, and the place was packed.

It was 1986, and I was twenty-six. As a single girl in Manhattan, it wasn't exactly Sex and the City, but I was having fun. I had gotten a good job as an office manager for a French product design firm that was expanding to New York and needed someone who was bilingual to set up and run their office.

It was Friday night and was planning on popcorn and some TV. It had been a long week.

Melanie had other plans. "Come on, we're going," she said, "I know the bouncer so we won't have to wait." So I put on my short plaid wool skirt, little red boots, black sweater and said, "I'm ready."

Rich had a strong chin, green-eyes, and an athletic build. He offered to buy us both Melanie and me a drink even though his eyes were on me.

While Melanie chatted with Rich's friend, Rich and I started the usual girl-meets-boy bar conversation. He was leaning against a column, vodka in hand.

"What do you do?" I asked, hating that meet-up question but going for it anyway.

"I'm a trader, on the Mercantile Exchange."

"Really?" I smiled, "So's my brother. I worked there actually, for a short bit after I graduated college." I started to show him my hand signals, which show the brokers the bid and asking prices occurring in the trading pit, flipping my wrist in rapid succession. He smiled.

"It was insanity," I laughed, "everyone screaming and spitting, and the trading cards flying everywhere!"

He was either impressed with my knowledge of what he did, or by how I looked in my short skirt and sweater, or perhaps both, because he stared right into my eyes with an amorous look. There was an immediate attraction.

We continued to chat. I told him about living in France, and he asked me to speak a little French. "Bien sur," I said and rattled off a few sentences. He seemed delighted.

"That's so great you know a second language, I've never been to Europe before," he said.

"Well, perhaps you should go."

We joked about the waiters and their Western-style holsters that held shot glasses and the ridiculous over capacity of the room. We discovered we both grew up on Long Island, and we shared about common places we both went to in our childhoods.

Rich was easy to talk to.

"What's your last name?" I asked him at one point. When he told me "Brownstein," I knew he was Jewish. I was glad because I liked him. After growing up a Conservative Jew, meaning I attended Hebrew School three times a week for five years, and knowing how important it was to my father, and thus me, I wanted to marry someone Jewish. Also, in those days, there was much less inter-marriage. Even Alain had been willing to convert for me.

After about a half hour or so of more conversation, Melanie nudged me. "I think it's time," she said.

"Of course," I answered. She had been kind enough to wait it out while Rich and I chatted.

"Can I have your number?" Rich asked before we left.

Normally uncomfortable giving it out, this time I was happy to oblige.

A week later, the phone rang. It was Rich, asking me out.

When the first date came, I was nervous because he seemed to have it all: smart, handsome, and a trader, something that was familiar to me. I didn't feel confident that I had as much to offer. Since I returned to New York from France, my insecurities were popping up like a whack-a-mole game, with me trying to strike them down.

But in spite of the straw getting stuck up my nose when I leaned in to take a sip of my drink that first date, he called for a second one the next day. That went well too. Other dates followed. In spite of being nervous, I felt comfortable with Rich.

He lived in an apartment on Central Park. I didn't know anyone near my age that could afford such luxury. It was actually decorated in the teak Scandinavian style of the time, rather than having the usual jumble of piecemeal stuff most people I knew had. It was also strewn with newspapers, magazines, coins, glasses, used tissues, belts and disheveled clothes on all of its surfaces. Neatness was obviously not one of Rich's virtues.

There was also a sarcastic side to him, one that I did not appreciate and fought back against, but for the most part he was attentive and caring. I came to consider him my "diamond in the rough."

When we were finishing dinner one night after about a month of dating, I left to go to the bathroom as the check arrived. When I returned to the table, Rich was gone. I waited, thinking he had also gone to the bathroom. Fifteen minutes passed. Confused, I grabbed my coat and left. Rich was standing outside with his hands in his pockets, leaning against the wall. He smiled at me.

"You're out here? Why didn't you wait for me?"

"I don't know. I figured I'd wait out here," he shrugged.

"So you just up and left without telling me?" He said he was sorry, but I didn't know if he really got it. Was he that clueless? Or maybe he didn't like me enough to care, the insecure voice that lived inside me whispered in my ear. Maybe it was more than that. Maybe as an adoptee, abandonment issues lived deep in my sub-conscious.

As if in answer to my thoughts, Rich put his arm around me and gently kissed me on the lips.

His lack of etiquette that night, and after, had nothing to do with his feelings toward me I soon discovered. He never had a role model. His father left his mother and his three siblings when Rich was just five years old. He married his much younger secretary and moved into Manhattan, visiting his children only on Saturday afternoons. Even that was accompanied often by a nap on the living room couch.

Starting down the street, Rich and I arm in arm, we approached a homeless man sitting on the ground in a dirty wool coat. Rich stopped and handed him a $20 bill.

"Twenty dollars?"

I didn't say it out loud, but that was four days food budget for me in 1986. "Yeah, well, there by the grace of God go I," he responded.

I looked at him, touched by his words. "You're so right, you know, by God's grace go *all* of us," I said. I was thinking, but didn't say of course, that it was by God's grace I ended up with the family I did and not with people who might not have taken such good care of me. I could have ended up on that ground too. Luck defines so much of where we end up, but for me as an adoptee, it was in my consciousness more than most.

One day, about two months in, I finally asked, "what's wrong with your ears?"

"My ears?" he laughed. "Nothing's wrong. They're cauliflower ears. I got them from wrestling. They're like a badge of honor to me!" It turned out he was a New York State champion in high school and an All-American in college. I, on the other hand, was picked close to last on sports teams. But while I might have been athletically challenged, I learned that Rich had never been exposed to art, nor did he have any interest. At the age of 28, he had never been to a rock concert while I loved music and had been to many. "I really love classic literature," I told him. He insisted he never read one classic because he was never required to.

"I grew up on the wrong side of the Long Island Railroad tracks," he joked, the side where many of his high school peers did not even go on to college.

So television was Rich's answer to culture, perhaps not unlike many young men his age from the Baby Boom generation. He laughed boisterously from under the quilt he dragged from the bedroom to the couch every Saturday morning to watch Pee Wee's playhouse.

"You're a cultural idiot," I teased him one day.

"Well, I guess I am," he chuckled, not caring. But our differences I believed, as is the case for many couples, made us more attractive to each other.

As nicely as things were progressing however, I was feeling my adoption status more acutely, that giant "A" pressing against me as we grew closer. Things were getting more intimate, yes, but I was far from ready to reveal my truth.

When Rich told me that he volunteered for the Big Brothers, and took a young boy out to basketball games and for meals, it touched me and endeared me to him further. His commitment stirred my own desire to go back to volunteering, something I had done in high school and college, but somehow dropped during the years I lived in France.

I decided to volunteer at the Jewish Home on West 106th Street in Manhattan. The woman they assigned me to was named Millie. We met once a week in a large TV room that reeked of cleaning fluid and stale body fluids. While the lifeless forms that sat in wheelchairs around us created a permanent inertia that was beyond depressing, I liked talking to her, especially since she had no family of her own. I held her wrinkly hand with its long arthritic fingers and listened to the small fragmented memories of her life she offered up in no particular order.

I wished so much she had her own child to sit there with her. I also began, for the first time since Albert's call, to think about the fact that I had a mother out there too, one who could be sitting just like Millie was, alone, with a stranger holding her hand. Did it matter if Millie and I were connected by birth or not? Later, I would read books about Buddhism, and its spiritual philosophies resonated strongly with me. I remember one said, "All strangers could be our mothers, or at least we should treat them that way."

So I did.

The crazy part was that she could have been.

"I want you to meet my mother," Rich said about three months into our relationship. He told he that when his father left his mother, he married his new wife only two months later thus was having an affair. It is a common tale now, but it was much more of a scandal in 1963, when divorce was still considered an anomaly and shameful. So his mother Carol was thrust into the job of raising her family alone.

We met his mother for brunch at Ratner's on the Lower East Side. It was one of Rich's favorites, an old-fashioned Jewish deli where old waiters in white aprons tossed plates brimming with bagels and smoked fish at the customers, and it always seemed like they were doing you a favor to serve you at all. But that was part of the charm.

All I knew was that I wanted Rich's mother to like me.

A petite brunette like me, she put me to the test. I felt like I was in a police interrogation.

"How did you meet Rich?"

"Where do you live?"

"Why did you go back and forth to France?"

"What were you doing in between?"

When the questions were finished, my coffee was cold. She got up to go to the bathroom, and I said to Rich, "Wow, your mother really grilled me."

"Yeah, well, that's how she is. She's very attached to me."

"I'd say." I rolled my eyes. Not too long after, I'd see just how much. It seemed she had a wall around her and her son, and there wasn't a window in sight for me.

"Maybe with you she feels threatened," Rich said as we drove out to the Hamptons shortly after to celebrate New Year's Eve at his friend's parent's house. "She sees it's more serious," he added, "and you know, she's had a hard life."

"Yes, she did."

"And we had no money," he continued, "So if we went to McDonalds we weren't allowed to order sodas. We couldn't afford to fix the washing machine so we went to the Laundromat. So when I started making money, I wanted to make my mom's life easier. I support her now."

Learning about Rich's family history helped me better understand his closeness to his mother. Both divorce and adoption could bring deeper attachments.

When I met Rich, he was already estranged from his father. He told me that his new wife didn't like him or his siblings, at least that is what he believed, and that she always found a way to push then away or be angry with them any excuse she got.

As for his dad, he rarely came to his matches, both in high school and college, in spite of his son's huge success in the sport. When Rich told his dad he wanted to go to an Ivy League college, his dad replied, "what does that have to do with me?"

So Rich ended up at University of Rhode Island, where they gave him a full wrestling scholarship, the only way he could attend college.

"But did he help you at all?" I asked.

"Well, he gave me a small allowance each week in college...which yes, I was grateful for," he said. "And he helped me get my first job."

"That was good of him...so he wasn't all bad?"

"No, but he took no interest in my life... "

I knew it was hard being pulled in two directions, just as I was as an adoptee. It was easier to negate what was uncomfortable for us, as I had negated anything positive about my own birth father.

"Are you ever going to talk to your dad again?" I asked.

"Not sure, but I don't think so." I felt sad. I remembered filling out financial-aid forms with my parents for college, knowing they would do whatever they had to so that I could go wherever I wanted. Saying no wasn't an option for them. In my mind I compared an uninvolved father with an overly doting one. It was one of those moments where I felt extra lucky for what I had.

Looking back at our relationship now, I think of something a dear friend of ours used to say. He was the son of a great jazz musician, adopted like me, and he traded commodities like Rich. He grew up with everything a child could want, attending private schools, travelling, and living in a luxurious NYC apartment showered with attention and love. He was an enigma to many who knew him however, a curmudgeon and the life of the party all rolled into one small package.

He and his adopted older sister wrestled with deep insecurities that he comfortably shared with Rich and me. I sometimes wondered if his complicated persona, his strong zest for life combined with his as strong displeasure of it, had a connection to his being adopted. He was the adopted son, not biological son, of someone talented and famous. Sadly, I never got to ask. He died at 45 before I started writing this memoir.

This friend was filled with pithy sayings, ones he either made up or repeated. "We are all broken cookies," was one he'd say, "some of us are just more broken than others." This one in particular resonated with me. Borrowing further from this simple metaphor, perhaps it was aspects of our brokenness that brought Rich and me together. Whether he realized it or not, Rich's life began to break apart when his father moved into the city with his young bride. More crumbs likely gathered with each of his father's absences, both emotional and physical.

My cookie began to break when I first found out from my neighbor that I didn't fully belong to my parents, and then crumbled more when Albert called to tell me "you are mine," letting loose the shameful secret that was buried inside me. Even though Rich and I were both happy and in love, I believe this inner sense of brokenness helped tie us together.

While Rich had revealed most of the reasons for his own insecurities, I had not yet revealed the source of mine. I knew I would have to finally come clean and let the chips, or should I say, crumbs, fall where they may.

⌒

"I want to fly to Florida to meet your parents," Rich said five months into our relationship. My parents had moved down full time. My uncle had wanted to expand his business to that warm climate, and my parents were just the people to do it. Soon they were settling into yet another new life.

"We're heere!" I announced as I pulled the screen open to enter. They approached us lit up, my mom first. Seeing her warm dark eyes, gray-streaked hair, and sun-spotted skin filled me with happiness. Even though I spoke to her every day, it felt good to be in her presence.

My dad came up behind her, his now balding head shining through the few dark strands of his thinning comb-over and his broad thin-lipped smile stretching from ear to ear. His Buddha belly, as my mom liked to call it, protruded over his "special occasion only" shorts, the one pair he hadn't purchased from the Marshall's sales rack. Because my father had survived the Depression, his frugality could border on the obsessive when it came to clothes and food, not unlike others from his generation.

I led Rich into the spare bedroom of their condo to drop our luggage. I suddenly became conscious of its contents: a twin bed covered by my old lightweight summer quilt, an inexpensive wood dresser, and an antiquated TV. I was suddenly struck by the difference between my parents' circumstances and Rich's plush apartment. My insecurities returned, this time the one that equated worth to worthiness. But it wasn't the bedroom decor that Rich noticed. "Boy, you don't look anything like your parents. I noticed that in the pictures you showed me, but now in real life, *really* not," he said. He was right. My mom was tall, big boned, with an oval face and black hair. I was petite, with a round face and brown hair. My dad had a large bulbous nose and thick lips; I had a small one and thinner lips. We did not look like we went together.

"Yeah, well…let's go into the kitchen!" I said, changing the subject. He followed me. My father stood with his apron wrapped tight around his extended belly and with a wooden spoon in his hand, mixing the meatballs he made with his homemade sauce.

He dished out a heaping plate and handed it to Rich.

"Wow, all that?" Rich asked and chuckle.

"That's nothing. There's more!" he said, explaining that he had simmered that sauce for hours.

When Rich finished all the food on his plate, my father was glowing. Later, when we said our goodnights, he hugged Rich tight. I wondered if my dad could become the dad he never had.

When our short visit together ended, I asked, "Well, what ya' think?"

"They're really nice, so so nice!" he said.

"Yeah, they're great."

"But I have to say, though, your dad isn't much of a looker." He chuckled.

"You're *sooo* mean, I can't believe you just said that!" I hit his arm.

"Just sayin'…but so nice…they're great."

It might have been a perfect time to tell him my secret, but I was still not ready.

At the end of that trip, Rich asked me to move in with him. I was thrilled.

Each day, coming and going, I looked around at the people on the street. I couldn't help wondering if they knew how lucky they were. I sure did. I couldn't believe I was one of them now, living in a doorman building on Central Park West with the most affluent people in the city. This new life, living in this spacious apartment with views of the park, dinners out at nice restaurants, and not having to worry about every dollar I spent anymore didn't seem real. My insecure self told me that I didn't belong here, that I didn't deserve it.

I couldn't help wondering, will it all vanish when Rich finds out I'm adopted? I had not told a soul other than Alain. He would also learn about my mother, the one my biological father had told me was "so ill I better not go there." He would learn that my biological father Albert is a strange Egyptian hairdresser-importer whose voice makes me cringe. He'll learn I'm not all who I appear to be, and I've kept this from him. And given all that, he may think I might be okay for a girlfriend, but definitely not for a wife.

I was not alone. Years later, I would read about others who feared they would be rejected. Joe Soll, a guru in the field, confessed in his book *Adoption Healing* that he could not bring himself to even tell his first wife and didn't tell his second one until years *after* they were married. Roberta Van One stated in an adoption book I read, "While I cannot remember being specifically told never to mention my adoptive status, I quickly became aware that this was a forbidden subject, never to be mentioned. And having finally unburdened this heinous secret to a psychiatrist in my thirties, I was then able to reveal it *at last* to my husband of ten years. He was shocked beyond belief—not at the fact of adoption, but at the fact of my secrecy."

Nine

A Ghost Made Real

I was like a newly caged bird on the plane to Florida. Rich was reading a book. I tried to do the same. My eyes darted over the lines without comprehension. Putting it down, I stared at the bottom of the plastic tray table folded up in front of me as if it were a magic mirror. What will the next day hold when I meet Albert, I asked it. How will my life change?

Just a few weeks earlier, I had finally gained the courage. Rich and I had gotten engaged after a year of dating, and it felt so late in the game to finally reveal my secret that my stomach churned on a daily basis. One Saturday afternoon, I walked over to the couch in our apartment and placed myself in front of him. Mustering up all my resolve, I blurted out, "Rich, I've got something I have to tell you."

"What is it?" he asked, looking past me at the television.

"There's something about me you don't know." I looked him directly in the eyes.

"Really? What?" he said, now more interested.

"Well," I took a long pause as my chest tightened, "you're not going to believe this, but…I'm, um…" I looked in his eyes, shaking inside. "I'm, a," I paused, "-*dopt*-ed."

"*Adopted?*"

"Yeah, *adopted.*" I looked away.

"How come you never told me?"

"I don't know, I guess I didn't know how you'd take it."

"What do you mean, how I'd take it?"

"I don't know. It's a pretty big thing." I held his gaze, waiting for his next sentence, but when he didn't have one, I looked down at my unsteady hands and cringed. I could feel his mind churning in those seconds that felt like minutes.

"Well," he paused, "I don't care. I'm just surprised that's all!"

"You really *don't care?*"

"No, of course not, why would I?"

"I don't know, I just thought you would."

"Well, I don't."

The intense weight of my secret suddenly lifted off of me. Could it be that this stigma that had affected me for so many years wasn't as horrible as I'd believed? I was so sure of it, even after having told Alain.

The rope of shame that wrapped around me, the one that squeezed on me since the day I learned the truth of my beginnings as an unprepared child and eventually becoming like a hangman's noose when Albert called me, loosened up with those few words. I was able to breathe.

"Have you ever met your biological parents?"

"I haven't met them, but I've spoken to my dad," I confessed, "a couple of times. He contacted me in college out of the blue, but I wasn't comfortable. So I told him I'd contact him when *I* wanted."

"And did you?"

"I made a couple of calls to him, but they were brief." I gave Rich the basic facts of the calls without any of the emotion, still scared to show my vulnerabilities. He asked about my mom. I told him she was mentally ill and my father told me it was better not to contact her.

He sat in thought. "So you don't know where she is?"

"No." He looked into my eyes, intent with curiosity. "Well, you have to meet him and then find her," he said with a smile, as if he was suggesting a trip to the grocery store. This was not what I was expecting.

"Meet him?"

"Yeah! It will be good." Good wasn't the word I was thinking of.

"I don't know about that. I haven't wanted to all this time because it's really emotional."

"Ok, well," he paused again, "then I'll go with you." I stared at him in disbelief.

"Well ... I guess I could call him this week and see what he says."

"That would be great," he said and then hugged me. He got up and strolled into the kitchen. I heard the refrigerator door open, ice clink and a liquid swoosh into a glass. Everything was normal to him. I sat frozen.

Meet Albert? Why? Because Rich thought it would be good for me? Or good for him? Did he need to okay Albert to okay me? I wasn't sure.

I knew I wasn't ready for this. But I had a phone call to make to my biological father whether I liked it or not. I didn't even think about saying no. Rich seemed adamant, and I was afraid he might not commit to me otherwise. Maybe there was also a part of me that wanted to finally meet Albert, to go where I was unable to go before, and with Rich by my side, would have the courage.

When I had to tell my parents that I was going to meet my birth father, the established villain of days past and potential spoiler of days ahead, my insides churned. I knew I'd be throwing an emotional bomb into their Florida condominium, the one Rich passed to me when he said, "You have to meet him!"

"You're not going to believe this, but we're flying down to Miami in a couple of weeks to meet," I paused, "*Al*-bert."

I could feel the stunned silence that followed. "Rich wants me, too. I hope you're all right with it?" Up until then, they must have felt beyond relieved that I had never sought out a relationship with him. Now with this announcement, everything changed.

"Well, I think it's," my mom took a long breath, " -- *good*. It's important for everyone to know their biological history."

What? Where was that coming from? Eight years too late. That was what I needed at 18. What happened to the mom who was so angry and who barely commented when I told her I spoke to him a few times? I was shocked by her change of attitude. Did time smooth her rough edges or did I misread her all those years? Either way, she seemed to have changed her feelings on the matter, and it gave me tremendous relief. I guessed she figured out that it is only human nature to want to know where you came from. Also, Albert was not the threat she once thought him to be now that I was grown. My father, however, was a whole other story.

"I don't think I'll tell dad," she added. I didn't argue.

We both knew that his ignorance, at least in this case, was his bliss.

⟶

*A*s Rich and me checked in at the hotel near the Miami airport, I stood before a woman who welcomed us with a voice that was monotone and humdrum. I thought my nervous energy alone might shake her from her torpor. I wanted to blurt out the reason for our stay, a confession to ease the pressure. The truth was pressing against my lips like an overinflated balloon. Of course, I only smiled and thanked her for the key.

"This is all so crazy. I can't believe it's happening," I said to Rich the second we turned from the check in counter.

"It'll be good." He leaned over and kissed me.

That night when I drew back the covers and crawled between the crisp white sheets, it was with the knowledge that I would not sleep. The bed didn't offer the kind of comfort I needed. I flipped my pillow and turned all night. Rich snored. At 3 a.m. I stumbled to the bathroom, turned on the light and looked in the mirror.

Who was this person looking back? Who will this person be tomorrow?

I would actually have a face to put to the ghost that had haunted me since that day in college, the one whose voice made me recoil. But it was more than that. He was the ghost that would challenge me to fit together the puzzle pieces that defined important parts of me, but the ones I lacked the courage to know because they scared me. Tomorrow the ghost named Albert would be made real.

The hot water hits me in the morning's shower, and I try to revive myself under its scalding stream. It is tough to apply my makeup with any kind of accuracy due to my shaky hands. Checking myself in the mirror, I adjust the new blouse I'm wearing. I rearrange my long bangs and tuck my hair back a few extra times, trying to take in the view the ghost will see.

Why am I so concerned with presenting a pretty picture? So he can be proud of what he created? So I won't disappoint him? So I can show him that life has been good to me without him? Do I need to impress him somehow?

Yes.

"Give me a kiss, it's gonna' be great," Rich says, "And call me from the lobby when you're ready."

"Sure," I say and exhale deep.

As I walk to the elevator, my armpits dampen. The other passengers gaze into the void, oblivious to what churns inside me. I am shaking while they are snapping gum.

I enter the lobby like a cautious soldier. I hone in on everything in my visual space, my head an anxious periscope. As I slowly step into the seating area, I see a man in the far corner start to rise from his chair. I stop. His face lights up.

It is the ghost. It is Albert.

I take him in, first with relief. He is presentable. He has thick dark hair and Mediterranean skin, and is of a normal weight. He has a larger and flatter face than my own but with handsome features. He is short, about five-feet-four. I suddenly understand my own short stature. It feels intoxicating to understand something genetic about myself for the first time in my life.

He wears a dark suit, a crisp white button-down shirt and polished shoes. Those shoes look awfully costly for a hairdresser. The thought comforts me. He too wanted to look his best for me. After we look each other over one more time, he throws his arms around me, as if it were his right. He squeezes me tight, too tight. My body tenses and his heavy cologne wafts into my nose with a heavy sweetness that makes me cringe. I know I have to allow him this moment even though I have no desire to feel him against me.

Albert steps back. He looks at me with a radiant grin as if I am the grand prize he has just won in the carnival of life. We both take deep breaths and sit down. He pulls his chair closer to mine and leans in. I squeeze the wooden arms of my own. I straighten my spine and look into his eyes, bracing myself for what is to come: the first chapter of the story of my life, as if I were hearing a storybook that begins, "Once upon a time..."

"I'm so, so happy to finally meet you Su-*zette*. You're beau-*ti*-ful you know," he says off tempo and then chuckles. It is that same reflexive chuckle I've heard on the telephone, which always feels like sandpaper against my nerves, but now it is happening alongside his wide-eyed piercing gaze.

"Thank you."

"I want you to know first off, even though I have said it before, that I never wanted to give you up. If the laws were different, I could've kept you."

"Yes, you told me that." I force a smile. Why is he telling me this again with such firmness? Perhaps he thinks I feel abandoned and wants to save me from that pain. Or maybe he wants to redeem himself in my eyes for having to give me up, letting go of whatever guilt he feels. Or could it be he just needs to remind me that I could have been his and should have been, so I should want him in my life? I have no idea.

"I have a picture of your mother I want to show you. It's the only one I have."

He hands me a black-and-white snapshot of a young woman. My stomach drops like an elevator cut loose from its cable. Something in her glance, her mouth, her face, *is completely my own.* It takes my breath away.

She wears a dark dress, cinched with a belt, with a flower on her shoulder strap. She has short hair brushed back, and there's a happy faraway gaze on her face. I'm not only bowled over with emotion, I'm overcome with longing.

Who is this woman in the photo with the smiling face? She looks lovely, and oh, she is my mother.

"She was very pretty," he says, "but I haven't had any contact with her since you were born. We were going to get married, and then she wouldn't talk to me. Well, what can you do? C'est la vie." He looks in my eyes and gives a sad chuckle.

There's something missing from the story. Why did she not want to marry him? Maybe he wasn't what she wanted, any more than he was what I want.

"I want to tell you about myself, my family," he begins. "I was born in Egypt as you know."

I can't hold back the huge question I've been struggling with all these years. "Can I ask you what religion you are?"

"Religion? I'm Jewish, of course. Why, what did you think?"

"I don't know, maybe Muslim, I mean, since you were born in Egypt."

"Oh, no, I'm very Jewish, my dear."

"I...can't believe I never knew that."

Monumental relief washes over me. The two trains charging down parallel tracks in my head, causing immense friction, merge together and become one smooth movement in terms of my faith, my Judaism. I am who I thought myself to be. I had not lived as an imposter in that regard.

"Our family lived in Alexandria before World War II," he continues. "The Jews who lived there did very well. My parent's divorced young and my dad remarried. I was their only child and lived with my mom, who became a dressmaker to make ends meet. But right after WWII, King Farouk who always got along well with the Jews went to war against Israel. It was a horrible time."

Decades later, with Albert in his eighties, he shared with me more about that time. He slept in the basement every night with his mother and grandmother. "It was very scary because you could hear the bombs coming down," he shared. "Obviously, my prayer was Shema Yisrael when I heard the bombs hissing...they hit so close to our house...the British discovered a crevice near our house with a bomb that had never exploded, thank God."

Another time, from his apartment window, he witnessed an Egyptian soldier behead an English one, and watched a group of them kick it around like a soccer ball.

"Suddenly, we were the enemy," Albert continues, "even though I was still a teen-ager, I was on their hit list because I was active in Jewish organizations."

"They were after *you*?" *Not only am I Jewish, but my father is a freedom fighter?*

"Yes, I escaped to France on a ship, leaving my mom behind, with many of the Jews that had to flee. I ended up in a refugee camp there."

Suddenly a childhood memory erupts in me. I'm sitting in our basement, on the old tufted burgundy leather couch from my parents insurance business in Bayside, looking at pictures of refugee camps in Life magazine. The smell of the musty leather, the smooth stiffness of the cushions, the chill of the cool basement air, and the big glossy pages that stick to my fingers return to me like I am sitting there once again. In the pictures, there are tents, dust, desperate eyes, barefoot children lined up behind Red Cross trucks, and men carrying bags of grains. The images are frightening, foreign, and fascinating.

I'd find out later that the refugee camp he was placed in was one of the nicest ones in France. He ate well and lived in a bucolic encampment in the mountains.

"I went to Israel after that and was put in another refugee camp, a detention center," he tells me. This one, however, was not pleasant. He found himself in a dreary abandoned British camp on the outskirts of Haifa, and "the conditions were atrocious…there were no sleeping facilities. I was forced to sleep on a wooden shelf with one blanket wrapped around me. You can't imagine how very sore I was in the mornings." During the day, he did hard labor, building roads and building pre-fab homes for the emerging state of Israel.

"One day, I was stopped by an MP and abducted into the army just like that. I served for two years in the Israeli military," he tells me. I sit up straight. A new sense of pride envelops me. My father fought for Israel! The ghost has morphed from a Muslim into a Jew into Moshe Dayan!

That brave soldier, I'd later learn, wasn't so brave after all. The training was so harsh that he couldn't keep up. His superiors realized that he was not a soldier candidate so put him in the mess hall to cook. But even that took its toll. "I became very depressed," he shared. "The doctors decided to send me to a rehab facility for a month. On my return, they decided that I should be released from the army."

Knowing the Albert of today, a happy-go-lucky man, it was clear that he just didn't have the stamina. He had done the best he could.

"What happened after that?" I ask him, shifting in my chair.

"Eventually, I went to live in Marseille, to be with my mother," he tells me. "She ended up there after the remaining Jews fled Egypt. It was a happy time. I lived there a while with her, then I applied for a visa to the U.S. with the help of my dad's brother who was here, and got one. I arrived in this country with very little money. I ended up bringing my mom here, too, some years later. Well, you know, *cherie*…a real immigration story."

Another chuckle, but now accompanied by the even more disturbing "cherie," that always made my hair stand on end during our phone calls. I was still not his "cherie."

"You know, you would've loved my mother, she was wonderful. She would've so loved to meet you, but she passed away last year."

"Sorry about that," I say, showing a sadder face than what I felt inside. She was a complete stranger to me.

But what did she think about me? Was I the irresponsible love child that she warned her son against? A grandchild she pined for? Should I feel more than I do that she died? She was my grandmother after all.

"I want you to know you were the product of a loving relationship."

Rather than a sordid one-night stand? And yet, there is comfort in what he is telling me. Some adoptees are even the product of rape, and that opens a whole other bag of difficult issues, ones I thankfully didn't have to deal with.

"I thought about you all the time. You know, Su-*zette*, you are a part of me and I am a part of you, always." I smile but inside I'm cringing. I don't feel like I'm any part of him, nor do I want to be. The closed system wall around me was still so thick that I couldn't even begin to process why it was so hard to hear that proclamation.

"Well, then I met my wife Betty. I got my beautician's license and worked as a hairdresser," he continues, wanting to reveal all of these details of his life to me.

"I thought you had an import-export business?"

"I tried while I was hairdressing, but it didn't work out." I don't want to tell him I am disappointed to hear he really is a hairdresser. Is it because of my parents' prejudices or my own from days of watching Tony, my mother's hairdresser? I'm not sure. Either way, it is not a thought I'm proud of today, that I cast such judgment on him then. We all don't get the same opportunities in life, ones like I did, and certainly Albert did not as a poor immigrant arriving in this country with no familial support. He did the best he could, like we all do, under the circumstances. In the end, he did well for himself. But I was too clouded to see it then.

"Eventually I was able to have my own shop. I'm very good at what I do." Another chuckle. "If you'd like, I'd love Paul and Pammy to meet you. They don't know about you, but I'd tell them if you'd be willing to get together. They'd be so surprised to find out they have a sister."

"I don't know. I don't think I'm ready for that yet."

"Ok, then, we'll see." He folds his legs and stares into my eyes with a longing that makes me uneasy.

"Why don't I call Rich down now and we'll go to breakfast?" Before he can answer, I lift myself out of my chair and walk to the house phone in a daze, my pants sticking to my damp legs. Suddenly, the other sounds and voices in the room switch on. I realize I have been oblivious to the comings and goings around me.

He isn't so bad. Certainly not as bad as I had imagined.

I pick up the house phone, dial our room number, and take a deep breath. "Rich, please come down, we're ready." Rich enters the lobby, wearing droopy shorts, a loose t-shirt and a broad questioning smile. I am happy he is here now to create a buffer, but I'm nervously anticipating what he will think, wanting to control a situation that I know I cannot. We enter the dining room and slide into a big booth. The waitress hands us the oversized menus and Albert begins to ask Rich a lot of questions. A lot more questions than he asked me, I realize.

Had he perceived I had a wall up around me, that behind my efforts to be welcoming and warm that I was really fearful and guarded? I suppose it was good he didn't ask me very much. What would I tell him? How much he had shocked and traumatized me? How angry my parents were? How much I tried to never think about him after he called me?

Small talk works fine. Albert asks Rich about his work and seems impressed with his business acumen. I guess it is much easier for Rich who is not carrying a lifetime of baggage. I occasionally add something, but I'm mostly lost in my own gyrations.

Albert's eyes continue to wander in my direction again and again, revealing a soulful desire that keeps me squirming in my seat. *I am no longer your child*, I want to tell him, but I know I still am.

We finish breakfast and make our way out of the restaurant. In the lobby, there are a few awkward moments. I am ready to say good-bye so I make the first move. "Well Albert, it was so great to finally meet you," I announce.

"Suzette, please, now that we have found each other, let's stay in touch. You're my family too, you know." I tell him I know, but knowing it and wanting it to be so are two different things.

The truth was I never thought about an after plan. It was only about getting through this meeting.

Albert embraces me. "Speak to you soon. Bye now," I say as I pull away.

"Love you," Albert says. All I can do is smile.

Rich puts his arm around my shoulder and kisses me as we walk back to the elevator. "You okay?"

"I don't know, that was sooo bizarre. I'm shaking."

"He seems nice enough, pretty harmless."

"You think so?"

Nice, yes. Harmless, I wasn't so sure. But Albert must have passed Rich's test, at least, a test perhaps I conjured up in my own mind.

On the flight home I gazed into my foldable plastic magic mirror and looked for more answers. The ghost was now a man. There was a face to the voice and a body underneath it. What now? How much do I need to embrace him moving forward? Do I need to make him a part of my life? Should I call him regularly? Should I visit him? What do I owe him now that we have met?

The magic mirror told me that I'd just survived some kind of identity storm. The longing in Albert's eyes to have me back as his child, my parents' disapproval of him, the taboo around connections between birth and adoptive families, and the years of shame I experienced left me confused and scared.

I decided it was best not to enter that place again for a while.

But how long before I enter again? I asked the mirror. No answer.

"You should find your mother now," Rich encouraged me when we were back home.

"Seriously?" I said. Was he kidding me?

"We'll see," I said, but thinking no way, at least not for now.

But I must tell my mother about meeting the ghost. She will be waiting to hear. And when I do tell her, she will try to be supportive, but I will hear a disdain in her voice, a more muted version than the one she had before but still apparent. So I minimized the impact of my reunion the best I could.

After that, I ended up putting Albert, the man, in the same place I'd kept Albert the ghost: buried deep, out of my consciousness. "It is not easy to hold on to a relationship that can potentially pack the voltage of an exposed electrical wire," Lifton stated. "Reunion can leave an adoptee not only stunned, but feeling even more fragmented and confused than before, not knowing yet how to incorporate this alternate reality into the adopted one." The adoption therapist A.R. Moran succinctly referred to it as the "paralysis phase." Lifton concluded, *"The adoptee may need to withdraw for a while."*

And that's exactly what I did.

Ten

A Tree, a Birth and a Wet Pillow

The high ceiling, large stained-glass windows and aged wooden pews of B'nai Jeshurun gave this Upper West Side of Manhattan synagogue a sense of timelessness that took my breath away. The congregation, founded in 1825, was the second oldest in New York. BJ, as it was called, was taken over in 1984 by the famous human rights rabbi Marshall Meyer who turned it into a vibrant and young synagogue. Prior to his arrival, Rabbi Meyer was head of a congregation in Argentina, where he spoke out vehemently against the military dictatorship responsible for killing tens of thousands of its citizens in the so-called "Dirty War." With his own life eventually at risk, he left for the United States.

Rich and I were amongst the rabbi's many devotees, but so was Betty Jean Lifton, the author of the book that awakened me to the closed adoption system. Of course, at that time, I knew nothing of her or what closed adoption even meant. Rabbi Meyer was her spiritual advisor and close friend. Wouldn't it have been nice if I could have spoken to Ms. Lifton at that time? I am sure I would have made a good case study on the "found" adoptee, a section that had only two short paragraphs in her book. Not that this was surprising given the sealed files that prevented birth parents from finding their children.

Before the wedding, Rich and I worked on our invitation list. I asked him if he would be inviting his father. He said no. "But he's still your father. How can you do that?"

"Because he has no place in my life," Rich stated flatly. The man who had disappointed him once too often would not walk his son down the aisle. I felt sad. I also knew then that any hope of their reconciliation would be gone forever with this decision.

At that point, only two of Rich's three siblings still spoke to his dad, but they were far from close with him. They all had experienced the same disappointment Rich had. I guess that each person's threshold is different. In my experience, expectations of other people are inversely proportional to happiness. Lower them, and you will be amazed at how more content you are. But doing so in terms of a parent can be a much harder challenge.

While I felt Rich was making the wrong decision, I wouldn't be inviting Albert to our wedding either, so in a way, who was I to talk. He was the Spirit of Secrets Past who had become real, but I was far from ready to give him a role in my life. This momentous event, my wedding, wasn't going to turn into a coming-out party.

While the reasons Rich did not want his father there differed greatly from my own, there was also a commonality: Neither of us was willing to examine the emotional dumpsters of our difficult and confusing feelings regarding what fatherhood meant.

"Well, why don't you at least write your father a letter and let him know how you feel," I advised Rich. The piece of paper he handed me the next night was a paragraph of unremitting anger, opening with "You were never a father to me."

"That's pretty severe, honey. Can't you rephrase it, in a nicer way?"

"No, why should I? It's how I feel," Rich answered. Feelings were neither right nor wrong. But how we express them can cause lasting damage. When Rich's dad received the letter a few weeks later, Rich's sister Casey told him that their dad did not understand the letter, not at all. Two opposite belief systems had collided head on. Rich didn't care. He had unloaded the monumental pile of bricks that sat on his shoulders, and that was all that he needed.

I cared. That night, lying in bed, I thought, Rich's father probably did not think he was a bad father. Maybe he considered himself far from great, but a bad one? Do any of us think we're "bad"? We all try to do the best we can, rationalizing our choices as the right ones, writing the stories in our heads that help us justify our feelings and actions. It is human nature. So I am sure Rich's father would have his own plausible explanation for his lack of involvement, one that made perfect sense to him.

I had to accept that Rich and his father were not going to even try to understand each other. Each had their own story, and they were sticking to them.

Rich's father was diagnosed with terminal lung cancer three years later. Rich reached out and called him. His father never returned the call. By then, I imagine that the divide for his father was probably too wide and too difficult to cross. I felt bad that he could not have given his son some parting words of caring and connection, however brief, before he left this earth.

On a chilly but bright November day, I arrived at the temple in satin and lace, my eighties bandeau headpiece in place. While all the guests were settling in, I sat down at a small wood desk where Rich and I needed to sign the Jewish marital contract, the Ketubah. The young assistant rabbi, Roly Matalon, asked me to first write my maiden name in English and then asked for the Hebrew names of my mother, father and grandparents. I looked toward my parents for help. Roly filled them in as Mom and Dad spoke the names. Much to my surprise, memories of a family tree assignment in fourth grade came back to me as I watched him carefully form the letters. My mother had spoken these names to me back then, and I wrote them down with great seriousness. When I handed in my poster with its carefully colored trunk, roots and limbs, I wanted to believe the information was as accurate as it was carefully rendered, but I knew that these people were not my true roots nor branches. It stirred uneasiness inside me as a young girl.

So there I was again, staring at another family tree of sorts, the stakes a bit higher, my Jewish ancestry being defined. At least I knew I was fully Jewish. Unlike in third grade, I was more choked up with pride than anything else. It came to me that while I may not have been born with these roots and branches, they were those of the parents who raised me. I knew they counted for a good part of who I was. And all trees, no matter what their seeds, need to be tended with care to grow, and I was, amply, more so than I could have ever asked for. I turned and looked at my parents with admiration and love. Having now met Albert, my gratitude to my adoptive parents was that much more profound, and I stared at them for an extra second before preparing to take my father's arm to walk down the aisle.

Rich and I were trying to have a baby. After our first try, sitting in the bathroom and a week late for my period, I was frightened. I held the plastic gizmo in my hand and waited. My mother's inability to get pregnant, then to have a child, came front and center in my brain for the first time ever. Would I follow in her footsteps? Was there some kind of phenotypical inheritance that Darwin missed? Would I be spared her anguish?

The line came into view. I was pregnant, just like that.

Overcome with disbelief and then relief, I smiled wide knowing my world, our world, was about to change for good.

A pregnancy of extreme nausea, anemia, gestational diabetes, a broken toe and a bout of wicked strep throat followed. I was far from the poster child for a healthy pregnancy. "Pregnancy is hard," Rich lamented throughout. I laughed at him and reminded him that it was me who was carrying the baby. He wasn't a huge admirer of the swollen female form either. "Can you put a shirt on?" he asked when I walked around the apartment with just a bra on. "You're a piece of work," I responded and laughed again. My diamond in the rough still needed some polishing, but I let such things roll off my shoulders. I knew how much he loved me.

It ended up that having a wife who swallowed a basketball and having that basketball in your arms were two completely different things. The minute we arrived home from the hospital, Rich said, "I'm going out for a little bit." Walking in a half hour later, he was holding a hand painted wood unicorn rocking horse wrapped in cellophane and tied with ribbons, with a huge grin on his face. This was from a man who hated to shop.

For my mom, the birth triggered a new confession. We were sitting on the couch ogling the baby one day. "So tell me again, you had an infantile uterus, and it would've been curable today, right?" I asked. Having just given birth, I was more curious about her experience.

"Yes, and I never told you this, but," she paused, "I was pregnant once after you and Oliver were born." My eyes widened. "You were in elementary school. I don't know if you remember that I went to the hospital for an overnight."

"Oh my god, yes, I do. I came home from school and you were in dad's lounge chair. I was wondering what the heck you were doing there. You told me you had woman problems and needed…some kind of *scraping or cleaning*, I think you called it. You said it was all normal woman stuff, not to worry."

"Yeah, well, it was a D&C, an abortion…the doctor said he guessed my infantile uterus had grown up since the pregnancy was holding."

My parents were ecstatic, bowled over by the thought of having another child, but their doctor didn't see it that way. "He said given my age, 44 at the time, the chance of Down syndrome was very high. Remember, they had no way to test for it. He then reminded Dad and me that we had two healthy children and asked us why we we'd risk disrupting our lives in that way."

I stared at her intensely, trying to process it all.

"'You should just be happy with the family you have,' he told us, "so after much deliberation, that's what we did."

⌒

That night, our first night together at home as mom and dad, we placed Brian into his white wicker bassinet next to my side of the bed. The warmth of our bodies together and the comfort of the down pillow under my head felt heavenly after the hospital. Soon, we were sleeping soundly. Twenty minutes or so in, the screaming began. Our heads popped up in unison.

"Jeez, that's loud!" I announced, my brain in forced wake-up mode. "What the hell did we get ourselves into?" I joked nervously, as thoughts of a lifetime of taking care of another human being suddenly came into focus. Rich shook his head and laughed, a nervous one, in a sleepy daze.

"He ate 45 minutes ago so he can't be hungry," I said.

"Just hold him then I guess." Rich dropped his head back down.

I lifted Brian up and checked to make sure his diaper was dry, not that I really knew what I was doing. There were no lessons on how to take care of an infant; you, everyone, just had to jump in the parenthood pool and learn how to swim. I held him against my chest and spoke soft words, and then instinctively began to shake him gently on my shoulder. When that didn't work, I walked out of the room to spare Rich the wails. Once in Brian's room, I slid the dimmer switch on the lamp with my foot to create a low level glow so I could see where I was going. I paced with him, back and forth, back and forth, my body tired but my brain awake.

Brian fell into a calm and blissful sleep in my arms. I lowered us both with care into the white lacquer rocker chair we purchased, taking him off my shoulder and placing him in front of me. The dimmed light cast a warm glow over the room. Shadows stretched across the carpet created by the crib, dresser and rocking chair, and I felt grateful for being able to have them all as I held my newborn son.

Fixing Brian's blanket ever so gently, I stared into his trusting cherubic face resting in the crook of my arm. I pushed off the ground, and we began to swing forward and back. I watched the slight vibration of his pursed lips and the flutters of his soft pink eyelids. I listened to his barely audible rhythmic breath. His innocence and sweetness filled me with wonder and love, a love I had never felt, that most new mothers probably feel.

Leaning my head back, I drifted into thoughts about his birth, the room, the nurses, and the sight of his face for the first time. I thought then about my own birth, twenty-nine years before, something I had never allowed myself to do. Had my biological mother held me like this? Was she filled with wonder?

Did she feel instant love? Or did she harden her heart and make them take me away to avoid the pain, needing to separate herself from the most primordial of emotions, a mother's love for her infant? I could not imagine in a million years someone taking this baby away from me. How could my birth mother allow that to happen, even though I knew it probably wasn't her choice?

As Brian and I rocked together in that moment, I made a decision. I was going to do what Rich always wanted me to do. I was going to find my birth mother.

⁓

I called Albert. I was nervous to ask him for help in finding Pearl.

"Find Pearl?" he hesitated, "well okay, I'll help." Maybe he still wanted to protect me from what he knew about her. Maybe he was worried that I would end up having more of a relationship with her than with him. I wasn't about to ask his opinion. I was just glad for the affirmative response.

"Your birth mother grew up in a foster family," he said first thing. I was shocked to hear this revelation. "The only contact I still have is a number for her foster sister. Her name was Florence… she's probably your best chance but I don't know if it's any good still."

"I'll take it," I said. I scribbled it down, my heart squeezed tight.

That night, gathering up my courage, I called. Florence actually answered.

"Hi. My name is Suzette, and I know this is crazy but," I paused, "I'm the child that your foster sister Pearl gave away…"

"Oh - my - god."

"Oh my god's right, I know, it's crazy!"

"But how'd you find me?" she asked.

"My birth father, Albert…"

"Oh yeah, sure, I knew *Al*." She didn't sound too enthused about knowing him, which pinched my heart.

She told me that Pearl, my birth mother, had been mentally sick over the years. "I feel bad to say this, but I don't think that it's a good idea for me to tell her about you or for you to meet her. She's doing a lot better now, but hearing from you, well, could…*set her back*," Florence said.

I was taken aback and deflated. Who was she to tell me this? I thought right away about hiring a private detective. But I would then be doing what Albert did to me, not respecting the wishes of someone who knew me best and calling anyway. As eager as I was now to meet her, the last thing I wanted was to create any further problems for the woman who bore me. Then again, maybe Florence didn't really know how my mother felt either.

When I asked her if Pearl ever said anything about me, she told me "no, never."

Florence was willing to meet me though, not ideal but a consolation prize. A week later, I greeted her at the restaurant in Lord and Taylor as she suggested, because it was near her work. The subway ride down had been fraught with apprehension as the car rattled and shook. What would I find about my past this time that I didn't know before? I gripped the pole tighter.

She stood up in the booth where she was waiting for me when she saw me enter. She mouthed my name with a questioning gaze.

"Should we hug?" I said when I arrived at her table.

"Yes," she said.

Well dressed, she was a full-sized woman with brittle blond hair blow dried straight and with eager, intelligent eyes.

"I have to say," she added, "I see some of Pearl in you!" My heart swelled at this connection. Sliding into the booth bench, she said right away, "I have some pictures for you." I was so excited to get this unexpected gift. It was no different than when Albert gave me his picture of my mother two years before. The woman who gave birth to me was before me again, yet I was still staring at a total stranger. "She was beautiful," Florence said.

Why did that please me? What if she had been homely? Would it have mattered? Or would I have thought her beautiful no matter what?

I pored over every detail of the photos, looking for clues about who she was in the thousand words each picture tells, my desire to meet her growing stronger with each flip of the pile. Florence shared with me, "All the boys loved her. She got a lot of attention from them." Staring at her face in each one, there was a disconnect. She looked so happy, so normal, which made me happy. Yet this was the same woman she said was too mentally ill for me to meet?

"We took Pearl in because my parents wanted to help a child," she said.

"I hate to pry, but I was wondering, was it financial too?" I mustered the courage to ask. I imagined that people took in kids for that reason too. "No, it wasn't that," she said. But their family consisted of she and Iris, who were two biological daughters older than Pearl, and a younger brother, so I wondered why they would want a third daughter, a fourth child, especially knowing it was the tail end of the Depression, and they had very limited means. I'd find out that many couples did take in foster care children to augment their income, and even if that were the case, it didn't mean that Pearl's foster parents weren't also giving and caring people. Florence wouldn't admit to any alternative motives, not that I would have judged them for it. What they did was a very generous act. I knew from the Cottage School that the world needed more foster parents than there were available. In my mind, they are our modern day heroes, not just talking the talk but also walking the walk in a profound way.

"Pearl had a good life with us. My sister Iris and I considered her a sister. My parents wanted to adopt her, but Pearl didn't want that. She always wanted to find her mother."

It was a physical effort for me to keep from tearing up at that proclamation. "Did she ever, find her?" I asked.

"No. At least not that I know of."

A black cloud moved over me. What could her mother's fate, my grandmother's, have been? It was a depressing thought, one I pushed away.

I also didn't even think about the argument I could have presented to her then. Since Pearl herself wanted so much to find her mother, why would she not want to have been found too, by me, the daughter she'd never met? Florence was being protective, which I understood, just as my own parents and brother had tried to protect me years ago from Albert.

I perked up when Florence filled me in on stories of Pearl's happy childhood, how "animated and sweet" she was, and how everyone liked her. After that though, she became unsure of herself and increasingly agitated as she grew older.

"She didn't love Albert," she offered unprompted.

"I kinda figured that out."

"She thought it best to give you up." I didn't probe, but it was clear he was not the man she wanted to spend her life with, even if it meant losing me.

I learned Pearl met her husband Martin soon after she gave birth to me and married him. He adored her. He stuck it out with her through all her years of illness. I tried to take in all these new pieces, fitting them together the best I could in the puzzle board I had started framing in my head, first with Albert's information and now Florence's. It was hard.

"Can you do me a favor after today…if my mother ever brings me up, would you at least tell her about me, that we met?"

"I will, yes, that I can do." I didn't have much confidence, but I felt glad at least for that. One thing was clear however; Florence was acting as the gate-keeper, and even after meeting me, she was not handing over the key.

A few months later, I was twirling the bottlebrush in and out of each baby bottle, getting them clean. Brian was sleeping in his crib, and Rich was stretched on the couch watching television. I was tired and planning to go to bed right after I finished. It was a mother's fatigue after caring for an infant all day.

The phone rang. I grabbed a dishtowel to dry my hands and ran to get it. "Suzette, hi, this is Florence, Pearl's Florence."

"Oh my god, Florence, hi! Long time no speak. What's up?"

"You're not going to believe this, but I talked to Pearl about you. We were talking the other night and out of the blue, I asked her if she ever thought about you, and much to my shock, she said yes, she does."

"Oh my god!"

"Yes, and guess what. She wants to talk to you. She's waiting for you to call her, right now if you want."

My insides froze. I dashed to grab a pen and paper. After writing down the number and a rushed goodbye, I got up and burst into the family room. I told Rich my news and he said with eyes opened wide, "Oh wow! Great! Call her!" I bee-lined back into the bedroom and shut the door. I was a sparkler on the Fourth of July! *What will I say? What will she say? How do you make up for thirty years?*

I picked up the phone and dialed the number, my mother's number. As the phone rang, my heart was like a jackhammer, beating out of my rib cage. One ring…two rings…I shifted myself on the bed, beyond excited inside but also scared. After the third ring, someone picked up.

"Hello?"

"Hello, is this Pearl Stein?"

"Yes."

"Um, this is unbelievable, I know, but this is your *daughter*, Suzette." My chest clenched in anticipation of her response.

"Suzette … *darling*, I'm *so happy* to hear your voice."

Awe and amazement flooded through every artery, vein and the spaces in between. This voice was my mother!

She had a thick accent that I recognized from the boroughs of New York. So in those brief seconds, trying to figure out the pieces right away, I told myself I would have been a borough girl, that I am a borough girl.

"I have waited for this for a long time," Pearl said.

"Me too," I said choked up. "I, I don't want to bother you or cause you any problems."

"You aren't. I assure you. I'm just so happy Florence told me."

"Where do you live?" I asked. I didn't even know where to begin.

"I grew up in Queens, but now I live in Brooklyn, sweetheart." *Sweetheart?* It seemed too endearing too soon, like when Albert called me *cherie*, but it did not bother me this time, did not feel inappropriate. It felt right, probably because of the mother-baby bond I had experienced myself or perhaps just because I held no animosity.

I tried to picture her in my head based on her voice, not as she looked in the photographs. She was more mature…and I imagined her sitting in a small narrow kitchen of an apartment, wearing a housecoat and slippers gripping the phone.

"You know, I wanted to keep you, I really did, but you know," she paused, "I just couldn't."

"I figured that, I really did."

"I've had a tough life."

"I know. It's okay."

"I met your dad Albert, you know, and well, got pregnant. He was very persistent. But I didn't want to marry him," she added.

"That's all right. That's fine," I said trying to alleviate her anxiety. I didn't tell her I already met Albert for fear it would be too much too soon. I also wanted to reassure her that she didn't have to go through the pain of a long explanation. At the same time I really wanted that long explanation.

"And when I got pregnant, I knew I couldn't give you a good life. I didn't want you to have a miserable one like mine. So I decided that the best thing was to give you to a family that could give you a good one."

Her words, *miserable one like mine*, knocked my heart on its side.

"I wanted to love you, but I couldn't."

"You don't have to explain. I've had a really good life," I said, wanting to give her at least that satisfaction. "You should know that."

"I'm so, so glad to hear that. You don't know how happy that makes me."

Some forbidden space deep within my core lit up.

"I always thought about you, always," she said.

"That's so incredible to hear."

"You know, I ended up with a wonderful man, Martin, and had three more children. But you know, sweetheart, I'm going to be honest with you. I suffered mentally all my life. I was a very sick person."

My heart filled with compassion hearing her confess this to me. "I'm so sorry that happened."

"You sound lovely," she answered.

I told her about Rich, Brian, my parents, and all the things she could be happy about, wanting her to know that it was all right. "Listen, what would you think about me coming to visit you?" I asked suddenly.

"Visit? I guess so, yeah, I'd be happy for you to." She told me that she was going down to Florida soon though as she and Martin had rented an apartment for the winter. He had just retired. I told her I would happily fly down there. I couldn't believe she was willing to meet me too.

I cannot even remember the exact farewell, but I do remember sitting and staring at the phone in its cradle for quite some time.

Who was this woman that was my mother and what was her life like? What would mine have been like? She obviously had a more difficult life than I did. I thought about the buildings I would pass in Queens along the Long Island Expressway when my parents drove my brother and me to the city for a museum trip or a baseball game. I would wonder about the people who lived in them and try to imagine what their lives were like. The world in those small identical attached homes and impersonal brick high rises seemed so far from my own life in the suburbs.

Now I knew that it would have been the world I grew up in had I not been put up for adoption. A girl that was "me" would have been there with a different name—but, of course, she couldn't be me. She would not have gone to sleep away camp, had a fashionably decorated room of her own, a grassy backyard with a swing set, a stingray bike to ride around the neighborhood streets and visit friends. The chances of her ever going to the University of Michigan or studying abroad were probably slim. In all likelihood, she would not have met a guy like Rich, gotten married in an elegant restaurant overlooking the city, nor be living in an apartment on Central Park West. At least not in my mind. With the truths of my maternal heritage now revealed to me from the lips of my birth mother herself, I felt an explosive bolt of gratitude for the life I was given.

I got up from the bed and walked out. "Well, I can't believe it, I just spoke to her. I think I need a hug," I told Rich.

"Come here," he said, holding out his arms. I lowered myself onto the couch and held on to him for a while. The real me, the adopted one, found it hard to let go.

That night in bed my mind was raging like a bonfire. Rich slept soundly. I thought about the young Pearl from the photos, then pictured her in the hospital bed giving birth to me. New images now formed where there were none before. There were nurses in white caps surrounding my mother in labor. A doctor pulls me out. A nurse wraps me and leans across the side of the bed to place me in my mother's arms, and she stares in amazement. It's a first-time mother's love. She looks up for a brief moment, but there is no one to share it with. She is alone. No adoring husband or family are there surrounding the two of us. She takes in my round face and full lips. She gazes at me and talks to me with soft words of longing, but overshadowed with ones of sadness and remorse. And then the next day, or two perhaps, the nurse takes me away.

I curled up on my side. Tears welled in my eyes.

Why was I crying? What the hell was going on? Shouldn't I be happy that I spoke to her?

I was confused. Big tears started to steadily drip, rolling across my face and soon covering the pillow against my cheek. Curling up into a fetal position and trying to suppress them, I was shocked that I was so overcome with emotion. I stuffed my face into my pillow as the sobs grew louder, not wanting Rich to hear. Then in spite of my efforts to hold them back, I cried aloud, in repetitive waves of heaving breaths. A loud ache escaped from my stomach, and I was no longer able to contain the emotion inside. What was going on?

But I knew.

I was crying for the mother who had to give me up, and then went on to suffer so much in her life.

I was crying because I lost something so important, and never got to know her love or been there for her when she suffered.

I was crying because of the pain of all the years I denied her and pretended she did not exist because of a system that taught me to do so.

I was crying because I felt some kind of guilt that I had the better life.

I was crying because finally I was in mourning, for a loss I never knew I suffered until that moment.

Eleven

TWO HEROES

*S*lipping behind the wheel of my mother's car, I straightened my linen tank top and matching shorts that I picked out that morning to make an extra nice impression. Twisting the rear view mirror, I tried to flatten my blow-dried shoulder length hair with my hand that was starting to frizz from the Florida humidity. I made sure my eye make-up wasn't smudged. Turning the car key, I inhaled deep. I was nervous. A nervous wreck.

On my way to I-95 to head south from Boca Raton to the town where Pearl lived, I pushed the air conditioning lever to full blast, aiming the vents directly at my face to get some relief. My body was clammy, not just from the heat, but from the sweat caused by fearful anticipation. Erik Erikson, the famous psychologist and adoptee himself, wrote, "A birth mother must make the baby into a non-person to give them up. Having done so, she will have a hard time when that non-person comes back looking for her." So as nervous as I was, I was sure Pearl was too.

"I just want to meet her," I reassured my parents in the foyer of their condominium before I left. It was just what I had said to them when I met Albert. When I called my mom to tell her I would be meeting Pearl before I flew down, I had left it to her to tell my father. I knew the initial distress he would feel would be more than I could handle. Reunions often bring adoptive parents back to painful thoughts of not being able to have a biological child of their own, on top of the threat and fear of losing their relationship with the adoptive child. For this reason, "as many as 50% of adoptees who search do not tell their adoptive parents until the search is over," Marilyn Schoettle, from the Center for Adoption Support and Education, stated.

The highway opened up before me as I pressed the gas pedal. The sun's intense rays blinded me, and I reached for my sunglasses. Even with the air on, perspiration continued to cover my body. I fiddled with the radio knob to find a song to calm my nerves. "Hero," from the movie *Beaches*, came on. I turned it up loud, as it was one of my favorites. I immediately became lost in the melodic sadness of Bette Midler's voice, and the words I knew so well took on new meaning in that moment. My voice rose to sing with the chorus, "did you ever know that you're my hero," and I wondered who my true hero was, Pearl or my mom. It never dawned on me that they both could be.

As I got closer, my anxiety level ratcheted up. The memories of everything I had heard about Pearl spun in my head…memories of Albert telling me that Pearl was not well mentally. Memories of Florence worrying Pearl wouldn't be able to handle seeing me.

If Pearl was "crazy," what did that mean in terms of me? She sounded okay on the phone last month.

I thought of the photos I'd seen of the young Pearl looking lovely and happy, a young girl with her whole future ahead of her. Could the ravages of mental illness have morphed her into a totally new being? My fearful imagination began to go into overdrive. The only image I had of mental illness at that time was from the movie "One Flew Over the Cuckoo's Nest." Would she look like one of those characters, disheveled and barely able to talk? Or maybe she would resemble the witch from my Hansel and Gretel childhood storybook that used to scare me. Would she have warts and missing teeth and stare at me with beady eyes and a devilish smile when she opened the door?

I shuddered.

I exit from the highway, taking deep breaths to calm myself. I pull up to an enormous intersection. My dad refers to these Florida lights as "lunch lights," because you could finish a meal in the time it takes for them to change to green, but today I'm relieved with the delay. I glance to a gas station on my right and watch people mindlessly fill their tanks. I envy their boredom. My heart beats fast.

I arrive at the entrance to her gated community, one of the gigantic ones in South Florida that caters to retirees from more limited means than my own parents. I roll down my window to a wall of hot humid air and say her name to the young man in the khaki shorts and button-down shirt at the gatehouse. He takes out his clipboard and pen, and with a serious expression, writes down my name after I spell it out slowly twice. He directs me to her unit, and I pull ahead.

I wind my way around the huge sprawling complex; there's not a soul in sight. The endless rows of bland cookie-cutter stucco buildings, lined with multi-level catwalks, holds thousands of people. My mother is one of them. Anxiety now paralyzes me.

Pulling into the parking lot outside her unit, I cannot move. I stare at the building and prep myself. "You can do this," I say out loud a few times. I finally open the car door and get out.

The intense heat hits me when I emerge. I take a moment to turn my face to the scorching sun and let it envelope me, hoping it will calm me somehow. It doesn't work. My heart pounds and sweat beads drip on my forehead.

I slowly climb the outdoor staircase that takes me to the second-floor catwalk where she lives. With steady steps, I mark the progression of numbers on each door, growing more nervous as I get closer to the one that I need. The one that belongs to my birth mother. Part of me wants to run away. Part of me wants to run to the door.

My heart is pumping. A piece of wood is all that now separates me from her. I raise my finger to push the bell but then hesitate. I take in air, shift my weight and exhale hard. I press the button.

Within seconds the door swings open and there she stands. In that brief nanosecond, a tidal wave of relief floods through me. She doesn't look like the Hansel and Gretel witch. She's not a monster at all. She looks normal. Actually, she's attractive. She could be any woman in line in front of me on the supermarket checkout line, and this is all that I need. I smile and my muscles unclench in shocked surprise. A decade of fear is laid to rest.

She has short silver-grey hair that is neatly cut and brushed back behind her ears. Her skin is pale and flawless. I can see that she has taken the time to apply mascara, eyeliner and red lipstick. Her nose, thin and pointy, is nothing like mine. Her face is square while mine is oval. Her startlingly blue eyes stare into my brown eyes, transmitting warmth from them, one that throws me off guard. Staring at her features, there is some resemblance – the nose, the eyes -- that jolts me. She looks like she could be my mother.

"Hi, Pearl."

"Hi, Suzette."

Instinctively I wrap my arms around her and she reciprocates. She then steps back and takes me in. "You're just beautiful. I can't get over it."

"I don't think so, but thanks…" I blush.

When I enter the small apartment, a tall portly man with olive skin and a full head of dark hair approaches me with a sheepish smile. Pearl introduces him as her husband Martin, and he tells me how nice it is to meet me. He seems perfectly normal, and I smile back. I wonder what he's thinking and feeling. Is he a reluctant husband trying hard to be kind to his wife, to put on a façade of support, while actually being displeased that this illegitimate daughter is showing up thirty years later? Or is he an open-minded husband who can't wait to meet a child that belongs to the wife he values and loves deeply? Or is he somewhere in the middle, where most humans live, conflicted by opposing emotions but trying his best to do what's right?

His face doesn't reveal much. Pearl grabs a camera off the cocktail table. "Let's take pictures. Go sit on the couch and Martin will take the two of us!" Surprised by her enthusiasm, I make my way across the foam green pile carpet and feel my insides trembling. Maneuvering around the glass cocktail table, I sit down on the stiff striped couch. There are few knick-knacks and photos. A moving company would take no time packing up this place. I'm relieved it's clean and not the den of trash and clutter my runaway imagination feared it could be.

"This is a short term rental, just for the winter," Pearl reminds me, almost on cue. She then tells me they will be buying a place there soon. Sliding herself close beside me on the couch, the hairs on my body rise up from some kind of genetic electricity shooting between us. Martin snaps the first picture. Musical chairs follow, with pictures taken of Martin and Pearl, me alone, her alone, and us together again.

"I guess you'll send me copies," I say breaking the silence.

"Sure I will," and then she says abruptly, "Martin is going to leave us now." I glance at her surprised. "Yes, it'll be better that way," she adds.

Why is that?

Martin walks over wearing a compassionate yet strained smile and gives me a soft embrace. "Well, I'm sure we'll see each other again," I say to him, not sure if that will be the case. He grabs his keys and walks out the door. As the door slams behind him, the vacuum of silence is deafening.

"Please come into the kitchen and sit."

I take a few steps over and take in the scene, thinking the surroundings might have some clue as to who Pearl is. An old toaster oven is surrounded by a few leftover morning crumbs and sits next to a sticky looking spice rack. Otherwise, it is clean. Pearl pulls out the chair across from me, sits down, places her small delicate hands on the table and with a deep breath looks right into my eyes.

"I want to tell you all about my life. I hope that's all right."

"Yeah, okay, of course. I want to hear." I didn't know it, but I was about to hear a very different story than the one Florence had told me.

She sighs deeply as if gathering strength and begins. "When I was a little girl, I lived with my mother in a one-room tenement on the Lower East Side. I have very few memories of that time in my life. My father wasn't there. My mother couldn't take care of me...I had no idea why. I do remember I slept on old newspapers. I remember drinking sour milk and being hungry. Then one day, people came and took me away. I remember the man had a gun on his hip. I was four, maybe five. They told me my mother was sick. I never saw her again after that. I tried many times to find her when I got older, but I never could."

"Oh my god, that's horrible."

"Yes, well...After that I remember being somewhere. I think it was a hospital. The ladies there took care of me. It was the first time I had a bed and real food. The ladies were so nice to me. Because they wore white, in my child's mind I thought they were *angels*, angels who had come from heaven to take care of me."

I shudder. While I imagined that stories like hers happened more than I knew, they were lives that I had never personally known, that were alien to my world. It would be fifteen years before I would start volunteering at the Cottage School, where Pearl's story would fit in well. But in spite of my lack of exposure or familiarity , this was now my world too.

"They put me with a foster family in Queens. That's Florence who you met. My foster parents took me in for the money, but I wasn't aware of that back then. They made me clean and wash and do all the things that the other two girls didn't have to. And if I didn't do what they asked, my foster mom would grab my arm and pinch it till it bled." She extends her arm on the table and points to different spots to show me.

I grimace. "Are you serious? She did that?"

"Yes. And she'd dress me in long shirts whenever the workers came so they wouldn't see the scabs. The ladies would always ask me if everything was all right, and I'd say yes, because I was scared to say anything bad about my foster parents. I didn't want to get them in trouble."

"Trouble?"

"What else did I know?"

Searching for someplace to look other than into her eyes, I look beyond her. I see silly magnets on the refrigerator door, but I feel queasy. I tuck my hair behind my ears, shift in my seat and tell her I need to use the bathroom. Entering the small space, I close the door and look in the mirror. This is a true-life Cinderella story, I think, as I stare at my reflection. Tears begin to form, but I wipe them away.

"I wanted to get out of there so badly," Pearl continues. "So when I was 15, I applied to a nursing program that would train me, the one at the Riker's Island prison actually. I found out about it at school. Ever since the days when I was little and those nurses took care of me, I wanted to be like them, and help other people. I sent away my application, but my foster mom wasn't happy. And then one day, a letter came…my foster mom opened it before I came home from school. I walked into the kitchen and she stood there holding it up for me to see. She told me, 'Your letter came and you were accepted,' and for that single moment, I thought I can now have a life."

I look at her with hopeful optimism.

"But then she said, 'You aren't going anywhere,' and tore it up in front of my face, letting it drop to the floor."

My eyes grow wide. "What?"

"Yeah, that's what she did." I drop my head to avoid her eyes.

"After that day, I was broken. I gave up," she says in a slow whisper. "I was a shell of a person." I bite my lip and my chest compresses. I look down at the table. A silence echoes between us. Words fail me. I sit in that silence. I know I should take my hand and put it atop hers, or do something, but I cannot move.

"Do you have a tissue?" I ask Pearl.

"I'm sorry this is so hard for you. I wanted you to know."

"No, I'm glad you're telling me."

The most probable reason as to why Pearl's foster mother refused to allow her to go to nursing school became apparent to me years later. A friend of a friend, one who grew up in foster care with the JCCA, not too long after Pearl did, shared her story with me. She was in a foster care home in East New York, a tough crime-ridden neighborhood. In spite of the difficult circumstances, she was graduating top of her high school class and was an excellent writer. Her high school English teacher recognized her talent and sent samples of her work to the journalism school of her alma mater, a very prestigious Midwestern university. She did not even know about it. The school offered her a full scholarship. When she went to her foster mother to tell her the great news, her foster mother said, "*You* can't go. Foster children aren't allowed to go to school out of state. That's the rules!"

She had no reason to question her foster mom. But as an adult, she found out that her foster mother lied. There was no rule like that. Her foster mom didn't want her to leave because she didn't want to give up the weekly check she got from JCCA for her care. And when the JCCA sent her to summer camp, her foster mother wasn't happy either because the checks stopped coming during that time. She would only allow her to go to camp for the shortest session even though she wanted to stay. Learning this, Pearl's story now made perfect sense.

"I finished high school and took a job as a telephone operator. I'd go every day. I still lived with my foster family, you know." I knew that back then that it was rare for single girls to move out before they got married.

"I worked but after a while, I found it harder and harder to get there every day. I was miserable. Then I met Albert. I was twenty-three. He was a house painter." She pauses as if she is re-living that moment in her mind. "He was very nice to me. He pursued me…and he was so persistent I let him take me out. But as I said, I was a shell of a person. So one night, I guess we were together. I was shocked to find out I was pregnant."

"When I found out I was pregnant, my foster mother sent me to a Jewish charity home, with other girls like me. And when I gave birth to you, a part of me wanted to keep you so badly…" she said and then paused. "But I also wanted to save you from the misery of my life. Then my foster mom told me to give you up, that I had no choice, it would be better, that the baby would be better off without me. So I felt I had to."

She looks away from me. There is thirty years of pain etched on her face. "I named you Charlotte, just so you know."

"Charlotte?"

"Yes, Charlotte!"

I have another name! The knowledge hits me like a deer leaping in front of my windshield. Suddenly, the reality of who I could have been becomes more real, a blurred image coming into greater focus. I had a beginning as Charlotte but then a life as Suzette? Is a rose a rose by any other name? What if it's tended to differently? I did not have any answers.

"After that, I tried my best to put you out of my mind and only think that you had a good family taking care of you and that gave me some peace. But it was very hard."

"I'm sure it was," I say. I can understand avoiding the pain. She locked her secrets up in her own little box because she had to get on with her life as best she could.

"After that I met Martin. We had three children together, Jeffrey, Alan and Stacy."

I nod my head. Where are they now?" I ask. She tells me Alan and Jeffrey, in their early twenties, are single. One lives on Staten Island, and the other lives in Bayside. Stacy is married and lives in Pennsylvania.

"Do they know about me?"

"I told them right after you contacted me. Before that, no, they didn't. They were shocked. Martin knew though. Stacy thought you might not be who you said you are, to be careful," she said.

"But you know that I'm your daughter, right? We went over this: Albert, my birthday?" Obviously, Stacy was concerned for her mother, but did she really believe I would show up *pretending* to be Pearl's daughter? To gain what? Maybe she thought entering their lives could mean something would change for *her* in a bad way, so she was scared. I had no idea.

"Yes, I know. Stacy also said she was worried that you could hurt me. That you could be carrying a weapon..."

"A *weapon?* That's crazy..."

"Yeah, well, I told her it was fine, not to worry. I don't think they're interested in meeting you though, honey."

"That's fine." It was more than fine. Pearl was enough.

"Anyway, I became sicker over time. I tried to go to nursing school again at one point, but it was too hard. I'd start walking to school and some days would have to turn around and go home. One day, I peed on myself. I'm not sure who knew, but I was humiliated. I never went back again. Time went by and some days I couldn't even get out of bed. They put me in the hospital many times...I had shock treatments."

Shock treatments? Images fill my head of people strapped down with leather belts on metal tables, wires stuck all over them, and convulsing off the table, again, based on my only reference point at the time, the movie "One Flew Over the Cuckoo's Nest." In those days, I later read, treatments could last fifteen minutes and were as brutal as portrayed. Nowadays, these same treatments are shorter, lower dosed and much more humane.

"Each time I returned home better, but after some time, it would just get bad again. And I'd go back in," she continued.

The worst then came. "At one point, I was really, really bad, sweetheart. And I'm going to let you know that I tried to kill myself, twice, by taking lots of pills."

I gasp. Her brutal honesty makes my stomach turn. I wanted the whole truth, and now I'm getting it. I am stunned. Back in 1990, I never heard of anyone committing suicide like is commonplace today. They say, "God doesn't give you more than you can handle," but I don't believe it. That is why people commit suicide.

"I wanted to die because I felt that my family deserved better than me. My husband could remarry and my children could have a mother who could really take care of them, and they'd all be better off. I didn't want to ruin their lives anymore. My children didn't have it easy. I survived for years like that. And then finally new medications came out. I started taking some pills and then one day, for the first time in my life, I woke up and heard birds chirping outside my window. I felt like life was worth living."

Pearl swallows hard. "And that my dear, is my story." She looks down at her hands. A heavy silence fills the space between us as the power of the revelations she made reverberate through us. Eventually, they settle down enough for us to resume.

"I don't know what to say. I can't believe what you went through." I shift in my chair and stretch my hands out to hers. Grasping them both firmly, I look in her eyes.

"I'm so sorry," I say. I want to hug her, but this is all I can manage. "I'm so happy that you're all right now. Thanks for sharing all this."

"Darling -- I hope you don't mind me calling you that -- I hope this wasn't all too hard for you to hear. But I felt like you should hear it. It's my story."

"I understand, I really do, it's okay." I pause. "It's really okay."

What else am I to say?

I tell her about my own life, which seems almost too good to be true now, trying to fill in the empty pieces of the Charlotte jigsaw puzzle that must have been living in not only her head but her heart, all her life. I embellish my happiness, hoping to reassure her that she had made the right choice in spite of her pain.

"I had a really good life, have a good life. You did a good thing."

"I'm so happy we met," she says again.

"Me too, you have no idea."

We stare into each other's eyes. I realize there's nothing left to say. I get up from the chair, and she does the same. We meet halfway and hug. The warmth of her body against me fills me with feelings of intense connection yet overwhelming grief. When she pulls away, I suddenly feel a need to leave, to exit that space, to say good-bye.

"We'll stay in touch," I say and smile with tenderness.

"Yes, sure...." she responds.

I walk toward the door, Pearl by my side. She turns the knob, pulls the door open and gives me one last sad but relieved smile. I return it, give her a quick hug and kiss her on the cheek.

Outside the sun jolts me. The fresh air and sunshine outside is as shocking as if I'd been trapped in a mine for days. I exhale for what feels like the first time since arriving. Squinting, I scurry along the catwalk and down the stairs. By the time I reach the pavement, I'm racing.

Sliding myself into the car, I feel the burn of the hot leather on my thighs. I let out a deep sigh and feel stunned. Turning the key, a hot blast of air shoots from the vents, burning my nostrils and lungs as I breathe deeply. I quickly crank the window open to get some relief, attach my seatbelt, and wipe my brow as the sweat starts to bead in no time. I back the car out of the spot as if I'm making a getaway. Once out of view of her building, I pull over, park the car and start to cry.

Pearl wanted to let me know who she was and wanted to give me an explanation for why she gave me up. Perhaps she wanted my forgiveness. But there was nothing to forgive. My mother had told me that giving up a child was the greatest act of love. It validated in my mind that my birth mother did love me. Some adoptees feel abandoned by their biological mothers, but I never felt that way. My adoptive mom's assurance that it was for the best and her admiration for what my birth mother did enabled me to not judge her for this act of relinquishment. Pearl had so little to give me, but she gave me something priceless and incomparable, even if she didn't have much choice in the matter.

As my sobs ebb, I put the car in drive and make my way out of the development. As the minutes pass, my head begins to clear slowly and my thoughts begin to solidify. I came thinking I'd hear a tale of insanity. Instead, it was a story of heartache and suffering. A story of being dealt one bad break after another, about having hopes and dreams broken, and of falling into a deep, dark well of depression.

I came fearing that I might find myself face to face with a witch straight out of my childhood nightmares or with the personification of extreme insanity. Instead, I'd met a woman who had aspired to emulate angels and sought to put her children's interests first, however misguided.

Twelve

A Courageous Man and a Storage Tub

T he experience of reunion, even when longed for by both parties, is still very charged. The one I had with Pearl did obviously not disappoint. I felt like I had been through an emotional cement mixer. Trying to process it in the weeks and months that followed were difficult at best. In spite of my relief and admiration for her, that she was able to survive, I wondered who I was in terms of this damaged genetic heritage, what my life should have been like, and how much of her genetics were in me, for better and worse.

Did coming from a damaged place mean I was also damaged, not from the secrecy anymore but from the truths of my lineage? The stigma around mental illness was very strong back then and the knowledge that it had a genetic component was clear. So the question of nature versus nurture gnawed like an angry dog at my sleeve, wanting to get to the flesh below. My identity felt more Rubik's cube than simple puzzle, the never-ending what-ifs circling around my head.

Due to this tremendous angst, I needed another "time out," just as I did with Albert.

I did not call her and she did not call me. However, I had no idea that fifteen years would pass before I would see her again. "Differences are discovered and magnified, emotions can become overwhelming and paralyzing, and many people put up walls after reunion and walk away, back into their limbo state," Jean Strauss wrote in *A Guide to Search and Reunion*. That described me well. I guess it was just too hard.

Because Pearl did not contact me, I took that to mean she did not want a relationship either. I guessed it was too hard for her too.

Years later, I came to better understand Pearl's reasons for not picking up the phone after the reunion. Carole Anderson, an adoption specialist, described it this way, "She [the birth mother] may have worked very hard at denying her feelings, at convincing herself that your adoption was necessary, at telling herself that giving birth does not make a woman a mother, and at pretending that she was not a mother and so did not lose anything. If she has succeeded at numbing herself to the pain by clinging to such beliefs, knowing you would remove the blinders from her eyes, exposing her to the full impact of all the years of loss and pain." It was heart wrenching, but it all made sense.

In Ann Fessler's book, *The Girls Who Went Away*, I learned about this time: the perfect storm that occurred in the fifties and sixties that brought on this phenomenon. Sexual mores had loosened. Sex out of wedlock became acceptable for many. With little accessible birth control and no sex education in school, young girls were getting pregnant in unprecedented numbers. Some were unwilling to marry in spite of parental pressure, and others were not allowed to marry despite wanting to. With abortions illegal, there were not many options. Being a "single mom" was not one of them as the stigma was enormous. Fessler documented the story of one woman whose parents hid her under heavy blankets in the back seat of the family car to sneak her out of the neighborhood, heaven forbid anyone see their daughter in that state. Pearl's foster mother, I remembered had told her, "If you keep this baby, you can't live here anymore."

So parents hid their daughters, telling friends and family they were "going away," to stay with relatives. The truth was that many were sent to homes for unwed mothers. Parents told their daughters, essentially, that they could come back when they were rid of their problem. There the girls lived, shielded from the world and filled with shame, until their babies were born. "Severe isolation was normal, as was withholding information from women about their pregnancies and impending labor like married women received from their obstetricians," Kathryn Joyce, author of *The Child Catchers- Rescue, Trafficking and the New Gospel of Adoption,* wrote.

When the mothers in these homes gave birth and saw their babies for the first time, many who had agreed to relinquishment wanted to change their minds. Social workers and parents went to work convincing them they wouldn't be good mothers and their babies would be better off without them. These admonishments made them feel unworthy, undeserving and unfit. "The pressure they encountered at maternity homes was harsh and unapologetic," Joyce wrote.

When the young girls went into labor they were rushed off to hospitals to give birth alone. The nurses and doctors did not treat them kindly, viewing them as sinners. The fantasy of Pearl being surrounded by caring nurses when they put me in her arms was burst for me the moment I read those words. Did they look at me with similar disdain, another bastard child? To add insult to injury, the mothers were told to pretend they were virgins when they went home; otherwise, men would not want to marry them. When many did eventually marry, they never told their husbands about the child they had, keeping it shameful secret for the rest of their lives.

When the girls got home, they were told that they would forget, "as if they had experienced nothing more serious than a nine-month stomach ache," one mother explained. Yet, they found "they could not go back to the life they had left behind because they had become different people in the process of becoming mothers," Lifton wrote. Carole J. Anderson, in her booklet *Eternal Abuse of Women: Adoption Abuse*, explains it another way: "Adoption is not the end of a painful chapter, but the beginning of a lifetime of wondering, worrying, and missing the child. It is a wound that time cannot heal." As Sorosky wrote in *The Adoption Triangle*, girls who gave up their babies "suffered terrible feelings of loss, pain and mourning after relinquishment that remained undimmed with time."

After relinquishment, the files were sealed forever. The "girls who went away" had "babies that were taken away" and never seen again. Later referred to as the "Baby Scoop Era," between 1945 and 1972, studies estimate that over a million and a half babies were given away, just like that, with no consideration that these young mothers might have just experienced the worst trauma of their lives. Is it no wonder that as a group, these women went on to suffer from high levels of depression, often haunted by tremendous guilt and sadness over the child they gave away.

On the flip side of the coin, of course, was Albert. He was desirous of a continued relationship. He called me right after Brian's birth. I was warm on the phone even though I felt uneasy. All the difficult and confusing feelings I always felt bubbled up in me as I listened to him speak through the handset. I was relieved to say good-bye.

In spite of that, when Brian was a year and a half, Rich and I went to Florida to visit my parents. I suggested to Rich we go visit Albert, surprising myself at the time. Thinking about my physical proximity to him as he lived only 45 minutes from my parents, and his expressed yearning for me, I felt it was something I should do. I pushed away the angst. He was my father after all, and I had opened the door between us when I initiated reunion the year before. Was it right to close it back again? Whether it was more guilt than a desire to start a real relationship, I did not know.

It would be an issue I would struggle with for years to come, the idea of what family really means.

That night, I was anxious about telling my parents, especially my father, that we were going. He had never mentioned a word to me about either reunion. He was not only the continuous ostrich with his head in the sand but the poster child for the closed system. "Gezunterheyt (Yiddish for "in good health"), *go!*" he said and turned away.

"To Albert, really?" my mom paused in surprise, "Well, if that's what you want …"

But I could read the curl of her lip and the stiffness of his posture. They were upset. Was I surprised? This was more than just reunion now; it was the potential start of a relationship. Having Albert in my life would also mean in their lives, and it was not in their playbook before, and certainly not now.

Nothing had changed. They still harbored enormous anger at this man for that call, the one my mother begged him not to make.

I wondered too if they felt a sense of betrayal from me that they would never admit to. Basically, weren't they enough? I was sure those thoughts must have danced in their heads, more so my father, who could never tease apart my quest to find my birth parents as separate from my love for him. It was not uncommon for adoptive parents from that generation to ask themselves, "What did I do wrong?" when their children decide to search, even if the question is often misguided.

My mother seemed to understand the difference, that I could love her and Dad but still want to connect with my birth parents. While she tried to accept my journey as natural, this doesn't mean it didn't pain or upset her. But she tried to keep her feelings under wraps even though I could read her so well. I was grateful for that.

When Rich, Brian and I arrived at the restaurant to see Albert and meet his wife Betty, all the unresolved feelings from the first meet-up bubbled up even though the shock value was gone.

I wondered too what his wife Betty made of me. A very thin petite woman with a pointy nose, angular features, and short, brushed-back hair, she was reserved. It was hard to get a read. At a minimum, I was sure she had to be ambivalent; it couldn't have been easy for her.

Nothing in her voice that day gave anything away. We spoke as if we were old friends catching up after a long absence, feigning the casualness that was required of us. Describing the mundane developments in our lives I knew was safer than touching on the underlying circumstances of the relationship. If truth serum had been in our food, I wonder what would have come out. Perhaps questions like, *How did you feel about being adopted, why did you wait so long to contact us, and what do you want moving forward?* Of course, nothing like that was said; it was only conveyed non-verbally in our mutual uneasiness.

"Did Pearl ask about me?" Albert asked about fifteen minutes in when Evelyn's attention was diverted. He knew I had met her.

"No, she didn't," I answered, wondering if I should feel bad about it. His face fell.

"Oh well…" he said, "What can you do?"

I shrugged.

"So how is she?"

"She's pretty good actually. She's married and has three children."

"Really?"

"Yes, and she's doing better now."

"Well I'm glad then," he answered, but I could see he was surprised.

"Oh, and she lives just fifteen minutes from you, one town over…" His eyes opened wide.

"Crazy, I know," I added.

What I didn't tell him was that she told me she never loved him.

The truth of Pearl and Albert's romance was quite complicated, as romances can sometimes be. While she did stop talking to him at some point early on in her pregnancy, plans were made for a wedding when she got pregnant and furniture was even picked out. When Albert showed me a photo of Pearl when I was in his house not too long ago, one he never showed me before, I turned it over and was taken aback to find a handwritten message on the back.

To the dearest, sweetest, and the handsomest man on earth.
Love, Pearl,
P.S. And the most courageous

What was this? She told me she had acquiesced to his demands for sex because she was a shell of a person. She told me she did not want to marry him.

"What did she mean by the most courageous?" I asked Albert, taken aback by her words.

"She meant that I never gave up trying," he explained, "but she *a-dored* me!" *Then why didn't she want to marry you?* I wanted to ask but held back. It was clear from her words however that he did make her happy after all, but not as a life partner. I can see now that the story was more like a jambalaya of facts, fiction, minimizations and wishful thinking than anything else, on both their parts. Sometimes we shape memory to make it fit the story we want to tell so we can get on with our lives. I am pretty sure some of that was going on.

Whatever her feelings were for Albert, he did not hear from her again until after she gave birth. He said to me once, "I was laying in my apartment in the Bronx. I was terribly sick, a horrible case of the flu, when my phone rang. It was Pearl and she said, 'I just want you to know that I gave birth to a baby girl,' and then she said good-bye." And that was the last he ever heard from her.

Throughout the lunch with Albert and Betty, Brian played with his Mickey Mouse rattle, a welcome distraction. I explained that we were moving to the northern suburbs of Westchester and had just signed a contract on a house. He was happy for us, of course.

Throughout the lunch, however, Albert's statements were interrupted by that same repetitive laugh that grated on me, as much as I was trying to be at ease. He was sweet and caring in his own way, yes, but oddly so, and it made it difficult for me to move forward in my acceptance of him as my father. On a visit to him years later, he insisted I take two tin cans of fava beans on the plane home with me because he wanted me to try them. He used to eat them in Egypt, he told me, and loved them. I told him it wasn't necessary, that I could buy these beans back home, but he would not take no for an answer. He insisted so forcefully that eventually I had to relinquish, walking out with two cans of beans in my hands. They still sit in my pantry unopened, perhaps a fitting metaphor for my relationship with him over the years.

I also remember he brought up his house and pool again, and he asked me many times to visit him there. I replied, "Maybe, we'll see." Strauss said, "Birth parents can make excessive demands; they have far greater expectations of their reunion than an adopted adult. The adoptee may just want questions answered, while they have painful memories of having to part with a child." I still wasn't sure what I wanted regarding Albert.

In the coming days, however, I realized that this little jump into "daddy-daughter bonding" would not be sustainable, whatever my intentions. My parents seemed so sad when I left for Albert's, and it pained me more than I would admit. I did not wish to upset them further. I also did not give much thought to the inevitable outcome of making Albert Poppa #2 to Brian, his wife Betty Nana #2 by default, and what that would be like moving forward. It didn't seem right. I already had a family. I was never looking for another one. So like with Pearl, I would not visit him again for a very long time.

About two years after this meet-up, however, I received a thick envelope in the mail and recognized the curly-cue writing as Albert's. Ripping it open, I found a handwritten note inside thanking me for the birth announcement of my second child, my daughter Mallory, who had been born three months before. Sitting in front of me in her infant seat on the kitchen table of our new suburban home, she was kicking and swiping at the plastic toys above her head. I stopped watching her and ripped open the letter.

Inside, for the first time, were pictures of him, Betty and their children. My eyes zoomed in, scanning the images with laser precision. Seeing his daughter Pam, thin and doe-eyed with thick wavy chestnut hair and eyes like mine, gave me a jolt. The one of Paul at his bar mitzvah, his curly dark afro and olive skin, while not a match, caused my chest to squeeze. He seemed really sweet. The last photo was of them as a family, all smiling, dressed for some special occasion. Having this visual smacked me with the realization that there was a whole other family out there, not just a birth father, that was also my own and where I should have belonged. It sparked a curiosity in me, yes, but more so an anxiousness, not wanting to go there in my thoughts. So much so, I don't even remember if I ever even called to thank him.

Mallory kicked, and I slid the pictures under a stack of papers on my desk hidden from view. I lifted her up from her infant seat and looked into her deep brown eyes. I kissed her on the forehead gently and held her tight, feeling comforted by the proximity of her skin next to mine. She is my family, I thought to myself.

Once I put Mallory down for her nap, I took the family photos I received from Albert, walked up the stairs to my bedroom and pulled out the plastic storage tub that sat in the far corner of my closet. It sat under the dresses, hidden from view, where no one ventured. In it were the mementoes of my life, the physical traces of an existence reduced to a 12 x 18 x 12 container.

I knelt on the floor and flipped through the files inside, first to Childhood, then High School, Michigan, Alain, Rich, and Children. In each were documents, cards, photos, and papers I saved, ones that were significant to me. The last folder was labeled Adoption. My chest tightened when I pulled it out. In it were the photos I had of Pearl that Albert and Florence had given me. I looked at them and was struck once again by her joyful gaze and her calm exterior, revealing nothing of what was to come.

I returned those photos and then added the ones Albert just sent me. Slipping the Adoption file back in place, I thought of the irony that both Pearl and Albert were now together again, at least as mere images in a manila folder in my closet, the only place on this earth where this could ever happen.

I slipped the tub back and got up. I knew the photos were safe here. No one would look, not even me, not for years.

Thirteen

TELLING

$\mathcal{M}$oving forward on the adoption playing board of my life, I was finally ready to advance to the next space, the one I dub "telling." It was 1990, and society was changing. It was becoming okay to reveal our long held secrets. Oprah and Donahue, magazines and self-help forums were paving the way. People were talking about all kinds of things that had once been taboo, like alcoholism, homosexuality and cancer. And I was along for the ride.

I am 30-ish. I sit with my high school friend Leslie in the bedroom of her new apartment in Forest Hills, Queens on a summer day. Brian is almost two; Leslie's daughter three, and both of them sleep soundly in their strollers. She asks me how my parents are doing. For the first time ever, something compels me to tell her. I have never told anyone other than Alain and Rich, although Rich has told his family.

"I never told you this," I say as my entire body clenches, "but I'm, uh… a-*dopt*-ed." The seven-letter word sticks to my throat like extra thick peanut butter. She looks at me with shock.

"So Sam and Evelyn aren't your real parents?"

"Nope."

"How come you never said anything?"

"I don't know. It was really hard for me growing up." I launch into the tale, pushing the sentences from my tongue while Leslie looks like a bobble-head doll nodding at each revelation. I find myself fighting back tears, and she hands me a box of Kleenex.

As soon as I'm done with my confession, I tell her I better get going, wanting to remove myself from my vulnerability left hanging in the air. She hugs me good-bye. When I reach the street, I stop and look up at the sky. I am actually amazed that no lightning bolts have struck and only a few tears were shed. I push Brian's stroller and start running with a bounce to my step. Somehow the stroller feels lighter.

In the coming months, I mouth the words "I'm adopted" to a few other close friends and Rich's family, wanting to free myself. Each time, the tightening in my throat diminishes. The weight of my secret lifts like bricks removed from the end of a seesaw one by one. People always seem surprised, repeating the word *"adopted"* back to me with wonder and round eyes, because they are not used to others admitting this to them. No one seems to judge me, or at least not as far as I can tell.

I am 31. At a family barbeque at my mother in-law's home on Long Island, I tell her about meeting Pearl, something I haven't discussed with many others. She responds, "Well, Suzie, you know, *my* mother, Pauline, was in a mental hospital, too." My eyes gaze in shock toward her. "Yeah, well, she had postpartum depression, and they sent her away. She never came back. My dad ended up marrying a woman named Rita, that's who Rich's named after… but before that happened, we lived with another family." I take a moment to absorb this.

"Wait, a *foster* family?"

"I guess that's what it was, but then my dad took us back. I was young."

Finding out that my mother-in-law had this difficult life astonished me, as did the parallels to Pearl. They both had been in foster care, had mentally ill birth mothers, and neither one saw her birth mother again. It was a pretty heavy load for a child to bear. However, Rich's mom talked about it so casually. In hindsight, maybe the 63 years had washed most of the pain away, not unlike the edges of the sea glass she collected in the jars throughout her home.

It caused a new sense of compassion for her to spring up inside me. It also helped me understand her close relationship with her son with new eyes. She could always depend on him to be there for her, unlike her mother and her husband who had both left her.

I found out recently that Rich's grandmother, Pauline, actually ended up in a place called King's Park, a sprawling asylum in Brooklyn that took in most of the city's mentally ill population at that time. In 1954, the patient census topped a whopping 9,303, all in one facility. The infamous Tower 93 was built to meet this growing need, rising up out of the ground like a dark and foreboding behemoth, something that looks like it is out of a horror movie in my mind's eye. By the time they were there, the old "rest and relaxation" philosophy, where patients farmed and cooked, were succeeded by more invasive techniques like pre-frontal lobotomies, electro-shock therapy and the administration of thorazine, a drug that turned patients into "zombies." Joe Kennedy himself, patriarch of the Kennedy clan, sent his own daughter Rosemary to be lobotomized when he could not tolerate her mental limitations, based on the doctors suggestion at that time. He also felt she would be a liability to the family's political aspirations, a telling indicator of how mental illness was thought of in those days. Becoming a near vegetable when the surgeon cut too deep, she was hidden away in a home for decades. What happened to her stayed a family secret until recent years.

With the advent of better medications and a collective social awakening to the cruelty of locking those who suffer with mental illness away, such institutions began to decline. Most of them ended up closed. Kings Park still rises however above the Brooklyn landscape, in ruin, an eerie graveyard to an inhumane past.

I am 32. I tell my very first group of strangers. At a UJA-Federation gathering in my new suburban neighborhood, the professional asks us to go around the circle and give the origin of our names, a surefire way to connect us to our Jewish heritage. When my turn comes I am nervous, still I push myself to say, "Suzette is after my father's mother Sarah…and Joy, my middle name is because my father was filled with such, um, joy when he *adopted* me." I cringe on the "A" word. The ladies stare at me, startled by such a secret in 1992. They soon relax and smile back. A few approach me after, telling me what a "nice" story it was. I start to think that no one will be talking about me negatively behind my back, at least I hope.

I am 34. I am standing outside my daughter Mallory's pre-school. I am talking with two young mothers I recently met, named Liz and Kate. Their daughters are in class with Mallory. Liz tells Kate, "Allison's adoption day is coming!" and they are "planning a big celebration." My heart skips.

"Allison's adopted?"

"Yes," she tells me so relaxed. "We make the day she came to us special for her!" I am in awe. How easily those words flow from Liz's mouth! That they celebrate her being adopted that much more amazing. This day is also affectionately referred to as "gotcha day," I'd learn later, in the world of open adoption.

"That's so great, Liz, that you do that and guess what, *I'm adopted too.*"

"*So was I!*" Kate chimes in, something Liz seems to already know. Kate becomes the first person I know other than my brother who is adopted. It feels amazing; she is bright and beautiful, a blond-haired blued-eyed Cali girl now living in the same town as me. An instant kinship is born.

A few months later, we have grown closer. I bring it up again, intrigued to know more about her experience in relation to my own. "I was fine with it. My parents were pretty open about it. I mean, we didn't talk about it a lot, but it wasn't a big deal," she tells me while we sit in the office of her home.

I tell her how I felt it was a secret in my house and about the stigma I felt. Envious of how normal and easy it was for her, I wonder in that moment how much of what I went through was about the secrecy and how much was about my own limited coping skills. I mean, why was I so troubled when she wasn't? Before beating myself up, I remind myself that she didn't get a surprise call at a vulnerable time like I did. Still…

She filled me in on some more details that fascinated me. When her second daughter was born, she had a minor medical condition. She asked her parents then for "the envelope," the one she knew they kept that had her adoption information in case she ever needed to know. Now she felt that she did. She knew handing it over would be hard for her parents, so she emphasized it was for medical reasons only. When Kate opened it, there was a small piece of white paper inside with the names of her birth parents written out in blue ink. She was amazed her parents had their names all this time and never told her, just as my parents had a similar envelope for me that held my adoption contract. I didn't know at that point that mine existed.

With the help of a professional, she found them. When she called her birth dad, she assured him that she didn't want anything but medical information. He wouldn't talk to her. "I'm sorry but I can't help you," he said. Then he hung up.

"Maybe he never told anyone about me and was scared. Maybe he has a wife and kids who don't know," she states trying to make sense of it. "But still, I only wanted *information*!" We nodded our head's in agreement. Looking back now, it is easier to understand how a man born in the 30s, from that era of shame and secrets, might not have wanted a child born out of wedlock showing up in his life, unless of course, I laughed to myself, that man was Albert. It made me feel sad for Kate that this man did not want to have anything to do with this beautiful and loving woman sitting in front of me.

Kate met her half brother and sister and liked them very much; however, her biological mother, Marilyn, would have some reservations about meeting her. She had to warm up to the idea. Her half sister told her "it would be too hard," alluding that it would be too painful for her to go back to that time in her life and meet the daughter she didn't get to raise. Kate got the impression that her birthmother was a little emotionally fragile.

Finally Kate's mom agreed to meet her, and she flew out to California where her birth family lived. Kate, her husband, Marilyn and her two half siblings all went on a picnic together for the big meet up. It seemed like an idyllic setting in my mind, the yin and yang of a tranquil setting against the potential reunion angst. It was a positive experience all round, Kate told me, but given Kate's upbringing and that she was now a grown woman who had initiated this meet up, I was not surprised. They shared stories and looked at family pictures. Most importantly, Kate got to do what she really wanted to do: to pull her birth mother aside and thank her for having her and tell her that she had a wonderful life.

After the reunion, it took Marilyn eight months to contact Kate. She wrote her a note telling her she was thankful and glad to have met her. But

Marilyn did not want to have an ongoing relationship, just like Pearl did not. Kate did not see Marilyn again for twelve years. When she did, she brought her two teen-aged daughters with her, and Marilyn seemed happy to meet them. She considered that visit a "bonus gift" she will always treasure, as Marilyn is now suffering with dementia. Marilyn was lucky to have their names. The birth parents of the "baby scoop" era are slowly passing on now, leaving a whole generation of middle aged adults who will never have the opportunity to set eyes on the people who created them.

A year later, telling ratchets up to an all-new level. Kate explains to me that she has started volunteering at a local adoption agency, Forever Families through Adoption, and asks me if I would like to join her on a panel to speak to prospective adoptive parents. I am taken with her involvement and confidence on the matter. "What exactly would I have to say?" I ask.

"Whatever you want. You just talk from your heart about your experience," she answers.

Soon I find myself in a large room filled with people sitting in rows of folding chairs. I am sitting next to Kate at a dais. I'm petrified when it's my turn to speak. People are staring at me with intense curiosity. I decide to tell the truth. My words come out shaky. I tell these strangers about growing up in the sixties and how my adoption was kept hidden. I admit how the secrecy eventually led to shame and feelings of being less than others. I can't believe these words spill forth, but I continue on.

"My parents did what they felt was right; they didn't know any better," I state. Then, inspired by my friend Liz who continued to talk so openly about her adopted children, and from what I believe to be right in my heart, I say, "Be open with your child about it, talk about it, and make it a positive part of who they are. You don't want them to think there's anything wrong with it."

Was it the right advice? I didn't know then that open adoptions were becoming the way of the world and that, yes, full transparency was the way to go. Couples come up and thank me for sharing. They tell me it was very helpful. I feel relief that I have not done any damage, at least none that I know of.

I see something else in these couples' eyes. It is a yearning. And it is mixed with pain. Just like my parents, they are in a world they never expected to be in. At least there is one consolation: They have an open and accepting forum to share their struggles and get support, while my parents had no one but each other.

On the drive home, I wonder: *What happened to the young girl who could never tell a soul?*

I think she is long gone, happily.

I wonder too about all the children who are being adopted now with open files, aware of where they came from, some even having a relationship with their birth parents. Their biological and environmental heritage molded together in one package, as it should be, no secrets, no shame. Still, did knowing who you could have been at an early age make it easier? Or is there a certain amount of difficulty no matter how your adopted parents package it?

Kathy Brodsky, the former head of Ametz Adoption for the JCCA, explained to me, "There are layers of complication no matter what the circumstances, closed or open." With adoption there is loss, loss for the adoptive parents who cannot have a biological child of their own, loss for the biological parents who feel they have to give up their child, and loss for the adopted child who is cut off in varying degrees from his or her biological heritage. The losses must be acknowledged and dealt with in an open way to maximize the chances for a healthy adoption experience.

But in spite of the losses inherent in the adoption experience, there is, of course, also much gain.

And with all the research that has been done, adoptive parents can enter the process well educated about the best way to go about it. They can seek out professionals if needed, get advice on blogs and websites, and share their experiences with others in a world that does not cast judgment.

I am 37. Telling leads to greater revelations. It's my first book club meeting in my new home. We have moved from our first suburban home to another more deluxe model in the same time. I didn't need it or want it, but he was on the current 1980's thinking highway that said bigger is better, so why not? I said okay.

I wondered, just like I did when I moved into Rich's apartment in the city, what did I do to deserve this huge home? What did anyone do to deserve it for that matter? People were starving all over the world, I would tell myself. Was it wrong to live this way? I was prepared to live in socialist France, happy and satisfied with a simple life and economic equality. Now here we were living the capitalist's dream because my husband was a talented trader. On top of that, I didn't earn a penny of it. It did not feel good.

But it was more than that. You see, rich people were always other people; now "rich people" was me too. It was like getting a fancy new suit that didn't fit right. Was it because Charlotte would never have had it? Or was it just an organic part of who I was? How much of my past affected my present? Sure, we gave a lot to charity, and this was a first-world problem, not a problem at all, but an amazing gift. So why was Rich's financial success so hard for me to be comfortable with?

I can see now that deep inside I had this belief that I was someone who should have grown up in a worn, cramped dwelling in Brooklyn where Pearl raised her own family. Thanks to Google maps, I was able to find their home: it was a small, dark and narrow two-family brick house on the corner of a busy street. And, while from my vantage point now, it was true that Charlotte might have risen up from her humble beginnings, gotten a scholarship, made it through college and had a stellar career in her chosen field, more so than Suzette did, I didn't even consider that possibility. The struggling Charlotte was all I could see, the one who didn't belong to this affluent life.

Don't ever get too comfortable, I told myself, because it could all be taken away in an instant, just like babies could.

<hr />

Since it was my turn to make a selection for the book club I joined, I recommend one called *Ithaka: A Daughter's Memoir of Being Found*, by Sarah Saffian. A few months before, while perusing the shelves of Barnes & Noble, the title jumped out at me like metal to a magnet. I took it in my hands and stared at the dark haired beauty on the cover whose piercing deep brown eyes stared back at me. I flipped to the back. I read that Sarah got a phone call out of the blue from her birth mother when she was just a few years older than I was. "The phone call, wholly unexpected, instantly turned Sarah's world upside-down, threatening her sense of family, identity, and self," it said. My heart dropped. *That was me, too!* Was it possible that someone went through what I did, being found, and was so negatively affected?

That night in bed, I gulped down the rest. Sarah was not only found at 23, but I learned how she struggled emotionally and how she did not know how to navigate both families. She also harbored a lot of pain and anger that her birth parents took the decision from her by contacting her when she was not prepared. It took her three years to even be ready to meet them. For the first time in my life, I did not feel alone. I knew that what happened to me happened to another human being and the traumatic upheaval I experienced was not unique. The validation at this stage of my life, 39 years old, was a mental-health remedy of the highest order.

When I recommended *Ithaka* to my book club, a group of women I had met through my work with UJA-Federation, I wasn't sure why I was steering these ladies into such sensitive waters. Being comfortable telling people I was adopted was one thing, but potentially sharing the gritty details with a group of ladies I barely knew was another. Also, this was a group of ladies that somewhat intimidated me: they were all attractive, impeccably dressed, wealthy and smart. My insecurities percolated up whenever I was in their presence. But feeling more confident with my adoption world, and having an inner need to move forward, I threw caution to the wind. I knew it would be good for me.

The women entered that night. Settling down in my library, they chatted and chuckled. My stomach squeezed. I was not only worried about making myself vulnerable but that the story held no interest for them.

"So everyone, what did you think…?" I asked them.

"It was *really good*," said one of them with her deep voice.

"It was such a wonderful story about what family really means," said another. The others chimed in. Each one had a positive comment.

"I picked this book, not just because I was adopted, as you know," I paused, "but because I was found by my biological dad, just like the author was."

All eyes lifted toward me. "Well, um, anyway..." I began, "Saffian writes that she knew that she was adopted but..."

"Wait, if you don't mind, we want to hear about *you*," another voice exclaimed. A barrage of questions followed, and I began to answer them all, egged on by their sincere and collective curiosity. It was scary to reveal so many intimate details. Would they think less of me? Would they judge Pearl and Albert? Were they wondering if I suffered with mental illness as well?

As I went on, however, I started to feel empowered by their empathetic fascination. My voice strengthened. I answered all their questions with brutal honesty, much to my own shock, and by the time I was done, there was a moment of silence. Take me or leave me, I thought, even though I was still fearful. I don't even remember if we ever got back to the book.

They all thanked me that night with hugs and smiles. After they all left, I climbed the stairs, slipped in bed next to Rich, and passed out. When the sun shone the next morning, I turned on the computer in my office. There were three emails from book club members.

Dear Suzie: Last night was so inspiring. We were all in awe of your story and so touched you shared it with us. It was truly one of the best book clubs ever. You have been through so much yet you come through with a big smile on your face, appreciative of your wonderful family. We all could take a lesson! Love, T.

I scarfed down the other two that were filled with similar sentiments, different versions of the same theme.

Something new dawned on me. Had I been thinking about it in the wrong way all these years? I mean, these women seemed to hold me in *higher* regard for my past, not less. Was it possible that I was better in some way, not worse, because of it? I did not know, but it felt great to receive such kind sentiments. No one can underestimate the power of kindness when we are feeling vulnerable.

elling now means it is time to inform the next generation, my children. I head down the steps to find Brian and Mallory eating cereal out of the box while watching television. My third child, baby Asher, is sleeping. He is one year old.

Before he was born, I asked my mother if she wanted to be in the room while I gave birth. As uncomfortable as I was with having my "down there" so exposed, I wanted to give her that experience since she was not able to have it herself. Her mouth and eyes stayed wide open while the miracle of birth was displayed before her. She was forever thankful to me for giving her that gift.

As I approach Brian and Mallory, I wonder if they will be upset to find out I was adopted. The world they were growing up in did not carry the stigma around it that mine did. Each had friends who were adopted. It was as normal for them as the air they breathed.

"Come here guys, I want to tell you something."

They come join me in the kitchen and sit down on the counter stools, curious. "I want you to know something about me…. well, that I was adopted." I say it in the most fluid, matter of fact tone I can.

"Wait, what?" Mallory asks, her six-year-old eyes growing wide.

"Yeah well, Nana and Poppa couldn't have children… so they adopted Uncle Oliver and me instead." I knew simplest is best, so I wait to see if they have any questions.

"So you have other parents?" Brian asks.

"Yeah, and so does Uncle Oliver, but we don't have the same ones. But they are just the ones who made us." They look at me a bit taken aback, but not upset.

"So Nana and Poppa are still our real grandparents, right?" I reassure them that of course they are. Memories of my parents reassuring me of the same thing, at about the same age, flood back. I knew it was confusing. "Okay," Brian says and gets up to chase after our tan shepherd mix, Sophie. Mallory looks at me, her brow scrunched.

"Well, I don't care," she adds in her high-pitched voice, shrugging her shoulders and running after Sophie too, her light blond hair flying behind her, the same blond hair she inherited from Pearl.

By the time I tell Asher that I am adopted, seven or eight years later, it is such a non-event that I can't even remember saying it.

⌒

"Telling," was something my mother would also do, but it would not be until a little while later. After six years in our more deluxe house, twelve in that town all together, we packed up and moved again, this time to the house and town in Westchester County that was right next door to the Cottage School. We wanted our kids to be in a better school district. Rich also bought my mom and dad a condo right near us as my dad's health was starting to decline. They sold their house in Boca and moved up from Florida full time.

After unpacking her boxes and settling in to her own new place, my mom walked into my kitchen one day with an envelope. "I have something for you," she said. She pulled out a sheet and opened it. "Do you remember this?" she asked me. The face of Dear Abby, the famous advice columnist, was on top.

Legacy of the Adopted Child
Once there were two women who never knew each other,
One you do not remember — the other you call Mother.
Two different lives shaped to make yours one.
One became your guiding star — the other became your sun.
The first gave you life and the second taught you to live in it.
The first gave you a need for love and the second was there to give it.
One gave you a nationality; the other gave you a name.
One gave you the seed of talent; the other gave you an aim.
One gave you emotions; the other calmed your fears.
One saw your first sweet smile; the other dried your tears.
One gave you up – It was all that she could do.
The other prayed for a child and God led her straight to you.

And now you ask me through your tears the age-old question through the years:
Heredity or Environment – Which are you the product of?
Neither my darling, neither –
Just two different kinds of love.
~ Author Unknown

"I do remember," I told her.

"I made this copy for you," she said and handed it to me. She then took out her wallet, slipped her finger into a slot and pulled out a very small piece of folded newspaper, one that was barely hanging together. "And do you remember this?"

I held it in my hands and read:

"Not flesh of my flesh,
Nor bone of my bone,
But still miraculously my own.
Never forget for a single minute,
You didn't grow under my heart
but in it."

"Yes, I do."

"I wanted you to see it again. I always have it with me" she said. Memories of her showing them to me as a young adult reappeared in my conscious.

"They're beautiful mom, I know…and both so true." I stared into her eyes.

"You know how much I love you, right, and feel like the luckiest person alive to have gotten you and dad as my parents?"

"Yes. You know you're my life," she said, choked up and beaming at the same time.

We embraced and held each other for a while. It felt fulfilling to have this moment with my mom, finally able to dwell on the significance of that winter day in November 1960 at the Louise Wise agency when I was placed in her arms.

She wiped her eyes and handed me the envelope she was still clutching. "These are your adoption papers," she said, "it's time you had them."

I never even knew they existed.

I took the envelope in my hand. It was yellowed and flattened thin, obviously from years of being squeezed in her file cabinet. "I'll take a look at it later, okay?" I said in a casual tone. I did not want to open it in front of her. I also did not want her to think having them was a big deal for me.

It was a big step for her to hand them over, I was sure. After all, she had hidden them for forty-five years. But how could I blame her for burying the evidence? It was the proof that I was not fully hers. Now her heart was ready, and I was amazed.

When she left, I picked up the envelope and examined it. The postmark was 1977, causing me to wonder why. That was my senior year of high school. I opened it and slid the papers out.

"In the matter of the adoption of Charlotte Kaminek..." *Kaminek?*

My last name was Kaminek? My stomach dropped. The reality of learning my last name too was viscerally overwhelming. The idea that I was once someone else, should have been someone else, gripped me once again in a powerful way.

I continued to read, "...by Samuel and Evelyn Gordon, his wife, duly verified before me the *13th of February 1962*...An agreement on the part of the foster parents to adopt..."

This detail stunned me. I was considered a foster child for the first eighteen months of my life. Thoughts of the Cottage School reverberated in my head.

I scanned the legalese of 1960's adoption. At the end it read, "And it appearing to my satisfaction that the moral and temporal interests of the minor, Charlotte Kaminek, will be promoted by granting the petition... Charlotte Kaminek shall be henceforth known by the name of Suzette Joy Gordon. February 13, 1962." And just like that, with the stamp and signature of a judge's hand, I went from being one person to another.

I reached for the second sheet in the envelope; it too was yellowed. It was the contract from Louise Wise. I scanned each line and stopped when I came to "Louise Wise Services has the right to remove the child at any time prior to legal adoption…. we will welcome the representative of [LWS] to our home, will keep her appraised of any change in our situation, and will consult with her on any questions."

A conversation with my mother that packed a truthful punch came back to me. "For 18 months after we got you and your brother, there was a trial period. They could've taken you back if they wanted. The social worker would come by unannounced. I mean, anybody can make a baby, but because we had infertility problems, we had to prove ourselves worthy of parenthood."

She was right. It wasn't fair, but was anything? Many of the children at the Cottage School had multiple full and half siblings, their parents abusing or neglecting them and a majority of them taking state money to live. My parents had to be under a microscope because they couldn't conceive.

Folding the papers back up, I headed up the stairs to our bedroom closet where I had installed a safe to contain all of our important documents. Opening it, I put the envelope inside and pulled out another one where I had written Birth Certificates in blue ink. I removed my own. An old fashioned copy, it had white letters on a black background and looked like a negative. I had not looked at it in years.

I looked at the names of my parents, their address and my name typed out. There must have been a previous birth certificate with Pearl, Albert and Charlotte, I imagined. What did the state do with that one? Was it destroyed? In her book *The DeClassified Adoptee*, Transue-Woolston explains that "adoptees are the only people in this country who cannot access their original birth certificates, and likens the amended ones to "hide your family drama" certificates. By the government doing such, she explains, it sends the message, to this day, that it's terrible to be adopted." I don't know if I would look at it that harshly, but it definitely wasn't right in the moral universe I lived in.

I further examined the part where it said I was born. *Staten Island.* I had seen that before but always chose to ignore it. All I knew about that borough were from my drives from New Jersey to Long Island when I was a college student going to visit my high school friends. I remembered mostly the many landfills. My eyes would watch the birds hovering over these giant heaps of refuse as the smell of waste circulated through my car and reached my nose. From my vantage point, it wasn't a pretty place.

How many times was I asked on documents to list my place of birth and wasn't sure. I'd fudge it by picking any one of the boroughs where I imagined my birth parents could have lived. I would never have asked my mom about it in those days, still in my adoption closet, the thought of it too scary. No one was going to call me on it anyway, I would say to myself. But I now knew that Pearl lived in Queens with her foster family. How did she end up giving birth on Staten Island? More answers led to more questions.

I heard Brian calling me. I quickly stuck the papers in the safe and turned the dial, locking up the documents with my thoughts on the matter, at least for now. Zapped back to my life where Charlotte didn't exist anymore, I headed downstairs to get dinner started. It was now as easy as turning off a light switch.

I telephoned my mother the next day, curious. I asked her how old I was when she adopted me. "You were three months old, your brother five."

"So where was I then during that time?"

"They had people who took care of you, of babies -- I guess foster parents. They wouldn't tell us who back then."

I asked her why. "I have no idea. And I didn't want to press the issue because I didn't want them changing their minds about us getting you."

After I hung up the phone, I was troubled. A movie played in my head. I was an infant in a battered crib pushed up against a wall of a dim room in a small dirty apartment. The bitter smell of fried food filled the air. The wallpaper was peeling and the rug was thin and frayed. There were three other babies in cribs pushed against the walls, sleeping. But I was crying. The floors creaked as an elderly woman came in and looked down at me. My face was bright red, raw and damp with tears. I couldn't make out the woman's face, only the brittle gray hair hanging from the back of her head and the thinned floral housecoat. She looked down at me and frowned. Then she walked away and closed the door.

Was this a memory? A nightmare? Or some combination of the two?

The belief at the time I was adopted was that infants were a "tabula rasa," or a "clean slate," and would thus have no memory of the early parts of their life. As long as someone was there to meet a child's basic needs, there would be no lasting psychological damage. Nancy Verrier, in her groundbreaking work

The Primal Wound, insisted that infants do experience a trauma when they are removed from their birth mothers. "The smell of her skin, the sound of her voice, and the visual imprint she makes are all engraved into a newborn's psyche," she states. The impact can reverberate for a lifetime. Whether this was true, that my brother and I were affected in negative ways, I do not know. At a minimum, neither of us will ever know who held us, fed us and cared for us in the beginning months of our lives.

I'd later find out that this "wait period" had a very specific purpose. Louise Wise wanted to make sure their babies were "normal" before adopting them out. I have no idea what they considered "not normal" or what they did with those infants. It was disturbing to me... very, very disturbing.

Fourteen

COTTAGE 10

It was the day of our very first lunch group with the girls. Rich and I were well settled into our new town that was right next to the campus. My girl-friends emerged from their cars with excited faces. Phina greeted the group and then led us up the three cement steps that led to the back door of Cottage 10. She took the key, put it into the knob, and pushed the heavy metal door open.

At the end of a pale green painted hallway, the ten of us entered a large room where fourteen teenage girls sat around round wooden tables. They stared at us as we entered. Their faces were as curious as ours were, but they were also unsure. So were we.

Phina announced our plan to the girls. "As it was explained to you ladies, these women live in neighboring towns. They will be coming to spend lunch-time with you each month and do fun things. Why don't we start by going around and introducing ourselves," she said.

The girls said their names, some barely audible, some with an edge, and some with enthusiasm. My friends and I went around and offered our names, with as much warmth and kindness as we could muster.

Looking at them I couldn't help but wonder what kind of abuse or neglect each of them had suffered, the tales they could tell, and how my presence, ours there, could possibly make any difference in their lives.

We began to circulate and say hello, one on one. Leaning over to be on eye level with them, each of us, all moms, started the task of trying to engage these young teenagers.

"Hi, my name's Suzie. What's yours again?" I said to one young girl, lowering my head to better see her face. She barely looked up at me. She told me in a meek voice that her name was Asha. Tall and thin with dark almond eyes, short black hair and a purple zip up sweatshirt, she hunched her shoulders and kept her head down. I laid the wood frame and a plastic white palette down in front of her. Squeezing paint into the small circular holes, I filled each one with a different rainbow color. I handed her the paintbrush and asked her to try. She did not move. I asked her again, saying, "Why don't you just give it a try," in an encouraging tone, and I held the brush next to her hand. She took it in slow motion, unsure, not lifting her head up. Barely dipping it in the paint, she then touched it to the frame.

"I love green too!" I said enthusiastically.

The edge of her mouth curled up a bit.

"Keep going, that's great!"

She started to move the brush back and forth over the wood surface. The other girls got to work too. I stepped back and announced in a loud voice, "When you're done girls, I'll take a picture of each of you with my Polaroid camera!" I held it up for them to see. "And in case you've never seen one, it spits out pictures right away so you can put them in your frame today!" There were a few nods and smiles. "Come to me for yours when you're done painting!" I added.

Asha dipped the brush in the water cup and then into a new color, lifting her head up a bit now. "Great job, there you go!" I said leaning over her and watching her move the brush.

The volunteers were hovering over the other girls doing the same as I was. Wherever there were free seats, my friends sat down next to them to be even closer to them. The noise in the room that began with a slow whisper started to grow to a gentle buzz. I heard my friends reassuring and encouraging the girls. Some continued to be quiet like Asha while others perked up with zest. The moms asked questions, and the girls started to answer. Eventually a chuckle or two broke through at the table to my left.

Phina came over to me and whispered in my ear. "This is a great project," she said, "because many of these girls have no photographs of themselves."

"I didn't even think about that," I replied in surprise.

"Yeah, well, who'd be taking their picture and developing them?" This was 2003, long before smart phones with cameras.

I looked over at Asha, and I felt good she was continuing to paint the frame. Her head was up now, and she seemed engaged. A tall, overweight girl with dark nail polish and enormous hoop earrings tapped me on the shoulder and said with hesitation, "I'm ready for my picture."

"Okay, what's your name?"

"Keisha."

"*Niiice* name! Come stand here against the wall." I grabbed the camera. She stepped in front of the wall and turned. "Smile!" I said. Her lips didn't move.

"C'mon, you need to smile. Can't I get one?" Her lips moved, a millimeter.

"Okay, *I know there's a smile in there somewhere!*" I blurted out with a huge one on my own face.

Her cheeks lifted and her teeth became visible. "There you go! Beautiful! You should smile more often!" I snapped two.

The deliveryman walked in with his large pizza bags. The aroma of tomato sauce and mozzarella filled the room. The moms handed out the slices on paper plates and filled the glasses with soda. They were moms being moms, doing what they do best.

When we finished the meal and our projects, I removed a sheet cake from its box. I took my icing tube and wrote out, "Happy Birthday Taweka," on top, put in the candles and lit them.

"Okay, it's time to sing happy birthday!" I shouted. Phina flipped the lights and my friends and I started singing while I walked toward the birthday girl. We circled around her. "For me?" she asked.

"Yes, for YOU!" we all yelled back. She blushed and looked at the burning candles, the flowers that adorned the perimeter in purple and pink icing, and the words on top.

"I never had a cake like that before," she said.

"Like what?" I asked.

"With my name on it."

We all looked at her, first with surprise, then with empathy. "Well, now you do!" said my girlfriend Lisa. Another friend encouraged her to make a wish. Her eyes opened wide, and she looked around the room at everyone staring at her. A sheepish smile grew on her face. It seemed to me that she was questioning whether she should allow herself to be happy or not in this moment. She took a deep breath and blew out the candles. Everyone clapped. Her face was now glowing.

I handed her a small wrapped box and told her to open it. Everyone was watching. Inside, there was a sterling silver necklace with a heart. Debbie managed to secure a bunch of them from a friend in the business. "Put it on, put it on!" a few of the ladies yelled.

Everyone told her how nice it looked as I closed the clasp. She touched it and looked at the group with appreciation. The impact of the gift was clear.

The hour ended in a blip. We wrapped our arms around each girl and said goodbye. Some kept their arms down. Some of them hugged us back.

The staff yelled out, "Thank the volunteers!"

"Thank you, thank you," echoed through the room.

"Will you be back?" one of the girls asked.

"Every month we will be here!" someone said. Her face lit up. Grabbing the large shopping bags from the kitchen, I yelled, "Wait, don't leave yet!" I handed out the soft beanbag animal pillows I bought. Even though they were teenagers, they started to clutch them as small children would.

"Oh, these are *soooo* cute," one of girls said with a huge grin.

"Time for school, girls!" the staff member bellowed, "leave your animals here please!" The girls put down their gifts reluctantly and shuffled out, one by one. The moms looked at each other.

"I think we did good!" Debbie said.

"Yeah, that was great Suzie," Nancy added.

"I want to remind you that these children have severe trust issues," Phina told us before we left. "All the adults in their lives have let them down or hurt them. So just be patient if some of them didn't seem all that interested.

They'll come around as they get to know you. And they know you were here for them no matter how they acted. I promise you, they won't forget it."

I drove away absorbing the experience. It was middle-aged, well-off white Jewish ladies mingling with traumatized poverty-stricken urban youth, trying to find commonality to bind us. Somehow I knew caring about them, in any small amount we could, would be the only commonality we would need, because it was what all of us need.

For me, however, it was more than that. Pearl was a foster child. She could have been in that room too.

Fifteen

CLOCK RACE

Intertwined with my story, of course, was the story of my brother Oliver. Eleven years after my reunion with Albert, he decided to jump into the adoption pool and begin his own search. It was the new millennium, Y2K, and while others worried about their computers blowing up, my brother worried about "the speed with which time was passing." With that, he explained to me, "there was a woman out there who never knew what happened to me. I was forty-four then, and I did the math...it meant she was getting close to her seventies, and I thought I better not wait any longer."

Married with three children, he had left his job with a bank to start his own trading fund and found himself with some free time, something he never had before. The timing was fortuitous. "I thought about her from time to time before that, fleeting thoughts, but it never seemed like the right time to search. Now it did."

My brother was also like many adoptees from the closed system that make the decision to search during middle age. "Having children of their own, middle-aged adoptees tend to reflect on their own birth experience for the first time and think about where they came from," Brodzinsky wrote in *Being Adopted*. Plus, it is a time in life when one is more settled, stable and prepared to deal with the emotional upheaval that reunion can bring.

Oliver called my mother for help, and she was very supportive. By then, she had been through all the trials and tribulations with me, so I imagine it was easier for her this time around. She gave him his adoption papers to help him. At that point in time, I didn't even know she had them, so I did not think to ask my brother how he found out his name; I just assumed my mother knew it somehow and told him. Maybe I was too scared to probe.

Oliver's adoption contract revealed that his birth name was Bruce Jacobson. At the New York Public Library where the records were kept, my brother spent hours combing through all the children born on his birthday with the name Jacobson, the only way one could search then if you were fortunate enough to know your birth name.

He found his.

He discovered his mother's name was Ruth. She most probably came alive to him in a deeper way, just as Pearl did for me when Albert uttered her name for the first time. He could not find any further trace of her after that in the records. He assumed she must have married and changed her name. The trail went cold. He did not go any further.

After he found his mother's name, my brother and I didn't speak about each of our adoptions again for a long time. Looking at it now, I believe we had some mutual aversion to it, at least one that I felt, all predicated on the way we grew up. Maybe it was just me who had the aversion actually, but he didn't bring the topic up either.

Ten years passed. By that time, our father Sam had sadly passed away. My brother renewed his quest. This time, he hired someone to help him. Her name was Pamela Slaton, an adoption sleuth, the Sherlock Holmes of her field. She found Ruth in two short weeks. She eventually wrote a book about her experiences in which she presented descriptions of some of the more compelling adoption reunions she facilitated. She included my brother's story.

When I picked up that book, *Reunited: An Investigative Genealogist Unlocks Some of Life's Greatest Family Mysteries,* I found out for the first time why my brother stopped his search after he found his mother's name in the public records. She quoted him as saying, "I thought about getting a P.I. back in 2000, but I knew my father would have been upset and I couldn't do that to him. I just figured somehow, if he found out I was searching, it would break his heart."

Oliver's words hit me hard. With them, I suddenly felt guilty about my own reunions, even if my first with Albert was not of my doing. They probably caused my parents more pain than I ever imagined, pain they must have shared with my brother but not with me. After what happened with Albert, it made sense that Oliver wouldn't cause them any more hardship in that regard.

Had I been selfish? Where was my allegiance? Or was it their problem, not mine? It was a delicate question, a balancing of scales; my conscience tipped toward reunion but Oliver's tipped the other way. But once my father had passed away, Oliver felt comfortable moving forward. He knew my mom would be okay with it.

I also wondered, after reading Slaton's book, if the desire *not* to hurt my father was the only reason Oliver didn't take his search further in 2000. In what I now know to be the challenging and complicated web of emotions that accompany the reunion experience, it is easy to understand why my brother, or any adoptee for that matter, might want to leave the door closed. If you open it, you might not like what falls out.

Even though I was now on the other side of reunion, and Pearl and Albert ended up being approachable and good decent people, it had been far from easy. Maybe Oliver sensed the "possible ego chaos that could be unleashed if he went further," as Lifton described it, and used our parents' feelings as a sub-conscious excuse. Maybe he did not feel that way. Maybe he did. Still, my brother putting our father's needs before his own, even if that was only partly the case, did make me feel badly about my own actions.

My mom called me and said with a muted enthusiasm, "Your brother found his birth mother! *And he met her!*"

I didn't even know he had made the decision to start searching again. Excited to hear all about it, I called him right away. Pamela Slaton found out she was living in a nursing home in Queens. He called her room immediately, but no one answered. He tried multiple times over the next two days. Scared that something bad had happened, he got hold of the director and explained his story. In spite of Oliver's heartfelt words, he wouldn't tell my brother where Ruth was. He started having heart palpitations and became frantic. He was afraid she would pass away before he had the opportunity to meet her.

He barked to the director, "Tell me or tell my lawyer!" The director relented. He revealed that Ruth was in the hospital and very sick with pneumonia.

"I realized I didn't have a lot of time...I literally got in the car and rushed to Queens to where she was," he told me. He also stopped to pick up a bouquet of pink roses along the way. And even though Pamela had made it clear to Oliver that he should call Ruth first, as she recommended to all adoptees before reunion, Oliver could not wait.

He walked into her room and smiled. He said, "These are for you," and handed her the flowers he had bought. He then said in a gentle tone, "My name is Oliver Gordon but my last name used to be Jacob. A long time ago I was given the name Bruce. I was born on Sept. 11, 1956. Does that ring a bell?"

Ruth looked at him and her face lit up.

"Ruth, I'm your son..." he said.

"I know," she responded, "I just needed to hear you say that. I'd always hoped you come and find me, but after all these years, I figured it wasn't going to happen."

My heart flooded hearing this. I tried to picture this scene, a woman with sunken cheeks, gray scattered hair and deep soulful eyes, her body lost under a pile of crisp white sheets, staring at this tall broad shouldered and handsome man who entered the room.

"She seemed sooo happy," he told me. I pictured their beaming faces, the initial spark of a mother and infant's love re-lit after fifty years. When reading Slaton's book years later, I learned more details that I hadn't known. Slaton wrote that Ruth told my brother, "I had a hole in my heart," and that "every time a man walked into my room in the nursing home or hospital, I wondered, Could it be him?" My brother had fulfilled her dying wish.

"Because she was really weak, she couldn't talk much," he went on to say. "I told her all about the good life I had." He held her hand the entire two hours that he was with her.

I asked him if he thought it was hard for her as well, to see him after all these years knowing what she missed out on, but he seemed to believe it was all positive.

"I told her that she did the right thing by giving me away. I was so glad to give her that closure."

"It must have been amazing for her," I said.

"Yes, it was…."

"And what about your dad?" I asked.

"It was a short fling when she was young…she never saw him again. She didn't even remember his name."

"I'm sorry…"

"Yeah, well," he paused, "but guess what, I have a half sister!" he happily exclaimed.

Ruth got married after giving birth to Oliver and had a girl she named Tracey. It ends up Tracey went to visit her mom in the hospital the day after Oliver had showed up. Ruth told her daughter about Oliver right away. Describing it to me after, he said "yeah…Tracey walked in and Ruth said, *oh by the way, guess what?* You have a half brother!" He half laughed and half shook his head while describing this to me, not believing the absurdity of it all.

Naturally, Tracey was in shock. Ruth had kept Oliver's birth a secret her entire life.

My brother and Tracey spoke for a good long while on the phone after that. She was happy to give Oliver as much of the family history that she could. He learned that Ruth had struggled all her life, and the man she married after having Oliver, Tracey's dad, walked out on them when Tracey was just two. It was a tough life for both of them.

As for meeting my brother, she decided against it. "I guess it was too much for her," Oliver told me. "She didn't want to have to explain to her husband and children who I was after all these years." That sounded just like Albert's words about his own children.

"But I'm okay with that…" he went on. Still, I felt sad for my brother that his half sister decided not to meet him. I also felt a loss for Tracey since she had no other siblings. It was all a reminder of the remnants of the closed system.

My brother finished the call by saying, "I'm going to bring Dawn [his wife] and the kids to meet Ruth next time!" He sounded so upbeat, exuberant, but I wondered if there wasn't a flipside—feelings of deep loss that co-existed with the happiness.

After hanging up, I wondered why I had never brought my family to meet Albert or Pearl since Oliver so freely did. I didn't want to compare, but I couldn't help it. I had come so far yet not as far as my brother, and he did so in such a short timeframe. I looked at the differences in our stories, which were enormous.

My brother read the draft of this memoir before publication. I was nervous handing it to him. He called me right after he finished it.

"It was so great...I learned so much!"

"Seriously? I hope things that were... helpful?"

"Well, let's just say I'm looking at myself through new eyes now... and seeing how being adopted probably shaped choices I made in ways I was never aware of."

Sixteen

WE ENTER

*W*ord began to spread about my volunteer lunch group at the Cottage School. My friends started telling their friends and like a snowball rolling down hill, soon I had three and then five groups. Cottages that did not have groups started asking, so I sent emails to everyone I knew to see if they would consider participating. Within five years, I had nine in all. I loved being on the campus for all of them.

The best part was that other women started their own groups. Eventually there would be over twenty, one for each cottage on the campus. I could not believe how one small lit match had turned into such a roaring flame.

The volunteer pool proliferated in other ways. Soon there were weekend groups of parents and children coming together. High schools started Cottage School clubs. Other charity groups, local universities and corporate groups started coming. The mentorship program, which was already in place, grew extensively. Thanks to the amazing leadership and hard work of Phina and her co-workers, Bonnie and Stacy, and eventually Sandi who replaced Phina, the program grew beyond what anyone could have ever expected. Today there are over 500 volunteers who visit the campus on a continued basis.

The presence of this enormous volunteer pool on the campus had a huge impact on the children. As our CEO Ron Richter recently explained to our volunteers, "Not only with your words and actions, but with your caring and love, you change their perspective on humanity. Their perspective has been very tainted. They don't know of trust and consistency and kindness. Some of them have had a few spurts of normalcy, but then horrible disappointments and traumas. You are a key part of our strength-based approach to their treatment. It's not about *what's wrong* with our kids but *what's right.* By being joyful, getting to know them and treating them like they are no different than other kids, you can truly make a strong impact in their lives." These words were powerful.

As for my personal motivation, it was more than just that. Each time I entered the campus, my mind went to the same place: *my biological mother was a foster child who could have been here.*

But at some point, I realized something further. Had Pearl not given me up for adoption, she would have been a single mom with no one to support her, something her foster mom made clear. Her debilitating depression would eventually have kicked in, so she could well have ended up unable to care for me and perhaps even homeless. Where would that have left me? There were a myriad possibilities but certainly foster care was a likely one. Perhaps I could have even ended up here on the campus. It was certainly a possibility.

So was I actually taking care of Charlotte each time I came here?

Yes I was.

But I was also taking care of Suzette, who was trying to find a way to make peace with her past by righting the wrong that was done to Pearl in some small way.

In doing so, the experiences with the children have left their indelible marks on my heart.

We enter Cottage 6. Deshon's eyes light up when he sees he's getting his own can of soda. "You mean I get to have the whole can for myself?" he asks me. I tell him of course.

We enter Cottage 8. Christopher wants to keep his paper Spider Man plate. "But it's covered in pizza grease. You sure you want it?" I ask.

"I don't care," he says, "I want to hang it in my room."

We enter Cottage Edenwald 7. Tyesha has never seen a birthday cake before. She is 11 years old. "What do I do?" she asks when the candles and cake are placed in front of her. We tell her to make a wish and blow. She accommodates, unsure, but then follows with a radiant smile.

We enter Cottage 7. Romaine, once the toughest and most defiant young man in the cottage, is now acting silly. He is hugging the volunteers and posing for pictures one of us is taking with her iPhone. When another boy gets too rowdy, he says, "Be respectful man! Stop acting like that around the volunteers." He wants us to know he appreciates our presence.

We enter Cottage 6. A new boy asks, "Why are you here?" He has no idea what a volunteer is. Many of the children don't when they arrive. A staff member explains it to him. He is perplexed. He cannot comprehend that people want to do nice things for him for no reason. He has grown up in a very different world than that, one where survival is the name of the game. Soon he sees he can accept the caring we offer and begins to talk and smile.

We enter Cottage 8. Desmond is buzzing as he paints the wood boxes we bring. He says to me, bubbling over, "My birthday's in May, my birthday's in May! I'm going to get a gift and cake, right?" May is five months away. "Of course!" I reassure him. I wonder if that is all he has to look forward to.

We enter Cottage Edenwald 8, the youngest boys. On the back wall, hanging up, are black and white photocopied pictures, ones that the boys colored in as a project. I cannot make out what they say so I go closer to look at them. They are all identical: a drawing of a small child leaning on his elbows with one caption above and one below. The top one reads, "I know I am somebody," and the bottom one reads, "because God don't make no junk." That such a poster actually exists astonishes me. I'm hit with the horror that many of these children might feel this way, that they are worthless.

We enter Gateways, the cottage for commercially trafficked girls. One fourteen-year old young girl tells us that she is looking forward to Thanksgiving on the campus because she hasn't celebrated a holiday in two years. It feels good to not be "thrashed" anymore either.

We enter Cottage 10. Keisha is sitting in a chair with her head bowed down on her arms. Soft sobs emanate from her. Two of us go over and ask her what's wrong. She does not lift her head nor does she answer. Later, the staff pulls us aside and whispers, "Her mother's been in jail, and Keisha went to court this morning. She relinquished parental rights...so now she has no one. She'll be put up for adoption." Sadness engulfs me. What are the chances of a teenage girl with emotional problems being adopted? Slim, I imagine.

In the state's quest to try to find families for these children, the NYC Administration for Children's Services (ACS) advertises on the local news twice a week, a segment called Wednesday's Child. Cottage School children are often presented. One day while making dinner in my kitchen, I hear a voice from the television say, "This is Joshua. His two biggest dreams are to one day become an engineer and to have a family of his own. This 14-year-old is personable, smart and is always willing to lend a helping hand...Joshua already knows his ideal family...one that will love and care for him." I stared at Joshua's big dark eyes on the screen. My heart sank. I hoped that someone would take him, someone braver than I.

Life is not equal. It is brutally unequal. Why did I get so lucky to not only be spared but also end up with a life I never dreamed of? Why did these children end up here and not me? But I have no answer.

⟜⟶

*J*ust two years after I started volunteering, I met Mark. Newly hired to be the VP of Fund Development for JCCA, he would later become instrumental in my search. At that time, he asked if I would be willing to run a fundraiser because "due to continuing state cutbacks, the campus was running at a deficit each year. Even though we have an endowment from our founding members, we can't keep using it. It's not sustainable."

Most social service agencies in the city of New York, I'd later learn, were in the same financial predicament as JCCA, then and today—only it's gotten worse. Most of them depend on government contracts to fund their work, yet what the government pays for that work does not meet the cost of providing it. According to a newly released report from the Human Services Council, "government contracts only pay 80 cents on the dollar of program costs," thus leaving agencies with a built-in deficit before they even begin. This leaves social service agencies struggling to fill the gap, and it is not easy. It requires intensive fundraising and many of them run at deficits. And to provide the quality of programming that the JCCA does, it becomes even more challenging. Sadly, the Human Services Council called social service nonprofits in this city a "crumbling industry that won't survive without fundamental changes in reimbursement models and regulatory burdens."

Interestingly enough, this report came out in the wake of the recent demise of the largest social service agency in New York City, called FEGS. It declared bankruptcy last year with a 17 million dollar deficit, even though many in the industry felt it was too big to fail. The government asked other agencies to take on their contracts, which meant growing their own deficits, at least in the short term. These contracts included housing and staff for the developmentally disabled, mental health services and case management to help the neediest people in our city acquire housing, food, jobs and schooling, to name a few. Crucial services that if not performed could leave a humanitarian debacle in the city of unprecedented proportions. The city would end up having to pick up the bill in other ways of course, with increased homelessness and incarceration. It is interesting to note that during the fiscal crises of 2008, the government looked at certain banks as "too big to fail," leading to their bailouts, while an agency that provided the largest safety net to needy New Yorkers was not rescued.

But when I met Mark, I knew nothing of these deficits or the intense challenges facing the social service sector of New York. I only knew that the Pleasantville campus needed help. How could I say no? I had never organized a fundraiser from scratch before, but I would do my best.

Mark went to work organizing a committee and chose two other co-chairs. We created an invitation list, brainstormed ideas and decided to hold the event on the campus so people who had never seen it would be able to. The group came up with the name A Tree Grows in Pleasantville, a play on the famous book, since a tree was a symbol of growth and stability. It was perfect. It was what we wanted for the kids in JCCA's care.

On a cold winter night in January of 2005, two years after I moved to the area, seventy or so people walked through the doors of the campus cafeteria for the first annual fundraiser. In spite of the bitter cold outside, the room soon became warm with curiosity. By the end of the night, it was also filled with deep interest and caring from all those who had never been there, awakened to the plight of these children who lived so close to them. Fast forward, and the event will bring in more than three million dollars over eleven years, run by different dynamic and passionate women in the local Westchester community, proving the saying that there is nothing a small group of motivated people cannot do.

A couple of years later, with my time and commitment to the campus growing, I asked Mark if I could join the board of trustees. Willing to present my name, he said, "Please send a short bio so we can review it at the next board meeting for approval." *Approval?* My insecurities seized me. I was not a lawyer, a finance executive, nor a commercial real estate broker, just a stay at home mom who ran lunch bunch groups and the fundraiser. Even though all this had given me greater confidence, I wondered what I could offer other than my financial buy in? The insecure little girl I still was became fearful.

A month later, I was approved. While I had never been on a board, I was eager to learn. Soon I would be engaging in ways I never imagined, my confidence building and my voice becoming stronger. Most importantly, it would bring me closer to this agency, to do whatever small part I could to advocate for children, children like Pearl.

Children that could have been me.

Seventeen

PAPER BRIDGES

I liken my years of "telling" to my "making peace with being adopted" stage. I was more than comfortable with everyone knowing I was adopted. The stigma and shame were gone.

That said, actually seeing Pearl and Albert again, let alone finding them a place in my life, was a whole other matter. I was not ready to cross that bridge.

I was also busy raising a family, and looking back, the demands of that were enough. It was easier to focus on the present where life made sense. Like all of us, I avoided what was uncomfortable and difficult.

But I could not ignore them completely. Since I was the one who had initiated the reunions, I did not feel it was right to completely close the door on them again. Blood mattered to me, even if a part of me wished it didn't. It was always confusing.

I asked a wise doctor friend his take on it, that I didn't want a relationship with my birth parents. He said, "you know *Suz*, the whole premise of honor thy mother and thy father is all from the Judeo-Christian ethic. It doesn't exist in nature. Animals have no allegiance to their parents. No one asks to be born. So let yourself off the hook if it makes you uncomfortable, you don't owe them anything."

"I guess that makes sense," I said. Still, I wasn't feeling it.

In my mind, I owed them something for creating me. Plus, I was part of their genetic thread, the one that connected me to generations that came before and generations that would come after on this Earth. I could not leave that thread completely broken.

So I opted for paper bridges.

I sent a holiday photo card each year to each of them that would connect me to them, yet keep me at a comfortable distance. I included a letter inside with a happy summary of my year, sharing milestones, leaving out anything that might spoil that message.

Because there was a photo of my children on the card, I felt good that they got to see their "grandchildren." When I got to the end each year, I wrestled with how to finish.

Should I write "Love, Suzette"? Instead, I always wrote, "Best Wishes, Suzette." It felt safer to keep that level of formality. Love was reserved for those I truly loved.

Albert did not stay silent however. He picked up the phone and called me every year or two during this time, usually after receiving my card. It was never a call I welcomed. When I saw his name on caller ID, my insides tightened up. Unable to answer right away, I usually waited a day until I was mentally prepared. "Greetings, Suuu-*zette*," he started each time with his singsong enthusiasm. I always responded in a perky tone, disguising my angst.

He filled me in on the basics of his life, and I told him how wonderful it all was, with an enthusiastic cheer that was forced.

I offered very little on my end over those years. He didn't ask either.

I continued to think him an odd man, or quirky to say the least.

Somewhere along the line, I don't remember when, he stopped asking me to come visit, resigning himself to the fact that it wasn't going to happen. I never had the guts to come out and tell him how I really felt, but instead skirted the request with "we'll see's" and "maybes."

Towards the end of those calls, he often added the phrase, "Su-*zette*, you know you are a part of me and I am a part of you."

"Yes, you are," I answered.

But which part and how much, I wondered after each call, having the nature-nurture question again thrown in my face. It unsettled me. It always felt like a Picasso painting when what I wished for was a Norman Rockwell.

When Albert finished those calls, he always said, "I love you." I never said it back. I did not love him and did not think he could love me; he still did not know me. Now I can see that what he probably loved was the thought of me, but back then I had little understanding of that. His avowals of love pushed me away rather than bring me closer.

Each time the phone clicked off, I tried to block out the swirling emotional sediment that this exchange always stirred up: the confusion of who I was, the lack of ability to integrate this odd man into my identity, the discomfort of my compromised beginnings, his longing for me that was so hard to take in, the scary what ifs if he had kept me, my parents angst over him potentially being in my life, and the guilt that I couldn't give him what he wanted, visits back and forth and a closer relationship. It was all mixed together in some turbulent whirlpool of emotions that continued to define my adopted life.

At least I knew it would soon settle...until the next call came from the man who only wanted to love me.

As for Pearl, for the first few times, she did not respond to my paper bridges. But one day, after my third child Asher was born when I was thirty-six years old, a note card came from her. It had a French impressionist painting on the front, and the quick brush strokes and dabs of color brought me back to my days studying Cassatt in Paris. It was of a mother leaning over a wicker baby carriage where her infant sat, her eyes aglow. I was struck deep by her choice of card, the coincidence of it, as if it was a cosmic sign we had always been connected whether I knew it or not, and that bond was important to her.

Just the fact that she was even able to go to the store to pick it out moved me.

Even before opening it, I got choked up.

Dear Suzette,

I received all your letters and pictures the last few years. I loved seeing every one of them. Thank you for allowing me to know how your life is progressing. I'm doing very well since they put me on a new antidepressant. My oldest son Jeffrey is getting married to a lovely girl. Thank you for the letter and the lovely picture. I'll treasure it for the rest of my life.

Stay well honey and enjoy all that life has given you. You're always in my thoughts and will be forever. You may continue to keep in touch about whatever is happening in your life. God bless you Darling,

Best regards and wishes, Pearl

I stood staring at it in its shaky script, my heart melting. In that moment, I felt connected to her through the miles of air and space that separated us, and it caused an unexpected longing to swell in the forbidden spaces inside me. I felt so glad she was doing better, but I also felt guilt. Given the poignancy of her words, I suddenly wanted to tell her that I wished somehow things were different, that I was sad that I did not go visit her again to get to know her better, even though I wasn't able to.

After re-reading it three times, I pulled out the plastic box in my closet, removing the manila file labeled "Adoption," and I stuck Pearl's letter inside. I did not answer her, but I continued to send my letter each year.

Three years later, I received a second note from her, also on a card with an impressionist painting of a mother and infant daughter. This time it read:

Dear Suzette,

I received your lovely letter. I'm so glad that all is well with you. The picture of your children is beautiful. Your infant son Asher Jordan looked just like you when you were born. I want you to understand that I recognize you and your husband and beautiful children. It embarrasses me to recognize that the only reason I had partial sex with your biological father was because it was my nature to please everyone but myself. Due to the incorrect information which I had obtained plus my generous nature, I got into trouble. Fortunately, for me, everything worked out.

During my lifetime I have sabotaged many lives or so I thought. I did save my foster mother's sanity plus her entire family. I paid a terrific price for all this altruism. But, life has given me blessings in return. My children and husband are fine. They never ask to meet you. Please don't feel offended. You have a wonderful life and I'm so very happy for you.

God bless you and your family. You will have a special place in my heart always.

Love, Pearl

Another confession?

A partial sexual encounter that she didn't even want to have? Obviously it was a full sexual encounter, although it might not have lasted long. One thing was for sure, it was time to tweak the film in my head titled "My Life," especially the opening credits.

Sabotaged many lives? Whose lives? I thought back at the purpose for her suicide attempts, to give her family a better life, that they would be better off without her.

Saved her foster mother's sanity? How? By not telling the social workers about the abuse she endured? Or that she did all the housework and chores, keeping the household running? Or was there more?

Meeting up with her son Jeffrey while writing this memoir, I learned that there was in fact "more." Jeffrey told me about the sexual abuse she endured by her foster father. His mother told him, "He touched me in places he shouldn't have." Distraught, I asked him if he thought it happened more than once.

"She told me it was only once, but it was probably more," he replied, "I mean, who knows about anything that went on in that household, or what she doesn't want to talk about."

I thought about the children at the Cottage School. I had been told that at least one third of the youth had been sexually abused, but those were only the ones they knew about. The numbers, the professionals knew, were much higher than that. Children are often hesitant or scared to come forward for obvious reasons. Pearl probably minimized the full extent of her abuse too. From spending time on the campus, I also knew what a heavy toll the abuse took on all children who were victims, and why the JCCA had opened a center of excellence for their treatment, the JCCA Center for Healing Sexually Abused and Exploited Children. It is hoping to become a model for other care facilities that deal with this insidious problem.

"Did her foster sisters know about it?" I asked. He seemed to think they had no idea. The younger brother left the family when he was 18 and barely spoke to them again, and no one seemed to know why, but it wasn't hard to imagine.

"And, Joyce, her little sister, got it worse," he added.

"Little sister, wait, what little sister?"

"Oh, they took in another foster care child after my mother...she tried to protect her."

The sadness of my mother's life re-ignited in my conscience. Her concern for the younger version of herself that had entered that household, and the nightmares Pearl and Joyce must have endured, real ones, bounced around in the dark corners of my troubled heart for days.

I'd find out later from Pearl's own lips that she protected this little sister in yet another way. Joyce got so angry with their step mom once that she took a scarf, wrapped it around her neck, and tried to strangle her. Pearl heard the commotion, ran over and pulled Joyce off. "I saved my foster mom's life that day," she told me. She also saved her foster sister's life by preventing this horrific crime from happening.

It also spoke to how broken a child can become when removed from a home, placed with strangers and then abused on top of it. The human mind is fragile and when pushed enough, is bound to snap.

⌒

Dwelling on Pearl's note and feeling bad, I decided that I'd write her and suggest that she read *The Girls Who Went Away*. If she understood the times she lived in, and that she was not alone, maybe it could offer her some relief. Isn't knowledge power? Can't the truth set you free? Or maybe at least remove some of the burden?

A month later, a note came back.

Dear Suzette,

Thank you for the book you recommended. I've read it and it's true. I realize that I cannot live in the past. My mistake turned out to be a blessing in disguise. I delivered a lovely little girl who was blessed with parents who loved her like their own. I was blessed because that little girl, through the influence of her lovely parents, turned out to be a gem. You and I should appreciate this and your wonderful parents, I know, and appreciate the fact that you turned out to be a lovely person. You may phone me anytime. Take care of yourself my dear child and I wish your family the same.

God bless,
Pearl

A sense of relief filled me that she was not only not disturbed by the book, but also actually thought it helpful. One part still bothered me greatly.

Dearest Pearl,

What you did, getting pregnant with me, was not a mistake. You gave me life and for that I am forever grateful. Please do not *ever* feel bad. I hope you stay well and healthy and I will call you soon. So happy you want to talk to me moving forward.

I paused before closing the letter, as I always did, wondering how to sign off.

This time I wrote:

With much love, Suzette.

Eighteen

CROSSING THE BRIDGE AND FINDING REDEMPTION

When I moved to my new town in 2003, it not only brought me next door to the Cottage School, but it marked the next pivotal stage of my journey, the one that brought me back to Pearl and Albert.

About a year after we moved in, a new friend came over and told me, quite casually, that she was leaving soon on her second trip to visit with her newly found family, her biological one. I did not even know she was adopted.

She told me that finding and meeting her "mom and sisters was incredible." Not only that, they all embraced her. "I even look like them," she lit up, "and I fit right in."

It all sounded like a Hallmark TV special. I made some reference to my birth parents, that it wasn't so great, but didn't say anything further. After she left, however, it got me thinking. Was there something I was missing out on? My half siblings were grown now, and they were separate individuals from their parents. Maybe there was something there, people I might like. Maybe I should meet them. Maybe if that meant seeing Pearl and Albert too, it wouldn't be so bad.

Maybe I had been ready to go back to the land of my adopted self for a while, and I didn't even know it. Maybe my friend was just the alarm clock telling me, "it's time already!"

My willingness to go there, looking back, I believe was in part due to starting to volunteer at the Cottage School. It had normalized my own compromised beginnings; in fact, it had made my own seem idyllic. Being with the children each week, their lives so much worse than anything I had ever encountered previously, made me wonder, *what are you so afraid of?* I was a grown woman, with three children all in school now, as Asher was in the first grade. I was settled in my life for the most part, more so than I had ever been.

I had also ready many books on the adoption experience that had validated so much of my struggle. They had given me greater clarity about my experience.

So with this friend's simple announcement, I made the decision to jump back into the adoption game, to take out the scary dust-covered playing board of what might have been, spin the dial in sibling world, and see where I landed this time around.

I told Rich of my plan, and he was more than supportive. "I think I'll start with Pearl's children first…they already know about me," I told him. What I didn't tell him was that something about sharing the same womb with them made me feel more connected.

Thanks to a people search website on the emerging Internet, I found Alan's number, the only one I was able to uncover. I was hesitant to call. *"Was I entering some private space I shouldn't be?"* I shared that worry with Rich, but he didn't think so. Fearing I might never pick up the phone, he called Alan a few days later without telling me. I could have been mad, but he did me a favor. He saved me from possible rejection.

Alan, he said, was agreeable to have me call him. I pumped him for more details, but in typical Rich fashion, there weren't many to offer.

I was scared to make this first sibling connection, not knowing what to expect. When I called, Alan spoke with such little affect that I did not know what to make of him. He did not offer much so I did most of the talking. Still, at the end of our short discourse, he suggested that I join him, his brother and Pearl for dinner the following week, just like that. His mom happened to be coming up for a visit.

"I'm not sure your mom will want to see me," I said to him, "Why don't you ask first?" Much to my surprise, Pearl agreed. So now, without even planning on it, I would be re-united with my birth mother too.

Before hanging up, I asked if Stacy could join us too. "Pennsylvania's far, so I doubt it, but I'll ask..." was his only explanation. I felt paranoid it was because of me, but I didn't dwell.

Rich and I drove down to the restaurant in Queens that Alan suggested. His brother Jeffrey lived there and that's where Pearl was staying. As Rich navigated the traffic on the main drag, I absorbed the surroundings under the night sky: the lit up discount stores, the old compact cars, the elderly women pushing grocery carts, and the dim side streets of attached linoleum and brick two family houses. I knew that Pearl had grown up in this borough, so I imagined that this was where I would have grown up too. The what-ifs of Charlotte's life began to emerge in techno-color. My heart beat accelerated and I took many deep breaths as Rich parked the car.

For all my nervous anticipation, Jeffrey and Alan ended up being nice, seemingly regular guys. Both had dark hair and light complexions like I did, but they were tall while I was small like my mother and father. Genetic checklist pulled out, it felt amazingly satisfying to compare myself to a "sibling" for the first time.

Seeing Pearl however was a shock. Sitting with her back to me when I approached the table, I placed my hand on her shoulder and leaned over so she could see my face. I smiled with all most warmth and caring I could muster.

"Hi there Pearl," I said and stared directly into her eyes.

"Well hello Suzette," she responded, smiling herself.

She looked different somehow. While I recognized her facial features, her complexion was paler and her lids droopier than I remembered. There was a frailty I did not see before. I found it difficult to believe, astonishing, that she was the woman who gave birth to me and whom I would have called mom, more so than on my first visit, when I was too emotional to focus on anything other than the words spilling from her mouth.

This time, my body was overcome with an unexpected and overwhelming wave of tenderness and caring, like she was some delicate creature that needed to be protected and cherished. A part of me wanted to curl up on her lap and be held by her, be the infant again that never got to do that, that primal bond drawing me to her with a strong force. But I squashed those thoughts right away. Instead, I held her hand off and on throughout the dinner, this small visceral connection giving me comfort and pleasure.

In her presence, my gratitude to her hurt my heart. That I missed out on knowing her hurt it even worse.

The conversation flowed that night, but I was nervous and uneasy. I could tell they felt unsure as well. Did they feel sadness that I was taken away from their mother or envious of the opportunities I was given that they were not? Did they feel sad they lost a sister years ago, or just happy to have a new one in their lives? Or did they not think much about it at all, not needing to delve into the what-if questions that haunted my own brain? Then again, they were not the ones taken away.

Pearl did not talk much, but she did tell me she volunteered at a hospice. "I sit with people and talk to them. My life's mission has been to help people. The priests there say to me, 'Pearl, you're one of a kind.'"

"That's wonderful," I answered.

"Well, there's a heaven on earth you know," she added. I nodded, surprised by this Christian religious comment. I told her that I just started volunteering too, at a place for abused and neglected children. She did not make any connection to her own past, nor did I bring it up. The volunteer work, something we both had in common, made me feel closer to her.

When the meal was done, my brothers and I exchanged phone numbers, talking of future plans in a hovering cloud of uncertainty. Now that I had met them, what did I want? Half my DNA yes but strangers too. Even though any potential relationship with them would not be as emotionally fraught and complex as with my birth parents, did I want to make them part of my life? Was it possible to make up for a lifetime of not knowing someone? It had been fulfilling to meet them, to add these two pieces to the puzzle, but did I need more? I had no idea.

I would not see Jeffrey again for many years and I would not see Alan again at all, at least at the time of this writing. I imagine that to them I was a non-existent person who appeared and then left, and became non-existent again.

I did not initiate contact either so I guess that I did not need "more." When I eventually did connect with Jeffrey in more recent years, it was only because he happened to be at his mother's house in Florida when I called her. He picked up the phone, which gave us an unexpected opportunity to reconnect.

As for Pearl after that second reunion, I would again need some space. Being in her presence was both a gift and an ache to my confused heart. I still did not know how I would fit her into my life, as I did not know with Albert.

I also did not know how she felt about it, whether my presence would be a blessing or a curse.

When I wrote her asking her if she wanted to continue to see me, she answered, "let's leave it alone."

The answer was clear. It was still as difficult for her as it was for me, even after this meeting. A part of me felt rejected even though I understood. Another part of me felt relieved. I did not know how to have two mothers.

Satiated for the time being, I moved on. I tried to retrieve the next puzzle pieces: Albert's children. I knew I could not go behind his back, so I sent him a letter asking his permission. I was too nervous to call and ask him directly.

Feb. 4, 2004
Dear Suzette,

I thought a lot about your request…I've decided that it is not in their best interest…years ago when you said you were ready to meet me, I was very excited… hoping that the meeting would result in our having a real relationship…however, in all this time you've never given me the opportunity to get closer to you…it now seems to me that you were merely curious…after we met, you curiosity was satiated.

You can't imagine the days and nights I spent thinking of you… I've heard from you only occasionally since then, usually around the holidays, although even that hasn't been consistently. Even though you told me your parents had a home in Florida…you never called or even indicated that you had been here…I'm not trying to put you on the spot, however, as a parent, I don't want to put my kids into the position of being "on display" and then dismissed. Therefore, I'd like to leave the matter on hold. I still want to hear from you and receive pictures as it gives me pleasure. I'm sure you'll respect my feelings about this, just as I've respected yours over the years by not intruding in your life.

Love, Albert

Not intruding in my life? What about the call in college? He was right about the rest though; I didn't want to have a relationship. But that decision was not for the reasons he believed, that I was just disinterested. I decided to respect his wishes even though he had not respected my mother's so many years ago. I pushed away the discomfort of his words, not ready to respond and put the letter in the adoption file in my plastic bin and closed it tight.

Two years passed, and I tried again. I felt a more pressing desire to meet my half siblings and complete the puzzle, which is best described in *Being Adopted*: "A person undergoes a subtle shift in her notions of time. While young, she views things from the perspective of the time that has passed since birth. In middle adulthood, her perspective changes to the time she has left (until death)...It brings on a new urgency to get things done—to solve the psychic issues that they (adoptees) have ignored for most of their lives." That was what I felt.

Albert wrote back, saying how happy he was to hear from me but surprised and disappointed that it took me so long to get back to him. He conveyed the same sentiments as before but added, "Had I not found you, you probably would not have found Pearl... it also saddens me that you went to visit Pearl, but never once had the kindness, consideration or courtesy to visit me the many times you've been in Florida...I realize that it wasn't important to you. However, I'm happy you connected with her and her children. You can give her my regards if you wish.

One thing I won't do is have my children being a subject of curiosity so I appreciate you not connecting with them. Additionally, I have to think of my grandchildren, and it would be most uncomfortable attempting to explain who you are to them…if I sound hurt to you, it's because I am, and frankly, I have no wish to be hurt more. I realize that this letter probably sounds harsh, but after your call, I wanted you to know how I felt. I would still appreciate receiving your holiday cards and notes, if that's okay with you.

Sincerely,
Albert Demachi

*O*uch, that was harsh. I stared in disbelief. I had no idea how much I hurt him, but what the hell? I only met Pearl that one time in Florida and that was hard enough in itself. Why did he assume I had been visiting her? What did he think, it was a pleasure trip? And now he was protecting his own children like my parents tried to protect me, and he didn't even see the parallels. I was pissed.

The next night I took a piece of paper and began to write, spurred on by his cutting remarks, to set the record straight. With a heavy hand, I vomited forth all my experiences and feelings, describing the secrecy, shame and stigma I felt and why.

"*When you found me, I became lost,*" I wrote.

I finished by suggesting he read *Ithaka,* so he could understand that what I went through wasn't an anomaly or unique.

It was difficult to make myself vulnerable to him, but I did so because I knew it was the only way forward. I also wanted him to know that I was not the villain.

I did not mean to hurt him—I knew that it really wasn't about him; it was about me.

He wrote back.

Nov. 26, 2006

Dear Suzette,

Although I received your letter in October, it's taken me this long to digest what you wrote. Your letter was very emotional and explained a lot about your feelings, both past and present, unfortunately, it never occurred to me years ago that my contacting you would leave you with negative emotional repercussions. Obviously I wouldn't have done so if I had had any inkling of what it might mean to you. I just assumed (rather naively as it turns out) that we'd be able to have a relationship that would grow (or not) over time. I certainly never thought that contacting you would be a negative experience and for this I apologize. It never dawned on me that, coming from a loving home and a good family there would be difficulties you might have to overcome as an adoptee. I can't help wishing you had your brother's feelings of not caring, as it certainly would have made life easier for you.

Now that you've enlightened me, I certainly understand your feelings of "shame" about being adopted. I grew up without a father in a time when divorce was unacceptable, which made me feel "different" and not as good as others my age.

When I first contacted you, it never dawned on me this could become a nightmarish issue for you. I was so excited to have found you, all I could think about was getting together. I confess I never even considered how you would take my getting in touch with you. I deeply apologize for not taking your feelings into consideration or even comprehending that your feelings might be different.

As far as meeting my children, I contacted you when I did so that they would grow up knowing and accepting you as their sister. While you chose to tell your children "at an early age" about me and Pearl, you were resistant, until now, to meet my children. It's interesting how life repeats itself, since now I'm the one who feels that your contacting my children would be shocking and open a "Pandora's Box" (to use your words) for them. I went along all these years to not contact you and respecting your wishes, and I hope you'll now respect mine. When I feel comfortable to share this information with my children, I'll let you know. So please be patient.

Fondly,
Albert Demachi

With his words, I felt intense relief. I had been vindicated, absolved, and understood. How could he have known what I experienced or how I felt? I had to understand it myself first, and then I had to be ready to share it.

What had started as a quest to meet his children turned into an unexpected opportunity for redemption with my birth father.

It was where I needed to go all along, even if I didn't know it at the time.

Re-reading his letter, I also felt empathy for him, his own contrition starting to melt away the animosity I held because of his last letter.

As for meeting his children, something I still really wanted to do, I reminded myself they were grown adults, both married now. As with Pearl's children, did I really need his permission at this point? Still, I would not betray him. I would wait. But I wondered if he really knew how they would feel when they found out they had a half sister they knew nothing about.

Nineteen

JCCA Surprise

It wasn't too long after settling in to their new condominium that my father started to succumb to the ravages of dementia. He was eighty. With it, he reattached the umbilical cord of his birth, but this time it was to my mom. Hating to be without her, he yelled for her whenever she was out of sight. When she left the house, he called her frequently, afraid she was not okay. The stress of being a caretaker was taking an enormous toll on her.

I decided to take her on a much-needed vacation, a break from my dad, back to Florida where she could visit with her beloved cousin Rose and her husband Irv. This was the same Rose who came to my parent's weekend freshman year at Michigan, the one that I did not remember even as having being there.

On the plane down to Florida, I thought about Albert and Pearl. I had not been down to Florida in years, so it seemed like an opportune time to make good on my decision. I was going to try to see them.

It had been seven or eight years since I had my second meet up with Pearl with her two boys, and even though she had wrote me "let's leave it alone," I was hoping that she might have changed her mind. As for Albert, it had been almost sixteen since I had him. I had no idea what to expect.

I told my mom, and she, of course, was surprised. She knew I had met Pearl and her sons with Rich years earlier, but I had not apprised her of my awakened quest to reconnect with my biological beginnings.

As for the possibility of meeting Albert, she said, "If that's what you want to do, sure, I'll go," looking a bit stunned. Still, I knew she would never deny me even this request.

After a pause, she added, "but I have to tell you…*I can never forgive him for what he did.*"

The harshness of her words confused me. So much time had passed and yet for her it was still all so raw, as if it were yesterday in my dorm room. I explained to her about my correspondence with him, that he was naïve to how the call would affect me, and that now that he was aware, he was sorry for it. She was skeptical. The truth was, even with his contrition, I was still not sure if I had completely forgiven him either. I was trying however to move on from perceived wrongs and no longer hold his lack of emotional intelligence against him. He had respected my wishes over the years, and I needed to move on.

As for Pearl, she perked up and said, "Yes, I'd like to meet her. You know, I always wanted to thank her for what she gave me, after all, *her loss was my gain.*" I smiled at this lovely thought, one she never expressed to me before.

But what would it be like for Pearl to meet my mom and be thanked for a sacrifice she was forced to make? To meet the woman who got to have the child she couldn't? Appreciation yes, but a stabbing dagger too, a place inside where one cannot live without the other. Maybe it wasn't a good idea, but I would at least call my birth mother and ask.

When we arrived in our hotel room, I anxiously picked up the phone and called Pearl. She told me, in a fragile and unsettled tone, that while she was happy to hear from me, she was not doing well. "I don't think it's a good idea to meet," she said. Then she hung up. My heart dropped. I was disappointed yes, but I knew seeing her again wouldn't be easy, especially with my mom in the mix. .

Albert, on the other hand, was delighted to hear from me. Plans were made to have dinner the following night. Since we had time to kill then before going to cousin Rose's that night for dinner, I pulled out the assignment calendar for my Cottage lunch program that I needed to work on. Mom was happy to click on the television and stretch out on the bed.

I logged on to my computer. There was an email from Mark, head of Fund Development. In it, he told me that the third annual Tree Grows in Pleasantville event had surpassed our fundraising goals.

I turned to my mom and told her about the success of the fundraiser. She lowered the volume on the hotel TV remote to hear me better.

"You know, mom, I was just thinking…about the Cottage School and Pearl," I paused, "and I had this crazy thought. I know it's a million-to-one, but by any chance could there be a connection to Pearl and the campus, maybe she could've been there before she was in foster care?"

"That's an interesting thought. It's worth pursuing, I mean, why not?"

I picked up the phone to call Mark. No time like the present, I thought. After some brief hellos and shared musings on the event, I announced, "Mark, you know I was adopted, right, just like you." We had discussed our mutual beginnings on a few occasions.

"I had this crazy thought -- maybe my birth mother could have been on the campus? I know it's probably ridiculous, but by any chance do you keep records from *like back in the 30s and 40s?*"

"Well, yes, we do." My eyes opened.

I wasn't even expecting that much.

He transferred me over to Leona, "the woman who takes care of all that." I explained to her the reason for my call, and she said she'd be happy to check. I gave her my mom's name and birthdate.

My mother stared at me, intent with curiosity. "They actually *have them* and she's *checking,*" I told her while I cupped the receiver.

I started to doodle on the small hotel note pad in nervous disbelief, my heartbeat accelerate, but still expecting nothing. After about six or seven minutes, the phone clicked.

"Leona?"

"Yes, it's me, sorry for the delay, but you're not going to believe this. Your mother's file *is here!*"

My mouth dropped.

"She wasn't on the campus but she was in our foster care program."

After a few seconds, I gathered my thoughts. "Wow, I *cannot* believe it! Can you send it to me?"

"I'm not allowed to," she answered, "because of the privacy laws, records are still sealed in New York."

"That's crazy, she's my mother!" I lamented.

Leona agreed that it was insane, but told me that she was, at least, allowed to tell me things in the file without divulging identifying information. This meant that she could give me details without the names of any of the family members involved. Since I already had my birth parents names, this was not an issue for me, and I told her so.

I then had another idea: I asked her if I could get a signed letter from Pearl that says she gives me permission to have the file, perhaps a way to circumvent this law. Leona told me that it wouldn't matter because the files were sealed to everyone.

"And you wouldn't believe the files we have here. We took care of thousands of Jewish children over the last hundred years, even children who came over during the Holocaust, and we're not allowed to divulge anything."

"So basically, you're sitting on a treasure trove of Jewish history and you can't do a thing about it?"

"Exactly."

Disappointed that I could not physically see my file, I was at least excited to get the information it held. I grabbed for the only papers in sight: the car rental confirmation I printed out, and turned it over to the back.

"Go ahead, shoot, ready."

She spent the next 15 minutes rattling off details. Details about who I was and would have been, and my hand moved furiously taking it all down, my mind a jumping bean, my heart a vise.

"Pearl's father was Polish, mother's heritage is unknown...Pearl's mother married twice, her second husband was Pearl's father, and he left her, she lived in Alphabet City, Manhattan...."

"Pearl's mother was so sick she didn't know how to raise her daughter... she left the house for long periods of time. There was no furniture in the apartment, just newspapers on the floor. She had no family or friends, but she did have a social security card."

"But there is no record of what happened to her in the file, so my guess is she probably died and was buried in a potter's field," Leona added on her own. My heart sunk. That was my grandmother.

Leona continued to tell me that Pearl's mother let her go because it was the only hope for her, and Pearl remembered seeing the officer's gun on his hip and being lifted up and going to the hospital. She had rickets. She thought the ladies who took care of her there were angels. As she read, I told her to "wait up" numerous times, lest I miss getting it all down.

At 6 years old, she's placed in various foster care homes. She ended up staying in one with two foster sisters and a brother and was picked for a training program at Riker's Island to become a nurse when she was 15. Her foster mother would not let her go. When she got pregnant, her foster mother told her she would continue to support her only if she didn't keep the baby. She was placed in Lakeview.

Years later while writing this memoir, I went back over these notes and looked at where I scribbled Lakeview. Thanks to Google, I found out it was a home for un-wed Jewish mothers built on *Staten Island*. Just like that, I knew why I was born there, this particular mystery from my birth certificate finally solved.

I was shocked to learn that the founders built it on Staten Island because there was no Jewish population there, thus minimizing the risk that the girls would encounter anyone they knew and experience the shame and disgrace. Making matters worse, the girls were not allowed to know each other's last names because they feared they would look each other up afterwards thus exposing their secret. The staff had them wear a wedding band each time they left the building, and they were not allowed male visitors, not even the fathers.

One of the most beautiful times in a woman's life denigrated to the most shameful. As a daughter of one of these women wrote, "There was no one there to say kaddish [the Jewish prayer of mourning], to the child that for all intended purposes, had died to them." In some ways, it was worse than death, because there would never be closure.

After giving birth, Pearl stated for the file, and I quote, "that she decided she didn't want to put you into a life of misery, so you wouldn't have to know all the things that went on in this world."

"Pearl stated she had a nurse's personality, wanting to be useful to people. And it ends there," Leona finished.

I put down my pen. Leona had confirmed so much of what Pearl had told me, cementing it in my mind, plus adding all this new information. My insides were scrambled.

Leona added, "You know, you can call Spence-Chapin adoption agency. They took over the Louise Wise files when they closed up, and they might have more information than we do."

"Thanks so much, Leona, I will. I just need to process all this."

I said good-bye and stared ahead at the sentence fragments in front of me, unable to move.

Twenty

ANGELS FROM ABOVE

$\mathcal{M}$y mother was snoring in the bed beside me, a slow consistent rumble. I did not sleep much -- the information I received from Leona playing in my head like a sneaker in a clothes dryer, bang-bang-banging throughout the long hours of the night. It could have been a novel but it was real.

In the morning as soon as I awoke, something inside me wanted to tell the story of Pearl's early life. It was more a need than a want, looking back now, to document it somehow. I decided to write my vision down, knowing it would be some kind of cathartic release of emotion through the writing process.

I threw on my jeans and a t-shirt, lifted my laptop and tiptoed out of the room, gently closing the door behind me. I sat down at a table in the hotel lobby restaurant and took a few sips of coffee to help my brain wake up. Opening my computer to a fresh Word page, I began to write how I imagined the sad life of my grandmother as well as the little child who would one day become my mother.

$\mathcal{T}$he wind whipped through her and yet she persevered. Her hunger was strong, and she knew what she had to do. She could not go home yet, but she could not be gone too long either. Up and down the street she walked, lifting up the covers on the garbage cans that lined the icy path before her. She pulled and pushed through the refuse, hoping to find something that would be enough for her and her daughter. She spied a chunk of bread. It was wedged between a brown bag and chicken bones and covered with coffee grounds, but finding it gave her a rush of relief. Quickly, she wiped it off and transferred the bread into the pocket of her coat, positioning it so it wouldn't fall out through the tear inside. She glanced up and looked around, rubbing her hands together for warmth. Whoever might be watching her, she didn't care; she had long moved passed embarrassment. She could not let her daughter starve. Yet, she would still turn her gaze downward to avoid other people's stares. Back down the street she ran until she arrived at the concrete stairs leading up to her apartment building. She climbed them quickly and opened the door to the dimly lit corridor. Up the staircase she pulled herself, tired and cold. The stairs creaked and her heartbeat quickened. Was her daughter okay while she was gone?

When she threw the door open her child ran to her, her face streaked with tears. The fright of being left alone was intense for the young child, and she wept every time her mother left. She fell into the warm embrace of her mother's arms, clinging helplessly, filled with the same euphoria she always had when her mother returned. Slowly her breathing calmed as her mother gently brushed away her tears and rocked her against her chest. Her beautiful blue eyes looked up at her mother and then her head collapsed on her shoulder.

The mother could feel the dampness of her face through her blouse. She lifted up her thin form, and walked across the bare floor to the stack of newspapers in the corner of the room. Gently she lowered the girl down on the makeshift bed, the paper crumpled from last night's sleep. The young child looked up at her mother, hopeful about what might be in her pocket. When she pulled out the half loaf, the little girl took it from her with appreciative eyes. Hungrily, she chewed in silence, gradually silencing her growling stomach.

"Wait right here, Pearl."

The mother got up from the newspapers and went to the door.

"You're not leaving again, Mama?"

"No," she answered.

Opening the door slowly, she quietly slipped out to grab the bottle of milk she had spied down the hall. Just as quietly she returned to the room and held the bottle up to her daughter's lips. She hoped the milk would soothe the child, but her daughter gagged when she tasted it. It had soured, and Bea pushed the bottle away.

"Drink a little anyway, you must."

"No."

"Come now, please."

"Noooooooo," the child replied recoiling.

"Okay, then I will give you some water instead."

The mother rose again to fill a sticky plastic glass with water and gave it to her daughter. When she finished drinking, the little girl handed her mother the glass and let herself again be enveloped in her arms. Together they rested on the piles of newspapers that gave a small measure of protection from the hard floor beneath.

How had it come to this, the mother wondered. Getting up she began to pace back and forth in the small room while her daughter's gaze followed her intently. She knew she couldn't do this anymore. The black cloud that had moved over her was growing darker and darker, locking her in despondency and despair. How would she survive another day? What would become of her and her child? Could she be going mad?

"It will be okay," she said to comfort her daughter, while she tried to clear her head and think. But she didn't want to think anymore.

The afternoon light slowly started to fade across the worn wood floor and her head felt heavy. Enveloping her daughter in her arms once more, the two fell into a restless sleep.

When she awoke, her child was standing over her. In that moment, how much Pearl looked like her father took her aback. She put the child on her lap and began to sing the Polish lullaby that her mother sang to her. When she had arrived on the boat to this country and saw the great statue in the harbor, like thousands of others, she had hoped for something better. But life had not given her any gifts. It had been cruel. She thought her husband would take care of her and their child, but instead he left them and never returned. She knew she had found it more and more difficult to cope during their marriage -- when he left, she could barely stand. Fear wrapped her in its terrifying cloak.

Quietly, Pearl joined in the lullaby, and their voices together were sweet and melodic. The mother stroked her child's hair and rocked her, the warmth of their bodies comforting to both of them, and when combined with song, bringing them momentary peace.

Suddenly, a heavy knock at the door intruded on the soft calmness. The forcefulness of the knock forewarned her of something bad. Her stomach dropped as she put Pearl down and pulled herself up slowly to answer it.

"Who's there?"

"The police, ma'am, we need to come in. Open the door please."

She got up abruptly, slowly unlocking and pulling the door open. Two police officers stood before her, their expressions grim and their faces tense. Next to them was that women, Mrs. Sands, the social worker who had been to her apartment a few times before. This woman had told her that she wasn't taking proper care of her daughter, but the mother had no choice but to ignore the warning. This time, though, the expressions on all their faces told her that something terrible was about to happen. She was filled with dread. Her heart pounded.

"Yes, what is this?"

"Mrs. Kaminek," said Mrs. Sands, "these officers are with me today because we must take Pearl away. She must have medical care, and then after, I 'm sorry to say, we will need to place her with a foster family that can take care of her. She will be leaving with us today, but you will be able to visit her once she is settled."

"You're *taking* my daughter?"

"Yes, ma'am," she will be coming with us now.

The officers' focus immediately shifted to the four-and-a-half-year-old child, who was peering out behind her mother, wide-eyed and afraid. The child could not have weighed more than twenty-five pounds and her face was gaunt and confused. Mrs. Sands continued clearly and slowly, "Mrs. Kaminek, do you understand what I'm telling you?"

"But you can't take her!!" she cried out.

"Mrs. Kaminek, we're taking your daughter now to help her get better. We don't know when she will be returning. That will depend on you. If your circumstances change, then you can get her back. I'm truly sorry, but we need to think about her life now."

Slowly the mother stepped back, stopping when she felt the wall behind her. She wanted to grab Pearl and tell them they could never ever take her child. She tried to speak, but no words came out. Her voice was crippled. Every muscle in her body tensed, and she stood paralyzed against the wall as if she were watching a scene outside of herself. She stared at her daughter in despair, knowing she had not properly provided for her. But she had tried. Her mind had not been her own for years now, and she had been unable to find or keep work.

She also knew Pearl wasn't well, but actually give her up? How could she allow this?

She stood there as the officer picked up her child, and Pearl began to kick and scream. "No, no…Mama, don't let them take me, don't let them take me!" she wailed, reaching for her mother. The child saw the steel and leather of the gun on the officer's hip and became even more frightened. She pushed and pulled with all her strength to free herself from the policeman's grasp. "Mama, mama, mama!" she cried desperately, but still her mother remained frozen and without words.

In an instant they were gone, and the sound of boots and heels pounding on worn wood stairs mixed with her daughter's shrieks soon faded away. The mother slid down the wall and sank to the floor. Her body convulsed until she could barely breathe. A huge moan of seething pain came from her, brought forth from the darkest despair of her soul. And slowly, but surely, her mind began to shut down. Her body went numb as she curled like an infant into a tight ball, hoping to somehow completely disappear, forever.

⌢

The officer lowered Pearl into the car and placed her on Mrs. Sands' lap. Pearl turned toward the apartment house door and banged with all her might on the car window, waiting for her mother to appear, but the door remained closed. The car took off and she continued to wail and fight, but soon she calmed from sheer exhaustion. Her body went limp and her sobs melted into a soft whimper.

"We're going to help you, Pearl. We're going to a place where they will take good care of you," Mrs. Sands told her softly. "Your mommy will get to see you soon."

Pearl sat there, staring ahead but seeing nothing, filled with fear and confusion. Why didn't her mommy come? What had she done wrong? What would happen to her?

The police car pulled up in front of a tall brick building with big white poles and a high door. The officer lifted her up and out of the car, carrying her through the door and into a big room filled with people walking and talking. They moved down a long hallway. A lady in a white dress and a white cap came out from behind a desk and took her in her arms. The lady carried her up the stairs and into a room where there were four beds, three of them filled with other children, all of them staring at her, the newcomer.

The lady told her that she was going to take off her clothes and bathe her. "Are you okay with that, Pearl?" she asked in a quiet voice.

Pearl nodded.

"Doctor Low, a really nice man, is going to look at you afterwards. He's going to help you get better. Don't be afraid."

The lady scrubbed and washed her, first her caked skin and then her matted hair, brushing it out with care, trying not to hurt her, and then put her in a soft white gown that she tied in the back. Pearl became less afraid, and when the lady in white put her into the bed and placed a blanket over her, she thought that she had never touched anything so soft.

The warm aroma of food filled her nostrils and she turned to see a tray by her side filled with all kinds of things to eat. The nice lady turned a crank on the side of her bed and it began to lift the bed up. It was some kind of magic.

"Is that for me?" Pearl asked in wonder, her eyes growing wide.

Then the nice lady in white began to feed her, and she eagerly chewed and swallowed, while the lady told her to slow down just a little.

The child was saved but the mother, no.

"Who are you?" Pearl finally managed to ask.

"My name is Frances."

"Are you an angel? An angel from heaven?"

"Oh, no," Frances laughed. "I'm a nurse, and I'm going to take care of you while you are here in the hospital."

The kind lady smiled broadly.

Pearl lay back in the soft bed and wondered when her mom would be coming to get her.

She would never see her mom again.

Twenty-One

"Dad" and "Mom" Meet

I was going to see my birth father again.

It had been sixteen years.

This time, my mom was sitting in the passenger seat next to me.

Albert was waiting in the driveway for us. My insides stiffened as he became real to me again. All the confusing feelings of him being my father but not, and the suppressed confusion over what he should mean to me in my life bubbled over me and seized me, although my feelings were not what they were the last time; that more vulnerable little girl was gone.

I tried to take stock of how he looked now as a man in his seventies. His features were still handsome, his height of course still small and his light olive-toned face did not hold many wrinkles. Time had been kind to him. However, his thick unnatural dark head of hair took me off guard: Vanity, thy name is hair dye.

"Please be nice," I said to my mom.

"Of course," she answered.

I emerged from the car first and walked toward him, my stomach in a knot. "Still *beau-tee-ful*, my petite Su-*zette*," he said and went to hug me. Like with my first reunion, I froze inside while he held me, and then I pulled away quickly.

He then looked over at my mom, his gaze turning cautious. "Hello there, Mom, can I give you a hug too?" he asked her.

"Suuure," she said while giving him a perfectly fake smile. Her body stiffened when he put his arms around her. I was sure her anger towards him was frothing to the surface, the first time in his physical presence. I imagined she probably would have preferred to push him down rather than hug him. After all, she had told me quite firmly on the plane that she would never forgive him.

She acted like she was happy to meet him, for me.

He lived in a tan colored stucco ranch with a two-car garage, lush plantings and a manicured lawn. As it ends up, Albert had done well in the stock market, and Betty made a good living with an elder care business she started.

Betty was waiting in the house. Just as I had remembered, she was a tiny woman, her angular features covered in make-up. I introduced my mother to her, and I gave her a hug and warm hello. "It's been a long time, I know," I said in a solemn way, wanting to acknowledge somehow that I knew my absence was hurtful to Albert, a feeling of guilt rising up inside me. I wondered if she harbored anger against me for it over all those years.

Once inside, I took in the large open spaces with modern artwork on the walls, decorative *objets d'art* all around, and the bookcases filled with works on Judaism and Israel. Artwork and cards by his grandchildren covered the fridge door and cabinets, and shelves had numerous pictures of them and their children. I was surprised how nice and normal it all was. I realized how little I knew about Albert, a sort of awakening that came to me in a compelling and powerful way, and for the first time ever, I wondered why.

The time in his house before dinner passed quickly, a round robin of small talk between the four us that touched on major milestones. There was a stilted politeness to it all. My mother's back stayed erect and stiff throughout. So did mine. She chatted more with Betty than with Albert, and I thought, *strange bedfellows.* I understood it was probably a more comfortable place for my mom to be.

Albert asked me if I had seen Pearl and if she ever asked about him. When I told him I had and that no, she did not ask, his face fell. It must have been sad for him, another blow to a wounded ego that perhaps never fully healed or a heart that never healed either.

After some wine and hors d'oevres, he walked me over to the kitchen table where a pile of all the holiday cards I sent him over the years waited for me. "*You saved them all?*" I asked.

"Of course!" he answered with a wide grin. He beamed at me while I leafed through them, as if to say, see how much you mean to me. As for his own grandchildren, he talked to me about them with deep love in his eyes, showing me numerous pictures. It was endearing.

When we went out to dinner, however, he parked in a handicapped parking space. I wondered how many of the seniors in this state took to doing the same thing, but it was horrifying to me that my birth father was one of them. His wife Betty did not seem too pleased either. My mom and I looked at each other and rolled our eyes. I admonished him in a gentle way, telling him it wasn't right. He didn't seem to agree. I chalked it up to another quirk of his character, one that I did not like.

While we ate salmon and salad and caught up on our lives, my heart was beating at an abnormal pace, a metronome set slightly faster than the music playing.

When we said our good-byes, my takeaway was that he was a loving grandfather and father, and he and Betty had a nice life together. Even though there was a lot of good there, I still did not like the gazes my way that were held just a little too long, just like at our last meet ups. His repetitive deep chuckle and sometimes simplified and naïve commentaries about life still made my eyes roll.

I still felt anxious even though I didn't want to.

From my vantage point now, I can see it was easier to judge Albert than to accept him for whom he was. It helped me keep a wall up, one that I obviously still needed at that point in my journey.

My mother had her own take away. When we got into our car and closed the doors, the first thing she said was, "I'm sorry, but I found him strange!"

"I know that, Mom, he is…but he means well at least." I was defending him now. "And remember, if it weren't for him, I wouldn't be here."

"Well, yes, for that I have to be grateful," she said. I knew she wasn't going to change the rest of her feelings, so I didn't even try. I knew what she was thinking, what she always thought before. He was the sperm donor, that's all, and the one who disrupted all of our lives.

She wasn't alone in her belief. Even Steve Jobs said of his biological parents: "They were the sperm and egg bank that's all. That's not harsh, just the way it was." But to me, it also sounded like another proclamation born out of growing up in the closed system that sadly gave no value at all to birth parents, even though they were people who were often coerced into relinquishment due to difficult life circumstances.

Twenty-Two

WHY A HISTORY MATTERS

The JCCA, founded in the year 1822, first began as the Hebrew Benevolent Society (HBS). The story went that members of the very first synagogue in New York, Shearith Israel, which still stands on the corner of 70th Street and Central Park West, raised $300 to help a Jewish veteran of the Civil War who lay critically ill in the hospital and was penniless and alone. When that veteran died sooner than expected, those men decided to use that money to create an independent Jewish charitable society, to "ameliorate the condition of the unfortunate of the same faith." Religious groups took care of their own back then, because no one else did.

By 1840, the increased flow of immigration from Poland and Germany raised the Jewish population to 15,000, and with it, the needs of the poor soared. That same year, Mordecai Manuel Noah, one of the first eminent Jewish leaders of New York, became president of this Benevolent Society and took action to fill this need. During Noah's nine-year presidency, "membership in the society soared, and the annual anniversary dinner became the social event of the year for the Jewish community. At first, non-Jewish political leaders considered it a duty to be present. Later they wouldn't have missed it for anything," Jacqueline Bernard stated in her book *The Children You Gave Us*. I thought of the A Tree Grows in Pleasantville event, and while far from the event of the year, it eventually drew a nice crowd from the Westchester community where I lived.

Soon the number of Jewish orphans began to skyrocket and the Benevolent Society knew they had to do something. Prior to that, dependent children were housed in "public alms" houses, "scary dumping grounds for adult paupers and the mentally ill," Bernard explained. Others were put on auction blocks and sold off to whoever bought the contract for their care. The famous orphan trains ran then, sending children from the city to join rural farm families. But these children usually became nothing more than free labor for the couples that took them in. Many were abused.

In April 1860, a three-story brick house was purchased at what is now West 29th Street, and it temporarily became the first New York Jewish Asylum for Children, separating them for the first time from the adult population.

By 1861, knowing the small asylum on East 29th was not large enough, the HBS received authorization to erect a building for 200 children on 77th and Third on land donated by the city of New York. The campaign to raise the needed funds was led by Albert Seligman, a friend of Ulysses S. Grant and soon to be known as New York's leading Jewish banker. The famous Baron de Rothschild also came to town and donated. The president of the New York Society for the Prevention of Cruelty to Children could not praise the Jewish effort enough and said, "I have yet to find any [asylum] which compare with those in charge of your people." A final move was made in 1880 to Amsterdam Avenue, between 138th and 140th Streets. There the number of its wards reached its peak at 1,592, all those children living in one behemoth large brick building, likened to an orphan city. It was from that orphanage that the children made their trek to the Pleasantville Cottage School in 1912.

Other Jewish institutions opened, with names like the Home for Hebrew Infants, the Hebrew Sheltering Guardian Society and the Hebrew Orphan Asylum. The Hebrew Sheltering Guardian Society, the HSGS, would eventually build the Pleasantville campus. Researchers finally began to understand that these large impersonal buildings that housed hundreds of children was detrimental to the physical and mental well being of their charges. In fact, "the average size for children by age in these orphanages was well below the national average due to malnutrition and disease," Bernard wrote. So Samuel Levy, its young president, persuaded his board to build a new type of orphanage that "combined the best features of both congregate and family care—the safety of the institution with the intimacy and individual attention only possible in a home." It was to be modeled after the one in England known as Barkenside, where "cottages" were built for orphan children that resembled homes. This marked the birth of the idea for the Cottage School and the origin of its name.

During this time, Jewish refugees were arriving from Eastern Europe to Ellis Island at the rate of 90,000 per year. Amongst those refugees were my own adoptive grandparents and my biological grandmother. My birth father did not arrive until many years later, at the age of 26. Many families broke apart due to the hardships of immigration and poverty, and there was no help for abandoned women. In fact, abandonment was referred to historically as the "quickie divorce," and my own grandfather, Pearl's father, did just that to her mother, one of thousands at the time.

So due to all this abandonment, Jewish orphanages were bursting at the seams. In 1901, specifically, "25% of all inmates of juvenile reformatories were Jewish against a population of only 19%," Bernard quoted. The well-known philanthropist and board member Jacob Schiff, stated, "I don't believe it is fully understood that this institution [HSGS] stands between Jewish honor and Jewish shame!" This was the kind of rhetoric that helped Levy raise the money to build the Pleasantville campus. Jewish philanthropists like the Carnegies, Lewisohns, Warburgs, Loebs and Schiffs were amongst the contributors.

While plans were being drafted, naysayers warned of "the destructiveness of Jewish children" and strongly doubted the wisdom of "surrounding the children of the poor with what appeared to be a relatively comfortable mode of life." Since there would be room for only 500 children, many of the older orphans were discharged and the ones under eight placed in boarding homes, which was the initial precursor to the foster care system today. Right now, children in New York City under the age of eight cannot be sent to residential institutions, but the Cottage School still receives them from Westchester

County. In my current Cottage Edenwald 16, and in the Start Cottages, there are sometimes boys as young as six, always an extra heartbreak to see.

In 1922, the Home for Hebrew Infants, the Hebrew Sheltering Guardian Society and the Hebrew Orphan Asylum all merged to form the Jewish Children's Clearing Bureau. Foster care was also introduced in a formal way at that time—keeping children who could not stay with their own families in the care of others, rather than institutionalizing them. In 1940, further mergers of Jewish agencies occurred with the Clearing Bureau, and its name was later changed to the Jewish Child Care Association.

The JCCA was the first in the country to have a psychiatric treatment clinic in child welfare, which was set up at the Pleasantville Cottage campus in 1925; the first to unionize their staff in 1946; and the first to start an experimental family day-care program in 1952, as women from struggling families started to join the work force under the auspices of UJA-Federation. More programs proliferated through the fifties and sixties as JCCA invented new and effective ways of helping traumatized children, including intensive diagnostic programs, regular and therapeutic foster care, supervised group homes, and halfway houses for children after discharge.

Finally, not to be overlooked, the agency helped rescue 600 children from Nazi Germany in 1934. A number of these refugees went on to work for the agency.

All of this history was fascinating to me. It was in many ways the legacy of my own salvation. These people and their passions had put a social service net in place for all those children who would have ended up homeless, destitute or dead.

In 1988, New York City Mayor Edward Koch came to the Cottage School campus to celebrate its seventy-fifth birthday, saying, "We needed you and you were here."

They were there for my mother. They were there for me.

Twenty-Three

A TINY MOUTH AND EARS

*B*acking down my driveway, I was heading to a UJA-Federation charity lunch. I stopped to grab the stack of letters inside my mailbox and spotted the words Spence Chapin on top. My heart skipped. Just like that, I was zapped back to the land of my biological self.

Taking Leona's advice, the woman who kept the files at JCCA, I called Spence Chapin Adoption Agency after returning home. Sure enough, my file was there, transferred from Louise Wise when they closed.

I held it in my hand. "Open me!" it shouted. But I did not have the time to read it. I knew that when I did, I would want to digest it slowly. I placed it down on the passenger seat next to me with the rest of the mail.

As I drove, I kept glancing at it. It pulled me like a moth to a flame.

Ten minutes later, on the highway, an exit approached. I put on my blinker. Seeing a garden nursery shuttered for the winter, I pulled in. My SUV bumped up and down on its rocky surface. I pulled to the end and parked to face the frozen farm field ahead.

I slid my finger under the flap, trying not to tear it, wanting to protect the sanctity of what it held. I saw right a way that there were no names listed as they explained would be the case, just as with my file from the JCCA. I took a deep breath and braced myself. What would I learn for better or worse that I did not already know?

Background

Your birth mother, who had been in foster care from the age of four and one-half, was referred to Louise Wise in February of 1960.

Just pregnant with me.

She was a single, Jewish young woman, born in 1935, and was described as an attractive looking girl who had dark blonde hair, blue eyes and a fair complexion. She was about 5'2" tall and usually weighed 118 pounds. She looked younger than her age.

My height and weight…and younger than her age…it took me a long time to get into an R-rated movie without ID…no one ever believed me. The ability to be able to compare myself to my birth mother on this specific level was so satisfying, as if the puzzle pieces that defined my heritage were flying down and finding their place in the empty spaces inside me.

At age 14 your birth mother had been in the ninth grade and a satisfactory student who was described as weak in arithmetic although obtained passing grades.

But that was my best subject.

"She was conscientious and was well liked by her teachers and classmates…and well liked when she went to camp. She liked swimming, skating, dancing, and biking."

I smiled. *She did have some pleasure in her life. How did she go to camp though? The family was poor…*

When I asked Pearl years later if she remembered going to camp, a huge grin formed on her face. "*Weeee*-ha-ha!" she rolled out with a singsong enthusiasm, as if for that brief moment she was back on those pleasurable grassy grounds. I couldn't help but smile. In 1917, I'd find out, the Hebrew Orphan Asylum opened two camps for their orphaned children, Weehaha for girls and Wakitan for boys, and they would become part of the JCCA umbrella when the agencies merged.

I pictured a little girl running down a wide dirt path, other little girls by her side, their locks flowing behind them in the warm summer breeze. The sense of freedom on their faces, her face, is captivating. I allowed myself to revel in the image for a few sacred moments before I went back to reading.

"At the beginning of high school, your birth mother was seen by a psychologist. She suggested that your birth mother pursue a commercial program.

She noted that your birth mother was somewhat anxious and could feel insecure. She wanted to feel accepted.

Wanting to feel accepted? Don't we all?

Regarding her emotional health, your birth mother sought counseling at a psychotherapy center starting in February of 1958.

A psychologist? Bold at that time. That was when she started dating Albert.

She realized she was having difficulty relating to young men, as her foster sister was getting married. She was feeling detached and without direction.

Sorrow filled me. Pearl was far from unique. Having problems with attachment and developing trust in relationships are both quite common for children raised in foster care. Former foster care children are almost twice as likely to suffer from Post Traumatic Stress Disorder (PTSD) as U.S. war veterans, according to a study released in 2005 by the Harvard Medical School, the University of Michigan and Casey Family programs.

Then it got worse.

"A social worker had a consultation with a psychiatrist about your birth mother in the spring of 1960. A note in the record said that the psychiatrist who saw her at that time thought she was borderline schizophrenic."

My heart dropped. I sat there trying to digest it, my mind swirling, hoping it wasn't true. How much did they know back in 1960, I wondered. Still, if she was, I realized I was beyond fortunate that neither my children nor I developed this debilitating illness. Having one parent who suffers from it increases the risk from 1% to 10%.

Interestingly enough, a number of lawsuits were filed against Louise Wise in the 1970s and 1980s because children adopted from there went on to develop schizophrenia. Their adoptive parents filed for "wrongful adoption," because the agency did not tell them the true medical nature and history of their birth parents. My own parents were never told about Pearl's struggles, only that I was "a healthy baby." My mother told me that the other details of my genetic history were left out.

The decision to not disclose any prior psychiatric history of natural parents in adoption was initiated because there was an uncertainty at the time as to whether mental illness was even inheritable. But the truth was that there were some studies that existed and had been released that made a clear genetic connection, ones that Louise Wise and other agencies chose to ignore.

Dr. Viola Bernard, who was the chief consulting psychiatrist at Louise Wise during that period, defended the practice by stating, "If you labeled a kid as being the child of a schizophrenic, there would be no hope for placing that baby. Any information that would be deemed to be destructive to the relationship between adoptive parents and children would thus not be disclosed." Their intentions might have been good, but in several cases, the outcomes were not.

In one tragic case, Michael Juman, a young man from Long Island, adopted in 1965, developed deep depression in his late adolescence. When his behavior grew more erratic, the Jumans went to Louise Wise for answers. They were less than helpful. In her 1999 *NY Times* article, "What the Jumans Didn't Know About Michael," Lisa Belkin wrote that Michael's birth parents were described to the Jumans as bright and accomplished, his mother the winner of a college scholarship, a woman who played the piano and helped support her widowed mother. All lies. The truth was that she was a lobotomized schizophrenic. His birth father also suffered with severe mental illness, and she had met him during one of her many years within a state institution. "Agency workers knew this when they placed Michael, and they also knew it when his psychiatrist called years later and asked for his medical history. But Louise Wise continued to withhold the information, admitting only to some mental instability." Michael was shocked to find out his real beginnings, and he ended up committing suicide in 1996. The family buried him at Long Island's Wellwood Cemetery, unaware that his biological mother, who died nine months earlier, was interred a few hundred yards away, another travesty of the closed system.

In another published case, Arthur and Barbara Ross filed a lawsuit for the son they named Anthony when Louise Wise did not disclose that the birth mother "presented as a girl who was failing in all her major adjustments to life," nor that the birth father was diagnosed as "a seriously disturbed young man." He too was a paranoid schizophrenic. In 1970, when the Ross's told Louise Wise that Anthony was experiencing "night terrors, cursed at the family, hit them and threatened people with objects," they were then only told of "some histories of emotional instability." No specifics were given about the schizophrenia. Anthony was taken to Bellevue, where he too was diagnosed as a paranoid schizophrenic, only after his father woke up during the night and found Anthony standing over him with a raised flashlight ready to strike. Sadly, there were other similar cases of such lies and deception, prompting articles and blogs online today.

The compounding evidence that mental illness had a genetic component led to a change in how adoption agencies viewed a child's medical history. In New York State, a 1983 law required agencies to provide adopted children and adoptive parents with all non-identifying medical information, including any drugs taken during pregnancy, any illnesses including psychological information, and anything else which may be a factor in influencing the child's present or future health.

We now know that most illnesses, physical and mental, are often caused by a combination of genetic and environmental factors, and it is the interaction between the two that leads to the onset of diseases in ways that are still far from clear. What Louise Wise and other adoption agencies did at that time was to rob prospective adoptive parents of their ability to make a choice. If the parents decided to adopt anyway, knowing the child had a specific history, at least they would have made that choice with full disclosure. No one can predict what a child's mental health will be, even if the parents are healthy themselves. But in this case, at least the adoptive parents would have been prepared and better equipped to deal with whatever symptoms emerged.

Ironically, a couple in Canada filed a lawsuit against Georgia-based Xytex Corp. and its sperm bank employees because the employees told the couple the donor sperm they were getting was coming from a man who was "smart, healthy and mature." They later found out he was schizophrenic, had dropped out of college and had been arrested for burglary. They are fighting it out in court for damages. It seems that the laws meant to protect prospective parents haven't caught up with the technology yet.

In fact, the entire sperm bank industry is opening up a new set of potential issues for the offspring that are similar to the ones relating to closed adoption: being denied one's biological identity, at least one half of it, and the consequences of not knowing.

I kept on reading.

Your birth mother's family

"Your birth mother's parents had lived together in a common law relationship for six years. Your birth mother's records state that her father had deserted her mother prior to her birth. Your birth mother's mother experienced difficulty in caring for her although she was described as quite attached to her… she was reportedly malnourished and neglected while in her mother's care. Her mother would leave your birth mother alone and did not follow up on routine medical care for her.

Nothing new, but "attached to her" vibrated through me. The story I wrote that evening in Florida suddenly became less fictional.

"Your birth mother was initially hospitalized in order to be treated for rickets and malnutrition. Her teeth were diseased; her tonsils were hypertrophied. Your birth mother remained in the hospital for eight to ten months.

That sick?

A note in the record states that your birth mother saw her mother once when she was 17 but that her mother was quite ill and did not remember her. This was understandably difficult for your birth mother.

Pearl had told me she never saw her mother again. Had she blocked out this painful memory?

I put the papers down to digest it. *To find her mother in that state must have been devastating.* I reached for the small package of Kleenex in my purse.

"She was in several foster homes prior to the family with which she remained."

The foster mother related that when your birth mother came to her home, although she was six, she looked like she was three.

Three?

She described your birth mother as a very sweet child who made many friends and was liked by everyone. She said that very early on your birth mother started asking, "Who am I?" and would look through the phone book for her name.

As often in my journey, I pictured it. A small girl sitting on the floor in front of a telephone cabinet, the door opened. She has pulled out the large phone book and is flipping the pages, looking for her name. Her foster sister stamps her foot and tells her, "stop already!"

"Mom, she's looking again!" she yells.

"Pearl, get her right now and set this table."

The little girl obeys. She doesn't want her foster mother to pinch her.

The "who am I" question that Pearl asked herself as she grew up in her foster home was no different than the one I was searching for. It haunted me even though the similarities ended there. I didn't experience the trauma of living with my mother for four and a half years and then being taken away, nor the abuse she endured as part of her foster family. But she was my mother, and the pain I felt for her was real.

"In the beginning your birth mother stated that, 'I had a wonderful foster home with foster parents that really took an interest in my health and welfare and gave me love, guidance and understanding.'"

This was in quotes? Yeah, like a child would say that?

Your birth mother's foster mother was described in the records as a warm and sensitive person, gifted in her role as a parent, who accepted your birth mother as part of the family.

Really?

From Pearl's own lips that day in Florida, I knew that this was not the case. I didn't doubt for one second that she was abused, nor did I doubt that her foster mom put on a good show for the social worker each time she showed up.

That said, her foster mother could not have been all that bad either. She did give her some semblance of a family life. She did want to adopt her.

However, as your birth mother worked with her social worker, she also spoke about some complexity in this family including saying that she had been physically abused along with her feeling that she needed to please the family and not complain.

She finally admitted it, good for her.

Your birth parents' relationship

The record states your birth parents met through a Jewish organization. A note in the record says that your birth mother's foster family did not approve of your birth father.

When your birth mother got pregnant, they spoke about marriage, but your mother subsequently chose not to marry. She did not feel she was ready because she did not have a firm sense of who she was.

You were born on September 18, 1960 at 8:34 pm. Your birth mother named you Charlotte. She told her social worker that you were a beautiful baby, and she spoke glowingly of you. You were described as having small, pretty features and quite fair skin with contrasting dark hair and eyes, which seemed to be turning hazel. You had a tiny mouth and ears.

She also said that it was hard for her to talk too much about you, however, as she knew that she would be planning for your adoption.

I thought of Erik Erikson's quote once again, "A birth mother must make the baby into a non-person to give them up." I turned to the next crisp white page, steeped in sadness.

Planning

A social worker that worked with your birth mother in the period following the birth described her as being depressed. She noted that your birth mother's sense of humor was a trait she used in coping. She had thought carefully about what would be best for you and her. She did not feel ready to be a parent. She did not feel she could care for you or support you.

A social worker met with your birth mother five months following the birth. At this time your birth mother spoke of how she still thought about you. The social worker felt that although your birth mother said things were going well, she thought that underneath she might be unhappy or depressed.

You think?

Updated Information

Your birth father had contacted Louise Wise in 1977 at which time he had spoken about wanting to include the child in his estate planning. He also spoke of wishing to meet you. Your adoptive parents were called by his intermediary and were told, and he subsequently called your parents directly.

That was my senior year of high school. Now the postmark of 1977 on the envelope my mother handed me from Louise Wise with my adoption papers made sense. They must have asked for my records again, to check for legal loopholes, perhaps a way to protect themselves from Albert?

Your birth mother again contacted Louise Wise in 1987 [I was 27 then]. She said she had three children from a marriage. She said she had a "nervous breakdown" some years ago and had been in the hospital several times. She also spoke of 17 years of shock therapy as she had major depressive illness.

This I knew...and yet, I felt like I was being punched in the same bruised spot again.

And just like that, the document came to an end. I held it in my hand and looked out the window, dazed. The sun was starting to peek out from behind overcast skies. I scanned the letter again trying to imprint the details in my brain under some inner file that said "Mother," under the one that said, "My History", under the one that said, "Who I Am," in a now deeper level of understanding.

Looking at the car clock, I snapped back to reality. With my heart in my stomach, I drove back to the highway, but I was in a daze.

It was as if I had just revisited the grave of someone who sacrificed so much for me, but whom I never got to know. I was filled with reverence and awe at the tragedy of it.

I drove the rest of the way in a daze as the sun started to burn off the fog around me. Pulling up to the valet parking at the country club, I left my car and entered the lobby. The gathering had already thinned, but I saw a group of friends standing there and headed toward them, plastering a smile on my face. "Hi guys! How are you?"

"Good, really good!" they responded.

"Any you?" they asked.

"I'm good!"

We proceeded to walk through the thick double doors together into the ballroom. Happy chatter echoed off the walls. I reached into the pocket of my dress and felt the tissues there that were still damp with my tears. I squeezed them for a good long time.

hree years passed. I had contacted the JCCA again to see if Leona missed anything from my file that day in Florida while working on this memoir. Oddly enough, the original paper file was MIA, probably due to Hurricane Sandy. The storm had flooded the basement storage area of their offices on Wall Street, and some paper files could have been files. But they found something on microfiche, new information I did not have.

"P earl's parents," I read, "presented as Mr. and Mrs. Kaminek, in an extra marital relationship, were receiving assistance from the Home Relief Bureau. Mr. Kaminek had been abusing her and taking most of the money they received, and she therefore wished to move to a furnished room and get assistance for herself."

"Throughout our contact, Pearl's mother gave the impression of being mentally disturbed. She changed frequently from sobbing to smiling and had an irrelevant stream of talk. She became emotionally upset when reference was made to her daughter. Although the mother was very attached to the child, she had so deteriorated mentally that she was unable to take care of her."

"She had no contact with Pearl and only upon Pearl's more recent request around wanting to know her identity was a visit arranged for the child to meet her mother. After meeting that one time, Pearl decided that while she felt sorry for this woman that was her mother, she guessed that her foster mother had served the role of mother after all."

"While Pearl always appeared to be a rather shy and conforming individual, she always had friends. In addition, she always managed to be popular with young men. Pearl herself seemed to prefer the boy or man who needed mothering or who seemed to the foster family to be emotionally disturbed. At 18 years of age, Pearl was discharged...the agency receives a letter from her in which she expresses her appreciation and thanks for helping her.

"I'd like to thank you, Mrs. Krider, [who I guess was her social worker at that time] and all my previous social workers for their guidance and understanding in helping me to help myself."

"She adds that 'when I get married, I hope to have a husband who is understanding toward children who are less fortunate than our own and who would consent to accept children from your home into my home.'"

After all she had been through…she thought to adopt a child.

From what I could tell from these records, it seemed that Pearl's overall experience with the social workers and staff at JCCA had been a positive one, although who could be sure? This was in spite of whatever abuse she might have endured. Back then, there were none of the extensive background checks, interviews, foster care parent training, and scrutiny that is in place today. The social workers did then, like we all do, the best they could. In spite of the horrors she endured, they saved my mother's life.

Twenty-Four

A Burial, A Bar Mitzvah and New Sibling Encounters

In 2009, my daughter Mallory was accepted to the University of Michigan, my alma mater. It brought me happiness of course but also angst. It meant I would have to go back to that campus, the place where Albert called me twenty-seven years before and upended my life.

When I went with her to freshmen orientation, the memories came back full throttle, as I knew they would. I saw the dorm where I lived, the libraries where I studied, the stores where I shopped and the paths that I crisscrossed hundreds of times, with the eyes of a now forty-nine year old woman.

Memories of the insecure eighteen year old that I was came flooding back, the one who was trying so hard to put the lid back on all the toxic emotions that had erupted out of her. I wished I could tell her it would all be okay, that she would be okay. To have done so would have meant putting my adult brain into my adolescent body, a nice idea but impossible.

With subsequent visits to my alma mater, another feeling would emerge: a sad regret for the college experience that was taken away from that young girl, the experience I now got to watch Mallory embrace with exuberance and confidence. Perhaps I even felt some shame, for having allowed that phone call to damage me so, for not being more resilient. It was a painful feeling. I knew I needed to let myself off the hook. Regret is not a land I wanted to live in.

Was I happy then too? I was some of the time, I was sure of it. Where would life have taken me if that call had never come? Of course, I could never know such things, the what- ifs that remain forever a mystery to us all. I received an unexpected bolt, the kind that knocks you down, leaving you dizzy, confused, and in pain. I stayed in that place for a while, not under-standing it. Wiser people than I have pointed out how these bolts can turn our lives in new directions, so maybe my experience turned me exactly where I needed to go. But when you're in the middle of a storm, it's hard to think that there might be blue skies ahead.

Just a few months before Mallory left for college, I went to visit my dad. He was sitting at the kitchen table, wearing his favorite cap that said Alaska, and his zip-up fleece, because he was always cold. He was eating the small cut up pieces of chicken my mom had prepared for him.

When I entered, he said hello but without his usual enthusiasm.

"Hi, Pop!" I said and gave him a kiss on top of his head. He smiled at me briefly. I stroked his bald head off and on, asking him about his day and how he was feeling. He gave me one-word answers. My mom and I chatted too.

Three minutes after I left, my cell phone rang in my car. I put it on speaker. It was my mom, distraught.

"You won't believe it," she said.

"What?"

"Right after you walked out, Dad asked me, who was that girl in our kitchen?"

My mouth dropped. My father always knew who I was, who we all were, before this moment.

"I told him, Sam…that was *Suzie!*"

He said, *'that was Suzie?*…well if I don't know Suzie, I don't want to live anymore."

I couldn't have imagined how it felt, for anyone with dementia for that matter, to know that you are losing the memory of the one thing that matters most in life —the people you love. I stayed in a fog the rest of the day.

A month and a half after Mallory started Michigan, my dad passed away. When we buried him on that warm October day in 2009, we placed his mobile phone in his casket, the one he clung too, the one that kept him connected to the people he loved. We laughed and cried that perhaps he would be able to use it wherever he was going. Judaism speaks of some kind of heaven where our souls reside. Buddhism tells us another body awaits our soul. Was it one of those or ashes to ashes, dust to dust? I wanted to believe he went somewhere, but I just felt cold inside.

We also placed with him an elephant figurine with the trunk up, one of the many he collected over his lifetime, because he was sure they were certain to bring good luck. Entering my parents' home, one would find framed pictures of our family along the shelves and the fireplace mantel but with an elephant in front of each one. The trunks were always turned toward the picture, because he wanted to direct the luck right into the people he loved. All one actually saw then were rows of elephant butts blocking the photo images. My mother did not dare move them.

We held each other as the rabbi recited Shema Yisrael, *Hear Oh Israel,* an essential prayer of the Jewish religion. It was the same one that Albert told me he used when the bombs were dropping around him during the Second World War while he cowered in the basement. It was also the one I recited standing next to my father in synagogue as a young girl, stroking the soft blue velvet of his tallis bag. I would hold it on my lap during services. Religion helped me feel connected to both my fathers in a comforting way, as religion can do.

We stood huddled as the workers lowered the casket into the hole. The rabbi told us that burying one's loved ones was the greatest honor you could give them -- to do what they could not do for themselves-- but it didn't feel like one to me. It felt horrible. We did what we were supposed to do, because that is what our tradition told us.

A few weeks after the funeral, an old work associate and close friend of my parents from London, named Keith, came to visit my mom and me. He had been overseas so was unable to attend. We went to the cemetery so he could visit my father's grave. He pulled a yarmulke out of his coat pocket. I was surprised because he was not Jewish. "Out of respect for your dad," he said. He knew that my father prayed every day with one on.

"You're a good man, Keith..." I said.

"Your dad was a good man," Keith said.

We started to tell stories, like we often do in times of mourning, to lift our spirits.

"One day we had plans for lunch," Keith told me, "you know, your dad and I often ate lunch out together. He walked into my office one day, and told me that instead of eating, we were going shopping."

I smiled.

"I knew not to argue with *Som*," he said in his British accent.

"He said he needed to get you an...I don't know, eye contraption of some kind."

I looked at him quizzically.

"Wait, I know, was it an eye brow pencil *sharpener*?"

"Yes, yes, I believe that's what it was...we not only missed lunch that day but the next one too, until he found one for you."

I blushed, embarrassed.

"Boy, he loved you, Suzie."

I knew the world stopped for my father when I needed something, but this was above and beyond. I smiled ear to ear, knowing how lucky I was to be placed in his arms eight-five years earlier.

⌒

We celebrated my son Asher's bar mitzvah only six days after my father's burial, the joy and sorrow of life squeezed into close proximity. Asher wore my father's yarmulke for the service, the one he wore to say his prayers in every day. It was one of those cheap nylon dime-a-dozen varieties, because my father was never one for fancy, and it stayed in the small drawer of the table next to his recliner. When my father recited his daily prayers seated in that chair, it was the only time in his life he would not accept a phone call from my brother or me. I envied his faith.

When the ceremony was done, Rich and I climbed up to the "bimah," the platform in a synagogue, to give our own personal words, as is the custom. "D'vor v'dor," I began, "From generation to generation -- the yarmulke you wear on your head is the one your grandfather wore...it is not only your connection to him, but to all who came before you, a 3000-year-old legacy of a people that has survived..."

When writing these words at home, the word *survival* echoed in my head. I thought of my grandparents who survived the Russian pogroms and Albert's father who survived the Armenian slaughter as a child. I thought of my father Samuel who survived childhood poverty and World War II. I thought of my mother Evelyn who survived verbally abusive parents and the devastation of infertility. I thought of my birth father Albert who survived World War II, displacement, sexual abuse and harsh service in the newly created Jewish state. I thought about my birth mother Pearl who survived severe childhood neglect, abusive foster care and sexual abuse. Here I was, with all the riches of life given to me, spared any such horrors. I had so much to say thank you for I didn't know where to begin.

As I sat in the pew and Asher chanted his Haftorah, the passage selected from the Books of the Profits that is part of the ceremony, I thought of my birth parents. I felt a small sense of loss that they were not there to share this with us. The closed system had set the blueprints a half century before, and we were still living well within its lines, at least I certainly was. Their presence here would have been too upsetting to my mother and too awkward for my children who had never met either of them. In a more perfect world, they would be here too, and their children, embracing us and us them, one big larger happy extended family.

The rabbi lifted the Torah to return it to the ark, and I stared at that sacred scroll. I took some weird comfort that Asher was fully Jewish, unlike what I had believed during those eight years after Albert's call.

I remembered the dogmatic and opinionated rabbi of our Conservative temple growing up, who had balked at my brother becoming a bar mitzvah, not convinced of his Jewish heritage. A neighbor of ours went and told him Oliver was adopted. Like some religious policeman, he felt compelled to warn him. He was also a "friend" of my parents that made it all the more disturbing. My father went in to the temple and had it out with the rabbi. He gave him "a what for," as my mom described it. Oliver got to have his day.

In my synagogue now, a Reform one, it wouldn't have mattered what my birth religion was. It would only matter what I identified as being. Still, it gave me a small sense of peace at the bar mitzvah, that all was aligned in these matters of heritage during this sacred moment.

Four years later, over a piece of poached salmon at a local restaurant in Florida, Albert blurted out, "You know, Su-*zette*, Pearl wasn't born Jewish…" He said it like he was giving me the local weather report. I looked at him astonished. "Yes, I'm sure of it. I remember I got her papers when I was looking for you," he added.

Where the hell was that coming from? And he waited till now to tell me?

"Then how did she end up at a Jewish adoption agency?"

"I don't know, well, they never knew what her mom was …and that blond hair and blue eyes…I'm sure, *very* sure."

"I don't think that's right, I answered.

"I'm telling you it is."

Suddenly, once again, my religious heritage was cast into doubt, but I was skeptical. JCCA only took in Jewish children back then, and they must have done their homework, so how would Albert know better than they did?

The funny part was that, at that point, either way, I didn't care. I was and continued to be Jewish no matter what Albert believed. It was in my heart and soul. That he chose to tell me this so many years after he met me, and in such a nonchalant way, irked me greatly. What's wrong with you, I wanted to say, knowing how important Judaism was to him in his own life. But I decided it wasn't worth the condemnation.

I chalked it up to yet another one of the off-putting comments that he made even though he didn't understand their impact. They were the ones that I took to define him in my mind even though I know he meant me no harm.

When dinner was done and my mom and I returned to our car, I took out my phone and called Rich. Sitting in the parking lot, I joked to him, "Guess what, honey, looks like you might be married to a *shiksa!*" I explained what Albert had said, but I was laughing now.

"I like that!" he responded, something I predicted he would say knowing his feelings on the matter. He was never a religious Jew, more a cultural one, like many of us, so whatever rules existed would not have mattered to him.

I also knew he would like to imagine me as someone new and exotic after twenty-five years of marriage, like he did whenever I spoke French to someone in his presence. So this was a new opportunity. We chuckled about Albert's comment for a good long time.

lbert came around and told his children about me. His son Paul exclaimed, "*I can't believe* you've been hiding a sister from me all this time!" I was delighted by his enthusiasm.

I flew to a suburb of Chicago, Illinois to meet him. He was warm, smart and witty, the perfect trifecta. I knew right away he was someone I would want to maintain a relationship with. I'd soon learn, however, that you cannot make up for a lifetime of not knowing someone, even if you really tried. It is a shared history that brings connection and creates a family, one we never experienced.

This did not mean however we couldn't make new connections and memories moving forward, and create a family in a different way.

I have since made Paul a "frother" of sorts, some combination of friend and brother that lives comfortably inside me.

When I first met him, he helped me understand two crucial things about Albert: first, that he was an incredibly stubborn man who put blinders on whenever he wanted something, thus shedding light on why Albert did not listen to my parents and called me. Paul was not in the least bit surprised when I recounted the story. Second, being raised in Egypt and then France, his cultural sensibilities were different from ours. From that, I extrapolated that closed adoption, perhaps even adoption itself, was probably a foreign concept to him, one he would reject given his upbringing. Both these admissions helped me step back and see Albert with a more objective lens. It helped me take a big leap forward in my understanding and acceptance of him as not only my father but as a man.

As for Pam, Paul's sister, she was the yin to Paul's yang. When I met her for dinner in Florida where she also lived, she was tight lipped and cool. While

I had my genetic comparison checklist out front and center, hers was seemingly stuffed away.

I emailed her about a year later looking for answers, finally having the courage to do so and telling her she could be "brutally honest." She emailed back, "it felt like you were on a fishing trip" and that "our meet-up seemed more like a chore for you than anything else…it would also be awkward to start anything at this point." I was shocked. I thought I had been enthusiastic, warm and gregarious.

Upset by her words, I sought to set the record straight. I sent her an email back where I opened up about the hardships of my journey, making myself vulnerable like I had done with her dad. "Being adopted in those days was hard for me…I am only now trying to put the pieces together…I really had hoped for a connection and a possible relationship moving forward, sorry if you thought differently."

I waited. Three weeks passed before she emailed me back. She wrote, "sorry but I've been away and busy with my daughters," and "I understand what you wrote and would be open to seeing you the next time you're in Florida."

Clearing out the vestibules of adoption mud stuck inside me felt good. In spite of that, I would not hear from her nor would she be available to see me on subsequent visits to her dad, proving that shared DNA does not also a sibling, nor even a "frister" make.

Tracey, Oliver's half sister, ended up not being much of a "frister" to him either. She told him that she did not want him at the funeral when her mom passed away. They both knew Ruth didn't have a lot of time left, and she wanted to let my brother know her wishes. At that point, Oliver had already been to visit Ruth four times. He also had brought his family in two of those times to meet her. As for her reaction when she met his children, he said, "she was beaming!"

Oliver explained, "she told me she didn't want to have to explain to everyone that her mother had a child out of wedlock, one she never knew about." Tracey must have discussed it with Ruth, he imagined, and he believed Ruth bowed to her daughter's wishes. He understood that Tracey's needs came before his own.

Accepting this, my brother said to Tracey, "How about if I stay in the back the whole time? I won't talk to anyone or tell anyone who I am, okay?" Still, she didn't change her mind. I shook my head. It didn't seem right to me.

When Ruth passed away a short time later, Tracey did not tell Oliver until after the funeral. He received an email from her. "It was as if she was notifying me that I had forgotten an umbrella somewhere," he told me in disbelief. "While I was hurt, sure, I had to respect her wishes. I mean if she couldn't even meet me how was she supposed to have me at the funeral?"

"But still…"

"I know."

"Have you had contact with her since?" I asked.

"I send her an email at holiday time." That sounded familiar. Paper, or in this case, electronic bridges to our birth worlds, worked well. In spite of his disappointment in Tracey, my brother, like me, felt the need to stay connected even if she did not. Once he had opened the door to his own blood ties, he could not close it back up. I understood all too well.

In the half sibling game, even Rich was confronted one night. The two sons that his dad went on to have with his stepmom were grown men now, married with families of their own. Rich had not seen either of them in close to thirty years. His younger sister, Connie, however, had reconnected with the brothers and established a somewhat close relationship.

It was at a JCCA gala in the city a few years back when Rich said to me, "come here, I want you to meet someone…" with a peculiar look on his face. I went over to where a tall and smartly dressed couple stood awaiting my arrival. "This is my half brother Mark," he said and paused, "and his wife Beth." My eyes opened wide. "Oh, wow!"

I smiled warmly at these two people in awe. They smiled back. A friend of theirs, one who was on the board with me, invited them to the gala. The JCCA had once again brought new familial connections in the most unexpected of ways.

We chatted for ten minutes or so in a circle of pleasantries. I liked them. So on the way home, I said to Rich, "they were so nice! Would you re-consider having a relationship with them? I mean, so much time has gone by…"

"No," he said curtly, with the small curl to the edge of his mouth that always told me "not up for discussion." So I let it be. I guessed it wasn't hard to imagine why though: seeing his half brother had to be a reminder of his dad's leaving him, and what his dad's new family went on to have that he and his siblings didn't, unconditional love and support. He didn't need to be reminded of this over and over again. Rich needed to keep his wall up, which I understood and had to accept, while I needed to break mine down.

To meet Stacy, the last of my five siblings, I reached out to Pearl first. I wanted to get a take on what she thought Stacy's feelings might be, remembering she had chosen not to join us that night in Bayside. She also had warned her mother that I might be carrying a weapon back when Pearl and I first met. I did not want to enter "Stacy-land" if Stacy was going to be hostile.

I was scared to call Pearl since the last time I spoke to her was the day she hung up on me in my hotel room in Florida, telling me she wasn't well enough to see me.

Sitting in my car outside the gym on a frozen winter morning, I took a deep breath and dialed. A younger woman's voice answered taking me off guard. I introduced myself in a gentle tone and the voice responded, "This is her daughter Stacy," a bit curt.

Didn't she live in Pennsylvania? I was fearful I had just stepped into a potential minefield.

She explained she lived with her mom now, moving down there after her dad had died. I wondered if her cool tone meant she was masking anger toward me for calling and intruding on their lives.

After that brief explanation, she said, "I'll put my mother on the phone."

"Thank you for calling," Pearl said, "but you know, I'm sick...the doctors think I have Alzheimer's now...I'm turning 73 in June." And then, as if a switch was turned on, she began to talk about the past, like she did the first time we met, as if she still owed me something. "You know, I remember when they put you in my arms, kissing you on your face and hands, and if I didn't accept giving you up, it would be terrible for me."

"I know. It's okay, you explained that to me when we first met."

"I don't know how I survived. I lived on sour milk. Who knows who diapered me? And then I was a *charity case* at the hospital…And my foster mother, well, she abused me." I tried to acknowledge each repeated declaration with as much compassion as I could.

"You're living the life I always wanted to live, I always dreamed of having. You're my inspiration. I save all your cards." My heart clenched and I was speechless for a few seconds. I then let her know how glad I was that they made her happy, that my life made her happy.

"You know I suffer with major depression. I carry around this book called *Lincoln's Melancholy.* It's about Abraham Lincoln. If you read it, you'll see what it's like for me."

My mother reads historical non-fiction? She is comparing herself to President Lincoln? I was shocked.

That I wanted to come down to visit her again and meet Stacy hung in the air unsaid as she said good-bye and hung up.

When I opened the tome, I searched for Pearl in every single page, trying to better understand who my mother was. I learned that Lincoln said, "I am the most miserable person there is," to a trusted friend. Another wrote, "He was the classic image of gloom." He often wept in public, and as a young man, he talked of suicide. When he grew older, he said he saw the world as hard and grim. It was an added compelling window into the depression that plagued my mother's life.

When I finished, eventually scanning through the second half, I was also amazed at her ability and determination to get through the 600 pages. It also made me feel good that, in spite of the dark clouds that circled around her, she sought to have a better understanding of her life as it was. She was a "seeker" in her own way, just like me.

A year later, I sent Stacy an email, rather than calling, to ask her if I could possibly come down and meet her. Much to my surprise, she said yes. "Are you sure your mom will be okay with it?" I chose to refer to her as "your mom," not to step on any sensibilities she might have had on the matter. She said it was good for me to come.

⌒⟶

𝒫ulling into the same community that I had pulled into twenty years before when I first met Pearl, there was a surreal sense of a time warp. So much life had gone by, and yet, she was still here.

Since Stacy was the only daughter of my birth mother, I realized that her life would have been the closest to what mine would have been if I had not been given away. So I was stepping into a world that had my first birth certificate plastered all over it.

The adoption jitters amped up as I drove through the community. Standing before her door, I paused and tried to look through the window beside me, to see if I might get a glimpse of them first. The window was opaque. And what if they had been looking out at me? I turned my head straight, took a deep breath and rang the bell.

The door swung open, and I stood before a young woman who looked so unlike me that I was startled.

Stacy had very dark, straight hair that was parted in the middle and hung close to her long thin face. Her thin nose did not match my wider one.

"Hi," she said with hesitation, but with a warm smile on her face. She wore lipstick, thick make-up and a matching jeans outfit with piping all over, something I would not have worn.

Even if we didn't live in the same make-up counter or clothes store, she lived in the same womb that I did once upon a time, and that was all that mattered.

I hugged her.

I followed her into the small eat-in kitchen. I took in the brands of crackers and cereal that were on the counter as we made pleasantries.

"Can I see the rest of the apartment?" I asked with as much warmth as I could muster.

"Sure," Stacy answered.

We walked into the main room that was dim and filled with heavy dark furniture. The dining room table had four mismatched chairs around it. Luggage was stacked in a corner and an old walnut wall credenza was over-stuffed with knick-knacks, picture frames and books. The couch was partly covered with a sheet, but beneath it I could see it was old and dated. Everything here was probably from their apartment in Brooklyn, purchased when she and Martin married a lifetime ago. It became clear that they were of very limited means, much more so than I ever imagined. I felt a sense of shock, and then quiet despair. It was hard to take in. The difference between their life and mine was staggering.

In the bedroom, I saw a picture of Pearl as a younger woman with Martin. I stared. "That was right after my parents got married," Stacy told me. Pearl looked happy. I took out my phone to take a picture of it. I wanted to have it, a small treasure I could look at whenever I wanted of Pearl after she gave birth to me.

When the three of us left to go out to dinner, a woman stopped us in the parking lot to say hello.

"This is my friend Mary," Pearl said to me.

"Nice to meet you," I said.

"This is," she looked at Stacy and hesitated, then shuffled her feet, "*these* are...my daughters."

"What beautiful daughters you have!" Mary responded. My heart squeezed for Pearl, knowing how difficult that must have been.

At the restaurant in the outside mall they took me to, Stacy was quiet throughout the evening, perhaps unsure of me and uncomfortable. Pearl seemed in a bit of a fog, and Stacy helped her with the menu. I found myself doing most of the talking to fill in the uncomfortable voids. I still could not get a read of what Stacy thought of me, but she was pleasant enough. I searched for topics that we could talk about, avoiding ones that highlighted the vast differences in our lifestyles, my sensitivity chip in overtime.

At the end, I asked Stacy if she thought her mom would be willing to see me the next day, just the two of us, while she was at work. I had no plans.

"What do you think Ma?"

Pearl hesitated at the idea. Then she said, "I guess it will be all right."

"Does your mom need anything, something I can buy her?" I asked.

"Actually, she could use a new pair of house shoes…you can take her back here, there's a shoe store."

The next day I picked up my birth mother, grateful to have a project to do with her. I was nervous about being alone with her. In the car, I tried hard to put her at ease with soft kind words. There was so much to say that neither of us could say.

Instead, a lifetime without a past together sat glaringly between us.

In the store Stacy suggested, the kind where the shoes sat in boxes along the wall, Pearl lifted one pair after another, examining each. She looked at the straps and souls, making comments, and I tried to help her. She shuffled back and forth in the same nervous waltz as the night before. "I don't know, well I don't know," she repeated over and over. I tried to show her the benefits of each pair, wanting her to try a pair on. Finally she said, "let's just go." I walked her out into the bright sunshine without a pair of shoes.

We strolled along the walkway with the sun blazing down on us. She clutched her bag tight to her chest, not saying anything. We looked in the windows of the shops we passed, many of them higher end chain stores, ones I imagined she had never set foot in.

I suggested we go into Starbucks for a cold drink. She had never been. Inside, she looked like a lost child. So I sat her down on a bench at a table near the register to wait for me.

Bringing over the drinks, I sat down on the bench next to her. In front of us was a young mother with her infant, a stroller parked beside her. She was cradling the baby in her arms. We both stared.

Pearl started to talk. She told me about how hard her life had been, and "that there are a lot of problems in my family, you know," with a shaky and nervous tone.

"I'm sorry to hear that."

She looked in my eyes.

"I never should have had children," she said.

"I don't think you mean that…"

"Oh, yes I do."

I rubbed her back and stared ahead.

I wondered if she was including me in that statement.

Twenty-Five

A FULLER TREE

*G*rafting, I remembered learning in some biology class, was the process by which detached branches are reattached to their trunk and actually grow. But only certain species can do it. I was wondering if homo *adoptive* sapiens can. Now that I had met all of my half siblings, I wanted to try to see if I could take these new branches, and we could grow together.

My desire to press ahead at this stage of my life was explained well in *A Bridge Less Travelled*, where Robert Anderson states, "Adoption is the window through which we view the outside world—if we take the time to open it more often, we will require fewer and fewer Band-Aids to repair the damage of just trying to plow through it as if it doesn't exist." It confirmed what I already knew, that I needed to keep jumping into my adoption pool if I was ever going to get used to the waters.

I headed to Paul's house in Chicago, the second time I would be seeing him, to start the grafting process. This time I planned my trip to be there when Albert and Betty would be too.

Was it a veritable family reunion? I wasn't sure.

The visit started off fine, although Albert smothered me right away with piles of pictures from his recent trip to Israel, seemingly oblivious to the fact that I had not yet properly greeted Paul or his wife. He was probably overexcited to have me there and wanted to engage me right away, but I got inpatient. When Paul suggested we move out to the backyard, I jumped.

Once in the fresh air, we stood there chatting about that and this, but mostly about Paul and his family's life, since I directed most of the conversation that way. At one point, Natalie, Paul's daughter, climbed on her toddler bike and tried to propel herself forward on the grass but kept getting stuck.

"Do you think she would like to take a walk down the street with me, in the push bike? I mean, only if you're okay with it?" I asked. Only one hour in and a part of me already needed a break. I wanted to feel at ease and was trying, but I just didn't. Being in the presence of this family that had shared a lifetime of history together, yet trying to fit myself in, was harder than I thought it would be.

Natalie smiled an emphatic yes to my offer, and Albert asked if he could join me. So before I knew it, the two of us were strolling down the sidewalk, side by side. A young couple passed by us holding hands, and we glanced at each other with neighborly smiles. They were probably thinking we were three generations out for a walk -- how nice. But wait, we *were* three generations out for a walk…

We continued to the corner, about a five-minute walk. Natalie was holding on to the small handlebars out front, turning now and then to take a look at me, the stranger behind her with her grandpa. Albert sighed and looked deep into my eyes. "You know, Suzette, I always loved you and I still love you, very much."

Not new to me, his steadfast stare and heartfelt words were not so irksome this time. It didn't feel like a premature invasion. Even if I could receive it, it did not mean I was accepting of it. I was far from ready to reciprocate the same feelings back.

"I wanted you to be a part of my life. But I guess you didn't want that. What can you do? That's life. But I'm glad now that you've met Paul and that we can see each other, hopefully a lot more."

"Well, yeah, of course," I said. I was not sure if "*a lot* more" was what I had in mind. While I had not thought that far ahead about the details, I knew that I would prefer to take it one step at a time and see how I felt along the way. Grafting would be a process.

We walked back down the street, my father and I. The plastic pink bike rattled over the cement walkway, bumping over the cracks and spaces where the roots of the trees had lifted the slabs. I heard birds chirping, and looked up to see them flitting in and out of the trees above us. The leaves fluttered in the soft breeze and the sun's rays filtered through the branches, creating an ever-changing glittering pattern of bright light on Albert, his granddaughter and me.

In that moment I saw a man who wanted only to love me, but I wouldn't allow to because of the wall I had built around me -- a 1960's structure that served me well. After all, I had been so young, and his abrupt entrance into my life after a lifetime of secrecy had been such a shock. I built that wall to protect myself so I could go back to the life I had, the one where everything made sense and I didn't have to deal.

But now that wall was crumbling because I was chipping away at it. Only time could have helped me arrive at this place.

⟋⟍⟋

When Brian came home from college that summer, I filled him and Mallory in on my visit to Chicago. I wanted them to be part of my journey now, to plant the seeds for their own connection to my biological past, which was their biological past too. For the first time, their ears perked up. They were growing up, after all.

"Wait, isn't your dad Egyptian?" Brian asked.

"Yeah, he was, an Egyptian Jew, but they had to flee when he was young."

"So that means if you're half Egyptian, I'm... *one-quarter Egyptian*, right?"

"I guess so."

"Wow, that's really cool!" he smiled.

"Glad you like that," I said. Mallory liked it too.

Shortly after, a small flat packet arrived in the mail, the ones with the bubble cushioning inside. I peeled off the string, curious. Inside was a stack of photographs, blown up to 5-by-7 black-and-white glossies and wrapped against cardboard. There was also a hand-written letter inside. The photos were from a time long gone but refinished. They were from Albert.

The first was of his grandparents in Turkey, two serious people cloaked in the thick dark garb of those days: my great-grandparents, staring like frozen statues from a world long gone but whose DNA still lived inside me. The next one was of his dad with his second wife and three children, casually dressed and smiling, with Albert not in the picture. After leaving Albert's mother, he moved far enough away from them that Albert had to walk an hour to see him. Soon, it was too much. Then the support stopped. A story similar to Rich's, similar to millions of others, but playing out in a different time and place.

The next photo was of Albert's mother with him as a toddler. She was dressed in a long wool coat cinched at the waist, and she wore a beret. Her cheek was pressed against her sons, looking at the camera with a lit-up smile, gazing out with love. On the back it said, "My mother, Adele!" I remembered back to the time he told me, "You would've loved my mother!" Seeing her image for the first time, I had to agree. The photograph caught an exuberant spirit radiating from her eyes, one that drew me right in.

Pictures of cousins, aunts and uncles followed, and I scanned all with scrutiny, my heritage now before me. The last was of a large group: about forty children of various ages lined up in three rows wearing sailor-type uniforms. The back said, "Guess who -- I'm here -- the answer -- the only handsomest blondest -- me, Albert!" Modesty was certainly not his virtue, I chuckled to myself.

The last photo mesmerized me. It was of a small boy wearing matching beige genie-style pants and vest, the pants cinched with a belt embellished with trinkets, and the bell-sleeved white linen blouse shaped to perfection. I gazed at the turban on his head with feathers that were attached in front. The boy's large dark eyes and soft features could be taken for a girl's. On the back, I read, "In the Purim costume my mother made me." I loved the photo. It would be hard for me to reconcile that this cherubic, angel-faced child named Albert would become the man who upended my life so long ago.

hen I opened the one-page letter that accompanied the photos, I learned that when my grandparents fled Istanbul to escape the slaughter of the Jews by the Armenians, it was a "run for your life or perish frenzy." Albert's grandmother, mother and aunt, all ended up in a refugee camp in Palestine, placed there by the British. The Red Cross moved them to Alexandria where his grandfather had gone, thus reuniting them, and where he grew up happily in spite of his parents divorce. At least he did until World War II broke out.

He finished his letter with this:

"I want you to know that I had quite a difficult life, but I've prevailed. I was able to overcome all of the obstacles that could have prevented me from finding happiness. I'm still working by choice, own a beautiful home, and my wife does well in her profession. In contrast to my childhood, I feel you had a loving family and grew up in a positive atmosphere, married well and have three wonderful children. The pictures I've included I hope will give you an idea of my background. Receive my great affection and regards to the family. Au Revoir, Albert."

It was so thoughtful of him to go through all that time and trouble. The lens through which I viewed my father broadened even further. I was able to see a lot of strength in him now, in terms of a history.

As for the pictures, I stared at them, over and over, a connection to a past that was mine too, one that had been denied me, and then I denied. I was finally ready to receive it as my own.

With these pictures, a different family tree, one that was true to my bio-logical heritage, started to take root in my head, with new branches and roots for all these people and histories intermingled with the ones of my adoptive family. Pearl's face was there too, but sadly not her mother's or father's, for now obvious reasons. This tree in my mind was bigger, fuller, and accurate for the first time, the one that defined who I really was.

When the framing was done, I hung up some of the pictures and placed the others on a buffet table underneath. I placed the enlarged profile shot of Pearl I had gotten from Florence between one of my mother and one of me as a child. I put the one of Albert in his Purim costume between the one of my brother and me as young children and my parents' wedding day.

The two heritages were now on display together for everyone to see. I no longer had to hide them. Still, my adoptive family was now mixed with my genetic one in photographs only. They were still not actively mixed in real life. They still lived, at least for the most part, as separate realities, and I was bouncing back and forth trying to figure out if still, and how, I wanted to weave them together in a way that felt right.

Twenty-Six

A HEART TO HEART, A "FUNNY" MAN AND SHOCK ABSORBERS

There was a part of me at this point that wanted to stop this whole journey, to place my adoption world in a box, tie it up and place it on some high enough shelf in my closet where I wouldn't have to ever look at it again. I had so many of the answers I wanted, more than I ever imagined I would. Other than Albert and Paul at that point, none of the others seemed to really care if I was in their lives or not, so why keep trying?

The answer was simple: At 52 years old, the peace I wanted to feel inside me was still beyond my grasp.

Rich had just bought my mother a condominium in Florida, to start spending the winters there near her beloved cousin Rose from Chicago, since both she and Rose had lost their husbands the year before.

Since I would be going to visit her each winter, it made it easy for me to visit Pearl and Albert. I didn't have to fly down exclusively for that purpose, less of a roadblock.

I knew that becoming more familiar with them and their lives, and the therapeutic value of the writing process, would be the only path forward to final acceptance. I decided to write this memoir. By putting the story on paper, I knew it would help me in my healing.

I carried down the draft of the opening chapters to show my mom my first time down. In an act of healing with her, I wanted to face the truths we had avoided, and the ones she might not have been aware of. I knew it would be hard, for both of us, but the only way forward.

"Well, what do you think?" I asked, after she read them. My insides were fluttering.

"I didn't realize how…*hard* it was for you growing up," she told me.

"Well, yeah, it was and it wasn't…"

We began to rehash the past for the first time in our lives.

"As you read, the secrecy caused shame, unintentionally," I said.

"I had no idea…"

"You wouldn't have had…"

"But we *did* talk about it, I mean, I did bring it up, not a lot, but I did."

"I don't remember you ever bringing it up."

"There was even a TV show on once we watched together on adoption," she countered.

"I have no memory of that either," I said in a soft tone.

But I knew that truth was not memory, and memory was not truth. I asked my brother after, to get his take. He also had no recollection of her or my dad ever talking about it, or ever watching any TV show.

She looked like she was going to cry. I knew in that moment she was overcome with tremendous guilt that she made choices that hurt me.

"I searched for books on the subject, but there was only one. It said to not bring it up."

"Well, that was the thinking of that time."

"And I really thought you were okay with it," she said, her face pale. She then shared a story with me.

"When Oliver was young and playing with Steven Weinstein [a neighbor], in our basement, I heard them fighting. They started to go back and forth loudly.

"Well, you're a*dopt*ed!" Steven shouted to my brother.

"Is that so?" my brother answered, "Well, at least my parent's *chose me*, yours got stuck with you."

"So I though you were fine too."

"I was, for the most part…until Albert called."

"I know…"

She shook her head, as if reliving it.

"When you called us after, you were so upset…we wanted to calm you down."

"I'm sure…understandable," I paused, "but your anger."

Of course she wanted to protect me. I understood that all too well now, being a parent myself. What she didn't realize then, however, was she also wanted to protect herself. I understood that now too.

"Listen Mom, you just did what all adoptive parents did back then, what I would've done. You didn't know any better…and I was really fine growing up, you know I've had a wonderful life. I don't harbor one iota of resentment. I just want you to understand why it played out like it did, that's all."

She nodded her head, her eyes wet.

"And that weekend we came to visit you, Rose and Irv saw it too, how withdrawn you were…they were worried too, but I didn't know what to say."

"Rose and Irv were there? I have no memory of that."

"Well, they were."

"I must have blocked it out…"

She looked at me, her lip quivering.

"And you know what the real truth is mom, even if you had talked about it more openly, who knows if that would have been more upsetting, making me feel more different given that no one else talked about it. I don't know if you could've won either way…don't think you could have."

She looked at me, shaking her head, trying to absorb that statement.

I walked over and took her in my arms and told her I loved her. Pulling away, I said, "You were, are, the best mom I could have asked for, you know that, I thank God every day that I ended up with you."

Her face lifted and her mouth curled up.

"There are no faults, just facts of how it was."

It was the closure we both needed, my mom and me. It is said that "to understand all is to forgive all," but the truth was, from that point forward, she only needed to forgive herself.

There was another hurdle she needed to overcome. She was still unwilling to forgive Albert, in spite of my efforts to convince her otherwise. It was an enormous stumbling block for me as well. "You know, they say forgiveness is for the forgivers, to heal themselves," I told her.

"I know, but I just can't," she responded. I wanted to help her, but I was out of words.

Together, we visited Albert for the second time after this heartfelt conversation. I wished it to be easier than it was. My mom was pleasant and nice, but I knew her so well. Her stiff body said, "I'm still angry, not happy with him." Her armor was still on.

As we went to say our good-byes, he said to me, "Maybe I'll come up to New York this summer to visit you," in the parking lot of the restaurant. This would be an enormous step forward, but I was not so sure how I felt about it.

"Sure, you can come," I responded.

The summer passed by though without contact from Albert, and he did not mention visiting me in New York again when he called to wish me happy New Year in September for Rosh Hashanah. I wondered if he too felt the discomfort of our adoption chasm...that it was too difficult and too late to cross. This parent-child reconnection business was not that easy for him either. I had given him permission to finally open that *let's all be together* door, something he yearned for his entire life, but he could not do it.

⌣

I timed my visit to my mother the following winter to meet up with my daughter Mallory who was coming down during her spring break of her senior year at Michigan. I asked her out of the blue if she would like to come with me and meet Albert. "Sure, why not?" she responded.

She also told my mom, "Nana, I don't think you need to go any more when mom visits Albert...she's fine...you don't like him, so why upset yourself?" I had never wanted to exclude my mother before, but Mallory was able to be honest in a way I could not.

"I don't need to go," she told me after, "I just thought that you needed me for support."

"You're always welcome, but I don't need you to come. I'm good going alone." The layers of confusion and complication were still playing out, even though we had come so far.

Mallory, on the other hand, wanted to come. I was excited. I was interested too to get her take on Albert.

The night was filled with banter. He was thrilled to have Mallory there, a precious gift I had brought him. At one point, he started telling us a story about being insulted by an Italian shopkeeper in France that did not know he knew the language. He proceeded to rattle on in Italian after the story was done, in a way that amused him, smiling ear to ear. He continued on for a while. "*We don't know what you're saying, Al,*" Betty admonished him. Mallory and I looked at each other and smiled.

Albert told us about a favorite recipe of his in great detail after even though we didn't ask, nor were discussing cooking, and he gushed about "how delicious it was." He advised Mallory, "you have to marry a man that treats you well," as if it was something she had never thought of. He told us about his housekeeper who was stealing from him, so he does all the cleaning now. He chatted on like that, mostly about his life, and we sat and took it all in.

When we got to the car, I asked, "so, what did you think?"

"He's a funny man!"

"You mean funny, as in witty?" I asked, unsure of what she meant.

"No, I mean funny -- like in odd. And you're right, he's off..." And for the first time in my life, I had validation that my opinion of Albert was not just shaped by the shame and stigma I carried with me for so many years, nor by my mother's disdain.

"But he's really sweet right?"

"Oh yes, very...." We smiled at each other. I was glad. I needed that too.

"Also," she went on, "it's like he has no concept that we're not really his family. Like, just because you were put up for adoption and lived separate lives doesn't mean that we all can't be close again. He asked me to visit him four times and told me he loved me three times."

I chuckled. "That's what he always did to me -- but only once this time. Guess you've taken my place!" I chuckled again.

"He's cute though, I mean, he's just a cute funny little man."

I smiled. That was a good synopsis.

⌒

The next morning, I called Stacy to arrange to see her and her mom. I asked her if I could bring my mom to meet Pearl. Stacy said, "my moms in a rehab facility. She's having bad circulation problems with her legs… so it wouldn't be a good time."

"Sorry to hear…"

"My brother's coming down tomorrow to take care of her, we have one night together before I leave to go up north. If you want to come with us to the rehab, I mean, you can…"

I was happy she invited me, and that I would get to see Jeffrey again after all these years. When I arrived at their apartment, she welcomed me with more warmth than the last time. Jeffrey and I hugged and looked at each other with curious grins, each of us acknowledging the craziness of it all.

Stacy chimed in, "let's take pictures!" and pulled out her phone.

She snapped like ten.

We piled in the car and headed to the facility. At the front desk, there was a sign in sheet where we had to put our name, the person we were visiting, and our relation to them. I hesitated on the last. "Daughter," I wrote.

I was glad I went last so Stacy couldn't see it. Maybe she didn't feel I deserved that privilege. I wasn't sure I did either.

As we walked down the hallway toward the elevator, her heels clicking on the tile floor, I asked her, "Do you think it's hard for your mother to see me?" I thought she could offer me some insights.

Stacy didn't seem to understand what I was talking about.

"Hard for her, you know, knowing she gave me away and all..." She looked at me blankly.

"Well, she did have three other children you know!" she answered sternly. I was taken aback but didn't say a word.

Could one child actually replace another? I wasn't going to start educating her. Maybe she didn't want to think too deeply about it. Maybe Stacy had it right, and I was my own worst enemy.

We found Pearl in a wheelchair in the hallway by the nurse's station. She seemed tentative when she saw me. She then asked Stacy and Jeffrey, "Do you know who this is?" looking my way.

"Of course mom, *she came with us*!" Stacy answered. In that moment, I realized dementia was starting to take hold. Pearl started rubbing her neck hard. She said she was having sharp pain. Her cheeks were flushed too. Stacy felt her head, and she was warm. Fearing she could be having a heart attack, the nurses called for an ambulance.

Stacy, Jeffrey and I piled back into Stacy's car to follow the ambulance to the hospital.

We entered the ER. The attending nurse stopped us and asked, "Are you all family?" We all nodded yes.

We arrived at Pearl's bed and waited for the doctor to arrive. She seemed to be feeling a little better, so I searched for things to talk about. After a while, I told her, "You know, my mother's turning 86 soon and is very healthy and active." I thought she'd be happy to hear it. After I said it, I realized it might not have been the most sensitive thing to say, to tell her, *oh by the way*, the woman who got to raise me is also having a much better life.

She answered, "Well, I picked you a good one, didn't I?"

I smiled but did not say anything about the fact that *no one picked anyone* at Louise Wise. If that story gave her comfort, who was I to burst her bubble. I was sorry I had brought up my mom.

Stacy left to see what was holding up the doctor. Pearl said to me, "You know, I never told Stacy, but I hear voices in my head...I had a schizophrenic mom, you know."

"I knew that about your mom, but you're hearing voices *too*?" I asked.

"Well, you know, people who hear voices do bad things. Did you see the movie a *Beautiful Mind*? Some murder people. Mine don't tell me to do anything bad though. I hear them when things are quiet. They repeat my name over and over, but not when people are around me. You know, I don't tell anyone, because people think you're crazy if you do, and then they ignore you. I told my good friend Mary though, and she said, '*Pearl, just tell the voices to shut up.*'"

"I guess that's good advice, I mean, if you can do that," I responded. Jeffrey, who stood beside me listening, said, "Mom, you never heard voices *before*…."

"Well I do now."

When Stacy got back, I told her what her mother said. She waved her hand, a bit dismissive.

"Believe me, she's fine," she answered. I suggested she take her back to see her psychiatrist, just in case. She did not think it was necessary. I did not know what the right thing to do was, what my place was, so I left it alone. Stacy certainly knew her best. But it pained me that she still suffered, still had no peace.

On a recent visit, she told me she still heard voices, but it was "talking in the background."

"Like a TV?" I asked.

"Yes," she answered.

"Is it okay, or is it, scary?"

"Oh, scary." I couldn't even begin to imagine.

Once the doctors figured out that Pearl was not having the heart event they feared, but probably an irritation and small infection from her dentures, she was transferred back to the rehab, again by ambulance. We drove in Stacy's car.

We waited outside her room for the ambulance to arrive. The paramedics finally appeared, and they wheeled Pearl down the hallway on the gurney and into her room. Jeffrey, Stacy and I watched from the doorway as they went to work. The nurses and paramedics got busy, taking vitals and filling out the necessary paperwork in a hubbub of activity.

One of the nurses stopped what she was doing and cooed, "It's so nice that you have your children here, Pearl," smiling at the three of us.

Pearl looked right at me. She lifted herself up in the stretcher. "Well, you see that one…" she said extending her arm and pointing right at me. The nurses and paramedics stopped and looked at me. "That's the daughter I gave up for adoption to a rich family. She was a lot better off than being with me."

They all stared in stunned silence.

Shock absorbers please…

"Yeah, well uh…that's…me," I said with a sheepish grin, wanting to hide. Thankfully, one of the nurses quickly changed the subject.

"I didn't grow up that rich," I said to Stacy and Jeff later walking out, needing to somehow soften the blow. "My parents had to borrow money to adopt me."

They shrugged. What were they to say? The truth was, I did grow up a lot richer than they did, and in many more ways than just financially. Not only did I have a nice suburban home to grow up in, summers at sleep away camp, an excellent education, and the ability to go to a great college, I also received, more importantly, consistent and stable love— the most importance treasure of all.

"What was it like growing up with your mom and her illness?" I asked Jeffrey when we met for coffee alone on one visit, wanting to know more about what my life might have been like if Pearl kept me. The "who I would have been" question continued to circulate in my head. He paused, and I wondered if anyone had even ever asked him that question before. "It wasn't easy," he offered, "but we had a lady who took care of us when my mom was gone. We didn't understand a lot, just that she was sick and that we wanted her to come back…it was okay, I guess."

I had convinced myself over the years that their lives must have been terrible, that my life would have been terrible with Pearl. Of course, her depression did not stop her from loving them. That in spite of whatever else she couldn't give, she was able to provide that, and amply so.

Jeffrey also explained to me that while his dad, Martin, was great with his mom, patient and loving, his aunt, his dad's sister, didn't approve of her. This sister let it be known any opportunity she got. Like the kids at the Cottage

School, Pearl was dealt a bad hand, and it perturbed me to hear that her sister-in-law was not more empathetic. It must have been so hurtful to be judged so. If she had struggled with cancer, would Martin's sister have felt different? Physical ailments often brought caring; mental ones often brought judgment, especially back in that era.

Ironically, the next year when I saw Pearl, I asked her about her sister-in-law, curious to hear what she had to say. Pearl stared blankly ahead so Stacy answered for her. She told me that since her dad's death, her mom hadn't heard from her, even though she lived in Florida too. Then, as if a light switch went off, Pearl blurted out, "Yeah, *she had a mouth on her, that one!*" I was delighted by her regained zest. It showed me that the stronger woman I met at our first reunion was not completely gone. I chuckled, wishing to have more of that woman back, even if she didn't appear too often in the years that followed.

I also asked Jeffrey about Stacy's life now, since in my mind it could have been my own. "It must be really hard for her," I said, "I mean, living in that elderly community and taking care of your mom."

"Are you kidding me?" Jeffrey said. "Stacy has the best deal! She doesn't have to pay rent and has no real household expenses. She's so lucky to live there, and my mom's good company for her too!" In that moment, I realized how much the life I had lived for 25 years married to Rich had colored my beliefs. It was all-relative, I knew that, but I was more spoiled than I liked to think. I had drawn conclusions based on my own reality, a warped one, not hers. It was time to re-adjust.

Once home from that visit, I told Brian that Mallory had met Albert.

"Would you like to meet him too?" I asked, not wanting him to feel left out.

"No, not really mom...I mean, Nana's my only grandma and Poppa was my only grandpa."

As Asher was still a teen-ager, I didn't even ask. Still, I wondered, while blood still held such weight in my world, why didn't it hold anything in theirs.

Twenty-Seven

TWO TEACHERS

I was sitting with one of my students in Mallory's eighth-grade class that we were co-teaching. Having graduated from Michigan, she was now working for a non-profit that partnered with inner city middle schools to help improve them. One of her jobs included bringing volunteer guest teachers into her classroom to expose them to different things. She asked me to be one of them, and I agreed to teach a weekly writing class in personal narrative. I was thrilled to not only put my new skills to work, but to have this experience with my daughter.

The student's name was Stephenie with an *e* in the middle. Two months into the semester, I was meeting individually with each one to discuss what they wanted to write about in their pieces. Mallory and I spent the first eight weeks teaching them the components of good creative writing. It had gone well—as did the grapes and gourmet Kettle Corn I brought to them each week. They all came from homes near or below the poverty level. Two of them had never tasted a grape and none knew what Kettle Corn was.

I placed two chairs facing each other in the back of the room to speak to each student in private while Mallory worked with the rest of the class on writing exercises. I was trying to draw out the most significant events in their lives, and since many of them were immigrants, that became the most popular subject of their work. Even though my story was so different from theirs, the feelings of belonging or not, as a general theme, resonated in my head. It was fascinating to hear their stories, a world I knew little about.

When I asked Stephenie what she wanted to write about in our session together, I expected her to tell me, "when I came to America," like the rest.

"I was in a psychiatric hospital," she said. Surprised by her candor, I paused. Her dark eyes were staring out at me, waiting for a response. I knew not to react from my years at the Cottage School. I nodded my head in compassion, wanting her to feel comfortable. "Go ahead," I prompted her with a soft voice.

She went on to explain to me she was having hallucinations and thus was hospitalized. Her mother was divorced from her dad, and he was living with his girlfriend, one that did not have much compassion for Stephenie's struggles. She told me they used to fight a lot. Her mom came in to the hospital where she was being treated one day unexpectedly, and she was called to the main office. Taking Stephenie aside, her mom proceeded to tell her that her dad had a fight with his girlfriend, and "he stabbed her with a knife and killed her...and then killed himself."

My insides fell to my feet. Stephenie looked down at her lap, her body curled, probably afraid to see my reaction. It took a few seconds for me to process it. "Oh my, I can't believe you went through all of that."

She shook her head up and down and didn't say anything, but then told me, "I thought it was my fault, because they'd fight about me." I wanted to hug her, to hold her, but given the rules on physical contact, I knew I could not. We could hug the kids at the Cottage School and did, all the time, and they hugged us back hard. This time, I sadly had to keep my distance. I knew she was lucky to have a loving mother, or else she would have ended up in foster care too.

I asked her how long ago it happened and she said, "just six months ago."

"Let me first tell you that you're very brave for sharing that with me. And a very strong person to have gotten through it -- and now look, you're here in school and *doing so well*."

"Thank you," she said.

"But are you sure you're okay writing about it? You don't have to."

"I do. I told my therapist about you and this class, and she thought it would be really good for me."

I was honored and amazed that she spoke of me with her therapist. "Okay then, that's great, and I agree that writing can help you heal." Then, given the poignancy of this now very personal and revealing tete-a-tete, I said, "You know, I was adopted and my birth mom suffered with mental illness. My grandmother was schizophrenic and my mom might have been also. It's part of my family history and something that's difficult. I'm writing about it too!" Of course, my upbringing was nothing like hers, could not even begin to compare, but I wanted her to know that even her teacher, indeed anyone, could and does struggle.

"Really?" she said as her face lifted.

"Yes, no one is alone in that regard. And writing my story helped me…so maybe writing yours will help you."

"Yeah, my therapist says it doesn't matter where you came from in life," she sat up and stated, "*it's what you do.*"

I looked into her confident eyes and smiled. "You know what, she's completely right."

Right there, from the words of this 14-year-old girl with the same name as mine, came some crucial information I needed to hear at that particular time in my life. I might have known it before, but now I was ready to accept it, now that the puzzle pieces of my past were finally in place.

"My cousin Karen, the one I've told you about before, from California…" my mom explained standing in my kitchen, "she's organizing a big family reunion upstate New York. Would you be willing to come with me?"

"Well, in all honesty, it doesn't sound that appealing, but if you want me to go, I'll go." They would be a bunch of strangers after all. But I knew it would be a chance for my mom to see and reconnect with some long lost cousins from childhood, something that would make her happy. Plus, cousin Rose and her daughter, Joan, who was like a sister to me, would be flying in from Chicago for it. Getting to spend time with them was all I needed to hear to be happy to go.

When October came, we all drove upstate to Saugerties, New York, having no idea whose house we were going to nor what to expect. We followed the directions that led us to a quiet flat rural street in the middle of what seemed like nowhere. I was relieved to see the lawns were mowed, the landscaping tended to and the homes in good conditon. There were no other cars parked outside when we reached the address.

"This is really weird," Joan said. I agreed.

Rose, in her headstrong way, snapped, "Don't be ridiculous, park the car!"

Joan complied.

Joan, my mother and I stood sheepishly behind Rose as she knocked on the door. When it opened, a 40-ish, heavyset woman with dark hair, olive skin, and an apron tied tight greeted us. "Come in, come in! You're the first ones here," she said with a warm smile. Entering with cautious smiles, we simultaneously made a visual sweep of the room. Seeing it was all tasteful and clean, we relaxed, finally.

On the living room wall, there was a twenty-five-foot-long family tree printed out, created by cousin Karen who had not yet arrived. Having never met her before, she ended up being an energetic powerhouse who spent two years researching and creating this enormous tree and putting this extensive reunion together. It was a sight to behold. There were hundreds of people on it, with a picture next to each name, ones she had collected or mined from the Internet. My great-great grandparents, the patriarch and matriarch, who arrived in this country in the early 1800s, linked all the branches.

Karen handed us plastic clip nametags with the "branch" we were from underneath our names, 1, 2 or 3. People started arriving in batches, introducing themselves to each other with curious wonder. The house soon filled to the brim with people from all across the country, a hodgepodge of shapes, sizes, socio-economic backgrounds and religions from inter-marriages, all bound by blood.

Everyone milled about, examining the chart, seeing where they fell in relation to others, trying to make geographical and social connections between people they never met. Looking at the black and white photographs from the earlier generations, I thought about the photographs that Albert sent me. This was a different "wall" of ancestry that was also my own. Where did I belong? Even after all this time, I still wasn't sure.

As the night unfolded, I decided not to tell anyone I was adopted. I was not in the mood to observe their surprised reaction or hear them say, "Oh, it doesn't matter, you're part of this family" because what else were they to say? Nor did I want to have to explain my story and the inevitable "Have you ever met your biological parents?" question that usually follows. I also did not want to do anything to cause my mother discomfort, nor make her think for one second that I didn't feel like I belonged there, because I knew how hurtful that would be for her.

"Isn't this amazing?" said one of my newly met cousins who approached me, with a broad grin, "I mean you have to know where you came from to know who you are, right?"

I smiled. "I guess you're right." I swallowed hard and walked away.

When lots of photos had been taken, bellies stuffed, and conversations exhausted, the reunion came to an end. It was a bizarre experience to say the least, wondering if I would ever see any of those people again. Once home and alone with my cousin Joan, I confessed, "You know, it was a bit strange for me there, being adopted and all." I had never once discussed my feelings about being adopted with her before.

I waited to see her reaction. "I imagine it would've been..." she responded right away. I felt surprised and comforted at the validation, versus a dismissal, which is what I had expected. While it felt good to have her say that to me, I wondered if she ever thought of me any differently as well.

"Technically, I really didn't belong there," I said.

"Well, that's true, but even if it's not your family genetically, it is socially and culturally."

I stared at her, the good teacher, as she was a teacher. "You know, you're right. It's a good way to think about it."

I realized that I did not have to figure out where I belonged because I belonged equally in both worlds. It was not an "either or" proposition but an "and" one. Sam and Evelyn were my parents just as much as Pearl and Albert were, only different. I had four parents not two, and I could embrace them all, a true blessing.

Twenty-Eight

FULFILLMENT AND FORGIVENESS

I wanted more than ever to give my mother the chance to meet Pearl. Her words from years back always echoed in my head, "I'd like to thank her for the gift she gave me." I was going to try my best this year.

My mother held the phone to her ears, and I stared at her face as Pearl spoke to her. She said and kept saying, "It's okay, don't worry, it's okay…" like she was talking to a small child that had lost its way.

"I don't want you to feel slighted in any way," my mom told me Pearl said to her over and over again after the call. Pearl was incapable of giving her an explanation for her refusal. We both knew why.

"Did you hear how fragile her voice was, how ill she sounds?" I asked my mom, trying to soften the blow, to help her understand what she was dealing with.

"Completely." With that, tears began to stream down her cheeks.

"Oh my, you're crying?"

"Yes," she sniffed, "Because I always wanted to meet her, but at least I got a chance to hear her voice. You have no idea how long I have waited for that and what it meant to me. You can have no idea how much I respect this woman."

The tears started to flow now, ones that had been clogged up for fifty years. I took her in my arms and held her. She apologized for crying, and I told her, "You never have to apologize. I get it. I so understand." She swallowed back her emotion and wiped her cheeks. In those tears, I knew was the guilt that her gain necessitated another woman's loss, the latter part of the equation now smacking her in the face.

"As sad as the story is," I said to my mom, "at least she got married to a man she loved and who loved her and who stuck by her through all her illness. And she has three children who love and care for her too. It could have been a lot worse. I take solace in that myself." She shook her head, wiping her eyes again, and we embraced.

"*L*et love in," said a rabbi I knew. Could it be that simple when it came to Albert? The writing process was certainly helping me heal. I learned so much from the many self-help books I had read over the years, accept what is, face your fears, let it be and let it go. Sometimes easier to say than to do, but in the case of Albert, it was actually becoming easier.

On a recent phone call, he asked first thing "Can you do me a favor?"

"Sure," I said, wondering what it could be. "There were three guys sitting in a bar." This was a favor? I guess that meant listening to his joke. "A fairy came in and told the first guy he can have any wish he wanted. He asked to be 25% more intelligent. The fairy hit him with his wand and *poof*, he became 25% more intelligent. The fairy then asked the second guy. He said he wanted to be 50% more intelligent. So the fairy hit him with his wand, and *poof*, he became 50% more intelligent. The fairy asked the third guy. He said he wanted to be 100% more intelligent. The fairy hit him with his wand, and… poof, he turned into a woman." He then started cackling wildly.

"That's cute! I guess that means you think women are smarter than men then?" I asked

"Yes, I do," he said. I laughed. I didn't know many men who would ever admit to that but Albert wasn't like most men. I focused on the humor and tried not to dwell on the awkward timing.

On my very last visit to him, we sat around his kitchen table.

I allowed myself to take in all the good in him, not judging the parts I might have in the past or stopping myself when the inclination came. I enjoyed his company more than I ever had.

On our way out to dinner he said, "I hope you'll start calling me more now! Will you?" He must have noticed the significant change in my attitude, that I was more gregarious, relaxed and accepting.

Was it simple as the saying, "If you change the way you look at things, the things you look at change?"

But when we were walking to the door, he took my arm and yanked me closer to him, throwing my body off balance for a second. I was taken aback by this assertive maneuver. "Do you really mean it, that you'll call more often?" he asked staring into my eyes. I grinned and removed his hand from me, stepping back. "I really, really will! *Okay?*"

I did not cringe, roll my eyes, or become angry, as I always had. I was in control, physically and mentally. I shrugged it off as a manifestation of nearly forty years of frustration bottled up since the first time he called me. I would always be the infant he didn't want to let go of, even at 54 years old, and I could accept that. And when he told me, "You'll always be my baby doll!" I just told him, "I know," and smiled a genuine smile.

"This place where I live is Shang-ri-la!!!" and "I hope to live another 75 years," he said at some point that night with an infectious energy. I grinned in delight. Who couldn't love that kind of enthusiasm and optimism?

He told me he went to a spin class almost daily, and since I loved spin too, I chuckled as to whether there was a common gene for that particular exercise that he passed on to me. He was artistic too like I was. I made connections to our genetic similarities in ways I never allowed myself before.

"You know," he said before we left his house for the restaurant when Evelyn wasn't listening, "I go to the community where Pearl lives every week. I still do someone's hair there. Every time I go, I look for her."

I had no idea. This information was surprising. I smiled, but rather than thinking boy, he will never let it go, I said, "You do? Well, maybe one day you will!" and felt empathy.

Sadly, however, Pearl had never once asked about him, and I never brought him up, sensing it would be difficult for her.

However on my very last visit to her, I asked her if she would like to see pictures of my children. She had never asked before.

"This is Mallory, Brian, Asher..." I said, holding my phone before her.

"Very nice," she answered. She did not ask any questions.

I then took a chance. "Do you want to see a picture of Albert? I have a recent one."

She hesitated.

"Well, doesn't cost anything extra..." she chimed.

I smiled. That was the zippy Pearl I loved. She was having a good night.

I swiped and found the image of Albert and me from the last time we had dinner together.

"So, do you recognize him?" I asked with a huge grin.

"No, I don't."

"Not at *all*?"

"No."

Stacy, who was with us, asked, "Can I see him?"

She looked at him and nodded her head. She handed me back my phone.

"Ma," she said, "if you want to see him, I can take you...I mean, we can meet for a drink somewhere..."

Pearl did not answer.

"Ma, do you *want* to see him?"

"No, Stacy."

Stacy looked at me, grinned and shrugged. I grinned and shrugged back.

"Not happening, I guess." I answered.

I changed the subject.

In some perfect world, I imagined, it would have been nice if we all could be together just one time, to hug each other and marvel over the journey, the one that finally brought us together after fifty-six years.

I drove down the highway to see Pearl alone that night, happy that my mom got to talk to her but sad I would not have her with me. I really had wanted to fulfill her lifelong desire. Given her emotional state after the phone call, I was grateful that my mom had her cousin Rose, her daughter Joan and my mother-in-law Carol, all there to be with her while I was gone.

My mother-in-law and I had become close over the years, whatever insecurities we both had during my early years with her son long buried in the past.

She and my mother had also established a close relationship.

This past Christmas break, we were all together in Florida chatting in her condo apartment after having dinner. She too now spent her winters in Florida, in the same community as my mom.

Carol started talking about her beginnings to my Mallory and Asher, who were also down with Rich and me. It was a story I knew, had heard years ago, but we hadn't discussed in a long time, that she had been in foster care herself for a few years after her mother was institutionalized for depression. She went back to live with her father when he re-married, where she remained until she married.

Mallory was asking her further questions about it.

I had a light bulb moment. "Mom, do you remember where you were back then? You didn't last time..."

"Actually, I think it was called the *Hebrew* something..."

"Really?"

Once home, I emailed the JCCA once again, as I had did with Pearl, giving them her name and birthday, and asking them to check the files. I doubted it was possible. But I was wrong:

Hi Suzie,

Good news! We were able to find your mother-in-law's records on Microfilm.

My jaw fell.

Both my maternal grandmother, at least by birth, and Rich's maternal grandmother had been institutionalized for acute depression, that was old news. But
now my birth mother and Rich's birth mother were both also in foster care
with JCCA.

When I told her that I could access her file, she was shocked. "It's insane
I know, first Pearl and now you. Who would have ever thought?"

"I can't believe it. I have no memory of those days of my life," she told me,
"and now I will get to read all about it…I'm so…*happy*."

There were over a hundred pages of notes on my mother-in-law Carol and
her three sisters from the social workers, much more than I had received on
Pearl's time in care. I had them printed and bound for her. She read them in
small spurts, needing breaks in between, sometimes teary.

"I hope you' re not sorry I gave it to you."

"Of course not, I've been crying yes, but tears of joy too. I'm finding out
who I was."

To be able re-visit her early life in such detail was a powerful gift. She was
able to shine light on that part of her childhood that had long been cut off
from her. She also got to know her father in ways she could not as a child…
how he worked so hard to oversee their time in foster care and get all his
daughters back. She had always loved him, but now she had new levels of
admiration.

*O*n this trip to Pearl, without my mom, she was the quietest I had ever
seen her. But there were moments of great lucidity too.

When she got out of the car on the way to a restaurant that night, I
took her arm and held her up as we headed across the lot. She did not need
my assistance, but it felt good to have her near me.

"I worked in hospice for years," she said as we walked.

"I know, you told me that once before," I smiled.

"I was good at it you know…because I'm so comfortable with death."

I paused, wondering what to say next.

"That's a good thing to be," I responded.

I wondered if all the suffering she had endured in her life made her well suited for this task.

I felt proud that she did this vital work, in awe of her ability to give of herself in that way.

While I was attentive and doting as I could be, trying to draw her out, she was often unresponsive. Sometimes I just got a nod of the head or a one-word answer. She did not smile once.

I thought about the words Pearl uttered, marked in the Louise Wise files, when she was finally reunited with her own mother at the age of 17, the one she was taken away from at four and a half years old. Pearl's mother had not recognized her. "I feel sad for this woman that was my mother," Pearl told the social worker after. I felt the same now too, in this moment, about mine.

Pearl turned to me after we were done and in a nervous tone said, "Your mom could've come, you know, I, I...don't want to exclude anyone." I looked at her with great surprise. I guessed Stacy was right about her mom. Day to day, but even moment to moment, you never knew what you were going to get.

The next morning, my mom approached me. "You know, I had a long talk with Rose and Joan," she said, "and they asked me why I was still so angry at Albert. They didn't understand."

"And?"

"I realize they're right. I need to work on it, I want to work on it... *to let it go.*"

I stared into her dark eyes with surprise. "Wow, Mom..."

At 87, the rock had finally split. I was flooded with relief for her and also for myself. Forgiveness can never come too late. She got to work doing just that with our rabbi, following up.

When my own birthday came six months later, this past September, Stacy called and both she and Pearl left me a phone message. Pearl sounded alert and upbeat, surprising me, her words clear and strong.

She said, "Happy birthday, Suzette, I love you dear, and I'm so proud of you!"

My heart flooded. I didn't know exactly what she was proud of though, except to think she thought I'd grown to be a nice person, which I guess was something to be proud of. It was also the first time she ever acknowledged my birthday. As a day that could only be fraught with pain for her throughout her life, remembering back to relinquishment, I felt glad she had reached a point in her own journey where she was comfortable enough to do so.

She too, at eighty years old, was moving ahead and old wounds were healing. I never thought about the fact that finding my own peace might also bring her some of her own.

⌣

*M*uch to my surprise, the following year the meeting would finally happen: my two mothers. Pearl had come around. She had agreed.

I made a reservation at a quiet restaurant in Florida. Mom, who came first, took a seat on a bench outside to wait, under the white lights that were strung along the trunks and branches of the banyan trees that surrounded the walkway to the restaurant. The irony of this abundance of trees was not lost upon me when I myself arrived, given my decades long quest for one integrated birth and adoptive family tree. It was a fitting canopy.

My mother told me after the dinner that while she was waiting on that bench, her insides were bursting with a lifetime of anxious anticipation. She watched as each car entered the parking lot, wondering if it could be the one that held my birth mother.

After about fifteen minutes, she saw three diners approaching. My mom knew right away that the older woman in this particular group of three had to be Pearl. "I saw you in her face right away!" she announced to me. It amazed her. She sat frozen for a moment's time. Walking side by side with Pearl was her daughter Stacy and Stacy's boyfriend Ray.

"I'm Evelyn," she said, very nervous. Pearl looked at her with apprehension in her eyes, my mom reported to me after. But then she extended her arm slightly toward her. Mom took her hand and asked if she could give her a hug. "Okay...sure..." Pearl said, but her body stiffened when my mom wrapped her arms around her. My mom quickly released, understanding the difficulty of it.

She introduced herself to Stacy and Ray. They walked into the restaurant together, through those trees, and took a seat inside.

Approaching the table, I glanced from mom to birth mom and back with an over-stretched inquisitive smile. Pearl was in full make-up, and she looked beautiful. So did my mom. Each had obviously taken extra time with their appearance. I knew that desire all too well.

I sat down next to Pearl. My mother sat on the other side of her. If Pearl was uncomfortable, I could not tell. I rubbed her back and smiled into her eyes as if to say, "You got this, it's okay." Rich got busy engaging us with his well-administered doses of small talk. Mom was talking to Pearl but I cold not hear what she was saying. Just watching this sight, my heart swelled.

It was a moment of karmic grace, amazing to behold.

At one point, wanting to put one issue to rest that always bothered me, I said to Stacy, "do you remember when I first met your mom and you told her you were worried I might be carrying a *weapon*...I never understood that."

Pearl looked up.

"That wasn't Stacy, that was my husband Martin!" she said. "He wanted to get the hell out of there. He wanted to have *nothing* to do with it."

"Did he actually think I'd hurt you?" I asked, taken aback.

"I don't know, maybe" she shrugged. "He thought you'd be really angry at me, that's for sure, and he wasn't sticking around for *that*..."

"Yeah, well, that was my father," Stacy chimed in. She then added in a sheepish tone, "I don't know...maybe I could've said that about a weapon. I was worried too."

I realized then that Pearl, Martin and Stacy understood something about adoptees that I did not even being one: that some might harbor extreme anger toward their birth parents for having been given up. How could they know that wasn't the case for me, that the opposite was true?

As we ate our meals, Rich started talking to Stacy and Ray about my volunteer work for a charity. My ears perked up.

"What charity is that?" Ray asked.

Rich answered "the JCCA."

Pearl's face came to life.

"J-C-C-A," she blurted out loudly, "they took care of *me*!"

"Yes, they did," I said, "*I know that*. I can't believe you remember…"

"I sure do!" Her face was glowing.

Thrilled with her positive response, and with this connection now out of the bag, I went on to explain about the campus and the coincidence of it all in an abridged two-minute version.

Then turning to Pearl, I asked, "Did they take good care of you?"

I braced myself for the answer, thinking that whatever she told me could affect my feelings toward the agency that I now so loved and was committed to, even though it would be irrational.

"Oh yes, they did!" she smiled ear to ear. I realized in that moment that whatever abuse she had endured at the hands of her foster parents had nothing to do with her care by the social workers at JCCA itself. Pearl was able to separate the two in her mind.

"You know, I was never supposed to see you again," she said shaking her head, "that's what they told me." By her tone, I was not sure if she was telling me she was relieved that I had entered her life or if all of this had been, and was still, too hard for her. I hoped it was the former. I thought it was.

"You know I was in an orphanage before I went to my foster family," she continued.

"That was probably the Hebrew Orphan Asylum," I told her, "which became part of JCCA." She did not remember that name, but then a disturbed look came over her face. "They had to tear me off my bedpost because I didn't want to leave there!"

Upsetting as it was to hear about yet another trauma she endured, it was not surprising. She finally had food, stability and people caring for her, and probably even friends. The known to the unknown, always scary for a child, was playing out then as it does now everyday in the foster care system.

When the dinner ended, Pearl got up and whispered to my mom, "What's your name again?" We followed each other outside, again finding ourselves cocooned amongst the banyan trees. My mother went to hug Pearl, but this time her advance was received with a different response. "She grabbed me and squeezed me so incredibly tight" my mom described after. "I was also quite amazed that this small woman could be so strong!" Pearl held onto her for longer than she expected.

"God bless you," Pearl whispered in my mom's ear.

I looked at my mom after she turned from Pearl to me. Her face was flushed and tears dripped from her eyes, although I did not yet know fully why since I didn't know what Pearl had said to her.

I put my arm around Pearl and hugged her myself, holding her small frame an extra few seconds.

The ghost of Pearl had finally become a living person that my mom could touch, hear, and see. It breathed new life into her in ways I never imagined as she approached her eighty-eighth birthday.

"I feel worse for her now than I ever felt before," my mother said. "And my gratitude, well…" her voice squeezed, "being able to tell her so, I can't even go there. It was I who should have said to her God bless you…"

"I love you more now than I ever have before," she told me the next day.

"What, why?" I asked.

"Because I saw how you were with her, how tender and caring, and I finally got it…why you would be, and what she means to you. And I was actually glad for you, for it. You know what, it made me want to be closer to her, too."

"Really, Mom? That's so lovely."

"And…I'm ready to share you," she said with a sureness I never heard from her before. "Before I was always scared that you would end up going to her… whenever you were distant from me I thought that."

"Wait, you actually thought that during my life, if I was in a bad mood or just going through my own stuff, that I might actually go to Pearl and pull away from you?"

"Yes. I never felt threatened as your mom, but I guess I was insecure about my place…"

And there it was. My mother had finally admitted what she could never before, that she lived with fear, just as my dad had. The rock had cracked again, and out of the fissure flowed an abundance of honesty and self-acceptance.

Her admission of vulnerability caused my own heart to expand, and my love for her deepened.

"Believe me, all adoptive mothers harbor those feelings. It's only natural and I'm so glad you were able to tell me that," I assured her.

"And I'm happy that you have this whole other extended family," she said, surprising me yet again.

"She said I could call her by the way, and I'd like to do that if you're okay with it."

"Of course I am," I said, "if she's willing to speak to you, I'm thrilled."

Was it possible that my mom could actually give Pearl some kind of comfort, a kind I never could?

I did not know, but it now seemed that just about anything was possible.

Twenty-Nine

FULL CIRCLE

"Shelter us under the shadow of thy wings, 1812" read the inscription hand-chiseled into the large dark marble slab. Standing at the entrance of a newly built garden and sitting area at the Cottage School, it was dug up by the construction workers who were amazed to have found such a treasure. No one had any idea it was there.

The JCCA had decided that it was important to have this space, a peaceful oasis for the children to visit with family members or staff in an otherwise open and minimally landscaped field. A talented designer and volunteer drafted the plans, and Mark got to work doing what development director's do, raising the funds to build it, just as they did to build the campus itself one hundred years prior. I had not been over to see this garden since its completion, but now I was here and present.

I stared down at the slab now sitting on a matching marble trunk that was built to hold it. Running my fingers over its inscription, a slight mist fell, and I thought back about the generations that came on this campus, all those who had suffered. They were all sheltered under the JCCA's wings, and if you believed, a godly providence.

With a deep sigh, I stepped around the trunk and raised my head to take in the American flag above me flapping in the cool breeze. I felt proud. I took in the well-designed area, the curved cement chess and checker tables, the floating iron lunch tables, the pebble paths and the greenery that enclosed it.

Looking down, I examined the pavement beneath my feet made up of hundreds of inscribed bricks, bought by people in the community to help raise the funds needed to build this space. I began to read them, one by one, moving forward in slow motion. I knew a lot of these people, so many of them had volunteered in the lunch bunch groups and gone on to do so in other capacities, their dedication and commitment strong. Each of them had not only enhanced the lives of the children who lived here but my own life, too. The relationships I forged here gave deeper meaning to my life, enabled fulfilling and rewarding connections to others and tied me to the heritage from which I came.

I saw the brick I bought in honor of my mother who had volunteered here in a classroom, as well as the one for my family, all of whom had come here in various capacities to give their time to the children. I thought of the opportunity I got to meet Rich's half brother and his wife, at the JCCA gala in the city, something that was satisfying for me even if hard for Rich.

I walked to the perimeter of the space, where small trees had been planted in people's names. I found the one for my father. The plaque read, "In memory of Samuel Gordon, Loving Father of Suzette J. Brownstein," with a tree design carved into it below.

I leaned down and pushed off the dirt that had partially covered it with my hand.

I admired the significance of the tree in the teachings of Judaism, a symbol of ancestry, growth, and renewal itself. The significance it had for me.

I lifted my head and looked out over the open expanse of the campus and paused, as I had thirteen years before. Life had come full circle for me in this place, the threads of my life weaving together here in so many ways and setting the stage for me to heal and grow. My heart felt full.

I inhaled and exhaled deeply and looked up at the sky and then at the woods beyond. I knew too that I was but one tree, and really part of the greater canopy that was mankind, and that is where I now wanted to look for meaning.

I took the keys from my purse and started to walk to my car, smiling.

Epilogue

As of this writing, I continue to visit Pearl and Albert each year, our relationship growing.

I am hoping to see Pam again one day. Every time I visit her dad, she has been unable to come. But I stay hopeful.

Paul and his family came for Thanksgiving dinner this year, the first time a birth relative has been to my house. He said before he left, "I love having a new sister."

Jeffrey invited me to his only child's bar mitzvah last summer. I couldn't attend but would have done so, happily.

Alan wishes me happy birthday on Facebook. I am sure we will see each other again.

Stacy and Ray have gone out with Rich and me as a foursome, in addition to my visits with her mom. She always takes pictures and posts them on Facebook with captions like, "Fun day with family."

It feels good to have gotten this far. I will continue to steer the boat forward, to whoever wants to get on board, sensitive to others feelings and to my own. The divide is dissipating fast. While this adoption stuff will never be easy, I am grateful for how far I have come. I will keep trying to create new memories best I can, even if in small little bits.

I know that family is what is given to us, but sometimes it is what is created too.

Suggested Reading

1. Pamela V. Grabe, editor, *Adoption Resources for Mental Health Professionals,* Mary D. Howard (New Jersey: Transaction Publishers, 1989)

2. Betty Jean Lifton, *Journey of the Adopted Self, a Quest for Wholeness (New York: Basic Books, 1994)*

3. David Brodzinksy, Ph.D., Marshall D. Schecter, M.D., and Robin Marantz Henig, *Being Adopted, The Lifelong Search for Self* (New York: Doubleday, 1992)

4. Jacqueline Bernard, *The Children You Gave Us, 150 Years of Service to Children, a History of the Jewish Child Care Association* (New York: Bloch Publishing, 1972)

5. Joe Soll, *Adoption Healing, A Path to Recovery* (Maryland: Gateway Press, 2005)

6. Arthur D. Sorosky, M.D., Anette Baran, M.S.W., and Reuben Pannor, M.S.W., *The Adoption Triangle, Sealed or Open Records: How They Affect Adoptees, Birthparents, and Adoptive Parents* (Triadoption Publications, 2008)

7. Nancy Newton Verrier, *The Primal Wound: Understanding the Adopted Child* (Kentucky: Gateway Press, 20013)

8. John Bradshaw, *Family Secrets-The Path from Shame To Healing* (New York: Bantam Books, 1996)

9. Marilyn Schoettle, "The Adoptee Search: Looking for the Missing Piece" (Maryland: The Center for Adoption and Support and Education, 2000)

10. Pamela Stanton, *Reunited: An Investigative Genealogist Unlocks Some of Life's Greatest Family Mysteries* (New York: St. Martin's Griffin Press, 2012)

11. Ann Fessler, *The Girls Who Went Away, The Hidden History of Women Who Surrendered Children for Adoption in the Decades Before Roe v. Wade* (New York: Penguin Books, 2007)

12. Kathryn Joyce, *The Child Catchers- Rescue, Trafficking and the New Gospel of Adoption, (New York: Public Affairs Publishing, 2013)*

13. Sarah Saffian, *Ithaka: A Daughter's Memoir of Being Found*, (Illinois: Delta Publishing, 1999)

14. Amanda H.L.Transue-Woolston, *The Declassified Adoptee: Essays of an Adoption Activist* (CQT Media And Publishing, 2013)

15. Robert Andersen M.D. and Rhonda Tucker, "A Bridge Less Travelled, Twice Revisited" (Badger Hill Press, 2000)

16. Carole Anderson, "Why Won't My Mother Meet Me?" Concerned United Birthparents Inc., 1982

17. Mirah Riben, *Shedding light...The Dark Side of Adoption*, (Harlow Printing Company, 1988)

18. Wisdom, Suzette and Green, Jennifer, *Stepcoupling: Creating and Sustaining Strong Marriage in Today's Blended Family* (Harmony, 2002)

Acknowledgements

I would first and foremost like to acknowledge and thank my writing teacher, Cullen Thomas. He was my mentor, and guide throughout this entire process. This book would not be what it is without his amazing wisdom and expertise in the art of memoir.

I would like to thank my early editor, Janet King, and my final editor, Jill Rothenberg, for their invaluable input.

I want to express my intense gratitude to the three women who took this writing journey with me: Sue Matthews, Janet Pfeffer and Lori Kaplan, who were all simultaneously writing their memoirs while I was writing mine. All your encouragement and feedback were priceless to me, as was your sharing, caring and friendship. Thank you, my beloved *Life Writers*!

Thank you to all my friends who gave me input and advice and editing help. You know who you are. I am humbled by it.

Thank you to Michele Kraushaar for the cover design and graphic art.

Thank you to the Pleasantville Cottage Schools, all the children and staff, who have given me the incredible gift of humility, gratitude, community and connection.

Thank you to the JCCA for saving Pearl seventy-five years ago.

Thank you to my brother Oliver for allowing me to share his story, giving me his thoughtful perspective and for aiding me in the memory department. I thank him too for his lifelong love and support.

To my father Samuel, I want to acknowledge how his unconditional love changed my life. He made me feel special every day, and for that, there are not enough words of thanks.

My incredible admiration goes out to my mother, Evelyn, who I forced to go on this journey with me whether she liked it or not (and sometimes she did not!). I knew it could be difficult for her, but she supported me along the way with grace, wisdom and strength. I thank her for allowing me to share her story in such an intimate way, for her invaluable insights on our shared experience and for helping me remember what was lost to me. This journey brought us closer in ways I never imagined, an added gift. I am forever grateful.

Thank you to my children, Brian, Mallory and Asher, who often asked, "Will that book ever be done?" Yes, it's done! I love you guys so much.

To my husband, Rich, I thank you for seeing me through the countless hours I spent at the computer, often neglecting you and sometimes oblivious to all that was going around me. Most importantly, thank you for setting me on this journey twenty-eight years ago when I was scared and unwilling, and then giving me the encouragement and confidence I needed to complete it. You were the rock that grounded me, and the foundation I needed to keep digging and growing. With deep love and devotion, I can't thank you enough for the opportunities and life you have given me and the life we have shared together.

Made in the USA
Middletown, DE
15 February 2018